To Gary

Good Luck

with Love ..

ADMIRAL OF THE FLEET
The Life of
SIR CHARLES LAMBE

ADMIRAL OF THE FLEET

The Life of
SIR CHARLES LAMBE

by
OLIVER WARNER

With an Introduction by Admiral of the Fleet
EARL MOUNTBATTEN OF BURMA

and a Foreword by
SIR STEVEN RUNCIMAN

SIDGWICK & JACKSON

LONDON

S.B.N. 283.35293.0

Printed in Great Britain
by Spottiswoode, Ballantyne and Co. Ltd., London and Colchester
for Sidgwick and Jackson Limited
1 Tavistock Chambers, Bloomsbury Way
London W.C.1.

CONTENTS

List of Illustrations

INTRODUCTION

by
Admiral of the Fleet
Earl Mountbatten of Burma

I FIRST knew Charles Lambe when he was a very small naval cadet at Osborne in 1914. In the intervening forty-six years I came to know him more and more intimately; and the better I knew him the more I liked and admired him. He became my best friend.

First and foremost he was a brilliant and outstanding naval officer. His qualifications for his final job, First Sea Lord, were unique. During the war he had commanded a cruiser and an aircraft carrier and had been Director of Plans at the Admiralty; since the war he had held a varied selection of the highest appointments in the Navy, especially in the Fleet Air Arm.

But he was a great deal more than a naval officer; he was a widely read, deeply cultured man with many outside interests and qualifications. He was a talented pianist; he took exceptional interest in his own 'Commander-in-Chief's orchestra' in Malta, and even as First Sea Lord continued to sing regularly in the Bach Choir. Latterly, in his flagships, he would have a piano in his cabin, and invite composer friends of his, like Lennox Berkeley, to stay with him on board so that they could enjoy the piano together. In Malta he played the piano in his own quartet.

He had also a great appreciation and judgement of pictures and was himself a competent artist. During the war, when in command of the *Illustrious*, he was one day apprehended by the Military Police sketching at the top of Table Mountain, in suitably bohemian clothes, without passport or papers—and for a long time was unable to convince them that he was the captain of 'that big carrier down there'.

He was that rare person, an 'all-rounder'; for as well as, and perhaps in contrast with, these qualifications, he was a great sportsman, a fine shot, and a fearless horseman. He played for the

Royal Navy in the Inter-Regimental Polo Tournaments at Hurlingham in 1930, 1931, and 1936. An accomplished pilot, he used to fly himself round the country.

In 1930, we were both in Deauville where the Royal Navy polo team was playing in high handicap tournaments. At a lunch party my wife placed him between Sir Thomas Beecham and Mr. Joseph Widener, owner of the Widener collection of pictures in America. After lunch his two neighbours approached my wife with the same remark: 'He can't really be a sailor or a polo player, he knows far too much about Music/Painting.'

Charles Lambe's great sense of humour and unfailing wit endeared him to all who served with him; and his deep understanding of men and their human problems, combined with a complete lack of any form of pretentiousness, made him accessible to all.

There was never a more unorthodox Admiral. What gave him his great strength in the Service was the breadth of vision acquired through the multiplicity of his outside interests.

The public may not have realized his immense services to the country, for he always shunned publicity but the Navy appreciated his value to the full.

His unswerving loyalty to those he served, and to those who served him, ensured that all who had the privilege to know him came to regard him with admiration and affection.

He was held in the highest esteem by the Allied Navies of SEATO in the Far East and NATO in the Mediterranean. But his greatest contribution was in the Chiefs of Staffs Committee, for here among the most outstanding officers of the other Services he stood out by his statesmanlike outlook and mature wisdom. His early death robbed the Services and the country of one of the really great men of our time.

FOREWORD

by
Sir Steven Runciman

I T IS often difficult to remember when and where we first met
friends who were later to play a part in our lives. But I still
have a vivid picture of the autumn evening in 1922 when I
was sitting, a young, shy, and awkward undergraduate, in my
rooms in Trinity, and the door burst open and in came a red-
haired young man who announced that he was my cousin. We
were indeed related; and he was pleased with me because, when
he told me his mother's maiden name, I could explain the kinship.
His mother and mine were second cousins, both of them descended
from a Norwegian pirate who made good at the end of the sixteenth
century. Old Andersen, the pirate, lent his ship and his services
to the Earl Marischal of Scotland when members of the Scottish
Court were wrecked off the coast of Norway on their return from
the wedding of James VI with Anne of Denmark. The Earl, the
head of the great family of Keith, rewarded Andersen with lands
in Buchan. My eldest aunt, who had married one of her Andersen
cousins, maintained on the flimsiest evidence that as an additional
favour the pirate's son was granted the hand of the Earl's bastard
daughter—and my aunt therefore christened her sons Keith and
Marischal. I hope that the story was true. I would like to think
that Charles added to his ancestry, however illegitimately, the
blood of the Keiths and through them of the ancient Royal House
of Scotland.

From that moment I was under Charles's spell. It was, I think,
his voice that I noticed first. It was a remarkable voice, deep and
mellow; very expressive, sometimes caressing, sometimes stern, but
never harsh and never over-rich. It delighted me whenever I was
to meet him. He had already an aura that combined the friendliest
charm with a certain authority. He was a little older than most of
us undergraduates, and much more a man of the world. But he

never patronized us. Instead, he somehow made us feel ourselves
a little older and wiser and more gifted than we were. The adjective
'life-enhancing' has now become overworked and trite. But it
exactly describes him.

I moved in those days in the bright young intellectual circles of
Cambridge; and Charles was at once one of us, and probably the
most admired. He had time for his studies and for his riding and
heaven knows what else; but I think that what he enjoyed most at
Cambridge was the chance to join in all the musical and artistic
sides of its life. I used to go to the concerts with him; and he was
then, as always later, the best of companions on such occasions,
with his love and knowledge of music and his high musical standards. He played the piano to us and he painted for us. That
autumn the Cambridge Amateur Dramatic Club put on a version
of *The Rose and Ring*, starring Cecil Beaton as 'Angelica'. (I was also
in the cast.) There was a competition for designing the scenery,
and the A.D.C. judges could not decide between designs sent in by
Roger Hinks, the future art-historian, which were in the best Lovat
Fraser tradition, and designs sent in by Charles, which owed more
to Bakst. In the end there was a compromise. We played Act I in a
neo-Georgian setting of perfect good taste, and Act II against a
riot of splendid colour.

After two terms he went away, leaving all his Cambridge friends
a little desolate. After that I was never to see him again so continuously for more than thirty years—not until I went to stay
with him in Singapore in 1955. His life inevitably took him to
different and often distant places; and I only met him at intervals.
But he was an excellent letter-writer; and I enjoyed writing letters.
So we were continuously in touch, and when we met it was as if
there had been no break. The spell that he quite unconsciously
exercised was never broken.

I have often wondered wherein that magic lay. He was extraordinarily gifted. Other people can write better than I can on his
gifts as a musician or as a painter, or as a polo-player. His whole
life was proof of his distinction as a naval officer. Whatever he
touched he did well. He could design a garden on a wind-swept
Scottish hilltop so that it was efficiently as well as beautifully laid
out. He could give an air of comfort as well as of style to any house
in which he had to live—and in this his wife, Peta, perfectly com-
plemented him. Even the uncompromising halls of Admiralty
House, Singapore, became almost cosy; and though the purist
might have gasped to see big Chinese paper lanterns hanging from

the ceilings, they were wonderfully effective. When he decided to take up needlework the results were astounding. He worked out elaborate stitches that he remembered being used by aged relatives. His entries won prizes at exhibitions (though he used often to enter them in his wife's name, to avoid sexual discrimination).

When anyone is so widely talented one is apt either to dismiss him as necessarily superficial or to feel too envious to allow him his proper appreciation. There probably were people who were jealous of Charles, but no one could deny his gifts. His friends could not but be grateful for them, for somehow he made you share them with him. He used sometimes to persuade me to play piano-duets with him. I knew perfectly well that I played the piano execrably, but his enthusiasm, his encouragement and his patient advice combined to enable me to play on those occasions far less badly than I ever played elsewhere. His painting was, I think, largely influenced by the water-colours of Edward Lear. He knew that I collected and loved Lear's work, and because of that he almost made me feel that I had a share in his painting. Whenever he told you of his work or showed you the results, he managed to convince you, quite un-justifiably, that you had been able somehow to help him. Charm itself defies analysis; but Charles's charm was vastly magnified by this affectionate generosity of spirit with which he indulged his friends.

It would be easy, but it would be wrong, to picture Charles just as a flawless paragon of virtue and talents. He was far too human not to have had faults; however, he kept them out of sight. He could be angry, and there were things that he could not tolerate: though when sometimes I thought him wrong-headed about people or politics and would argue with him, it was nearly always he who took the more tolerant and humane point of view. I was not always convinced, but I emerged wiser from the arguments.

We all, I suppose, have a list of friends who are dead, whom we are grateful to Providence for having allowed us to know. My list is not the only one that has Charles at its head.

Chapter One

SWEET WINE OF YOUTH

TO ANY boy born in England at the beginning of this century, assuming he grew to become sea-minded and adventurously inclined, there were few more attractive ideas than that of becoming an officer in the Royal Navy. Not only was it the senior of the armed services, it was incomparably the largest navy in the world. Moreover, it was regarded as something of a triumph in itself to be accepted for Osborne, the preparatory school for the Britannia Royal Naval College, Dartmouth, where more specialist work began. If the Navy was royal, so was Osborne, for this was the house where Queen Victoria lived and died. Part of it was converted, in the reign of her son and successor, to serve more mundane purposes than the private residence of a sovereign, but it retained a privileged atmosphere.

It was to Osborne, in September 1914, a few weeks after the outbreak of the First World War, that Charles Edward Lambe went, and from then until the end of his life he worked in an environment in which purpose was of the essence, that purpose being the defence of Great Britain and her interests overseas. In those distant days huge areas of the globe were coloured red on the maps, for this was the heyday of the country's influence. Although the period is like yesterday when seen against the background of history, it may seem almost as distant to the young of the present day as the pomp of Louis XIV. Yet the palace at Versailles is evidence enough that the King's glories were transcendent, while the imposing proportions of Dartmouth, one of the realized dreams of Lord Fisher, is proof that when Sir Aston Webb designed the building, he conceived it on a scale befitting the leading Navy.

Charles Edward Lambe was born on 20 December 1900 at Grove House, Stalbridge, which lies between Sherborne and Shaftesbury in the county of Dorset. His family were professional:

I

his father was a lawyer, his paternal grandfather a parson, and he had an interesting link, further back, with one of the more picturesque figures of the sailing Navy. This was Rear-Admiral Sir Thomas Louis, one of Nelson's 'band of brothers' who in 1798 won the Battle of the Nile. There was also a connection with the Mudge family, who had been close to the Johnson—Reynolds circle, and who in the eighteenth and early nineteenth centuries produced a famous succession of horologists and surveyors.

Charles was the only son of Henry Edward Lambe by a second marriage. He had one sister, Elizabeth ('Betty'), who survives him, and two much older half-sisters, Dorothea and Marjorie. Henry Lambe's first wife was killed in a riding accident. One day, in 1891, while hacking in Lord Bathurst's park near Cirencester, her horse shied at a steam-roller. She was heavily thrown, and fatally injured. Eight years later, Henry Lambe married Lilian Bramwell. She was one of the eleven children of John Byrom Bramwell, whose family has given so many eminent members to the medical profession. One of them married a sister of Admiral of the Fleet Lord Cunningham of Hyndhope, under whose command Charles was one day to serve.

Lilian Bramwell was musical and artistic; she was also long-lived, for she survived until almost the end of the Second World War. Henry Lambe, her husband, had extraordinary vitality and zest for life. 'He must have been the complete Edwardian "sportsman"', wrote his son in some notes he put together for his children, 'with absolutely no intellectual or artistic ability of any kind.' It is told of him that one day in the cubbing season, hounds met at 5 a.m. at Eggesford in Devon. Henry Lambe killed a cub, the hunt ending almost in a railway yard. He then caught the first train to Exeter where he breakfasted before going on to Torquay, where he had sent the launch of his steam yacht *Corinna* and also his racing yacht. He sailed the yacht round to Dartmouth, keeping the launch in attendance in case the event for which he had entered took too long for him to carry out the next part of his plan. There was, however, a fair wind, and having won his sailing race he boarded the launch, had a hasty lunch, and then steamed up the Dart to Totnes. There he won a steeplechase and came second in another.

After half a century of adventurous living, Henry Lambe was killed in a polo accident at Ottery St. Mary, when his children were still young. Seven years later, when Charles was at Osborne, his mother married a cousin of her first husband, Charles Laverock Lambe. He was then in the Navy, and had been one of the pioneers of naval flying. C. L. Lambe was Charles Edward's godfather as well as being his stepfather and cousin. He transferred to the Royal Air Force when it was formed, towards the end of the First World War, later becoming an Air Vice-Marshal and receiving a knighthood. He survived his wife by nine years, and lived to see the younger Charles a Vice-Admiral, and a K.C.B. like himself. His marriage led to what appears to be an oddity in reference books, where Charles Edward and his sister are recorded as being the children of 'the late H. E. Lambe and Lady Lambe'. Although this states what is a fact, that fact is itself unusual.

Charles Edward's paternal grandfather who was, originally, a clergyman, married, in 1856, Clementina Augusta Louis, the daughter of Captain C. B. Louis, Royal Navy. Captain Louis was the youngest son of Admiral Sir Thomas Louis, Baronet, who commanded the *Minotaur* in Nelson's victory over Brueys. It has long been understood that the admiral's father was an illegitimate son of Louis XIV of France: certainly he drew a life pension from the French royal family. The Lambe family were proud of this French descent. The future Admiral Lambe commemorated the fact later by calling his daughter Louisa while his son's second name is Louis.

Having the means to do so, George Lambe gave up pastoral work later in life, and set himself up as a country squire in a large house near Ivybridge in Devon. His father, Henry Lambe, generally known as Harry, married Elizabeth Symonds, who came of a family best remembered for having built the Falmouth packets, those fast-sailing brigs employed in the postal service that were designed to evade the French privateers which swarmed in Channel waters during the wars of the eighteenth century. Henry Lambe was a lawyer by profession, and practised in Truro. It is said that he bought a tract of land near St. Austell, intending to build on it. The discovery of the presence of china clay on his property caused him to abandon his original intention, and laid the foundations of the family fortune.

II

At the age of seventeen, Charles became a midshipman. Three weeks later, in September 1917, he was sent to the battleship *Emperor of India*, which was with the Grand Fleet, based on Scapa, and at that time commanded by Sir David Beatty. His ship was an important unit in the most powerful naval concentration which Great Britain ever assembled. She was then three years old, her sisters being the *Iron Duke*, which had been Sir John Jellicoe's flagship at Jutland the year before Lambe joined, the *Marlborough*, and the *Benbow*, in which Lambe was later to serve as a lieutenant.

The *Emperor of India* was large, powerful, cost a mint of money and never fired her guns in action, for she had been refitting at the time of Jutland, which was the only occasion when the Grand Fleet met the enemy. Beatty's force was a necessary bulwark, so long as the Germans possessed a surface navy, but by the time Charles was trained for sea, they were engaged in a campaign of unrestricted submarine warfare, which had already come so near to success as to cause the gravest concern in political as well as in naval circles.

Few officers of the *Emperor of India*, judges though they may have been of human qualities or promise, could have realized what an exceptional young man had joined the battleship. Charles was then of medium height; he was wiry, red-headed, hazel-eyed and freckled. Somewhat later, when he had finished growing, he nearly reached six foot. He was reasonably assured without being over-confident, and already had most of the attributes which he would in time develop as far as he could carry them. He had an aptitude for languages, encouraged when a child by the importation of a French governess, and this was never allowed to rust; he was a musician of promise, taste, and zest—always an asset in a ship's company; he was a reader; and he could draw. His fondness for music was very notable. He had a toy piano from the age of two, and had been taught to play by a Miss Urry from Stalbridge. He had an excellent voice as well, and sang solos both at Osborne and at Dartmouth.

Charles was insatiably curious about life in general; and he was so adventurous minded that he was already considering what possibilities there were of extending his activities from sea to sky: in fact within six months he had got himself attached briefly to a naval air station for a short course in 'free ballooning'. He had so quick a brain that even technical knowledge seemed to come easily to him, and it was not many years before he wrote in his diary:

Maeterlinck's philosophy leads me to believe that the only thing that matters in this world, are one's own relations to man. It is only a short step to go so far as to say that Heaven is the state of dying happy and contented with one's life, with the self-assurance gained by the knowledge that one has made full use of one's talents or powers. Hell is to die with the knowledge that one has wasted one's life, that one has failed, through lack of guts, to grasp that one huge opportunity that offered.

Charles's life and career is a commentary on that entry. With such varied capacity, and born to what are known as 'easy circumstances', it would have been tempting for him to flit and fritter. He continued many-sided, but he gave the best of his energy to his profession, which he took with the sense of responsibility that the naval life requires.

Charles had indeed shown responsibility very young. While still at the school at Horris Hill, near Newbury, to which he went before Osborne, he wrote to his mother, in answer to an inquiry as to whether he would like to try for the Navy, in the following terms —and he was at that time only twelve years old:

It is such a terribly awkward question for me to answer, since a good deal depends upon it. There is no doubt I should love to go into the Navy and yet I feel I ought not to leave you and Betty. Because very likely I should have to leave England to be abroad for a few years at a time. And then of course if I go to Harrow and Cambridge [as his father had done] I shall at any rate be able to look after you and Betty. But all the same the prospect of sitting in an office learning law *does* not attract me.

Again I am very fond of the sea. On the whole I should prefer to go into the Navy if it was not for that one reason. . . . Some of the pictures one sees as advertisements for the Navy simply make my mouth water. The other day I saw one of the workshops at Osborne which looked *so* attractive. And I should love to go to Osborne. Of course you must decide yourself whether you'd mind me going away, because if you did all the world would not make me go.

There spoke an only son to a fond mother. It was a relationship of affection, trust, and understanding which remained unshaken until his mother's death. Even after she remarried, she still remained Charles's most particular concern. On her side, Mrs. Lambe, though devotedly attached, was inclined, as was natural enough, to be over-anxious, but she never stood in the way of what her son really wanted, and as he always seemed to take the right course, she was fortunate.

Life on board the *Emperor of India* with the Grand Fleet actually offered less excitement in the way of enemy activity than was then being felt by his mother, who for a time lived at Dover and experienced a good deal of bombing, which, during the First World War, caused more alarm and casualties among civilians than is generally realized. Charles had occasional leaves in Edinburgh, and found plenty of opportunity for music—he was 'getting quite good' at Chopin waltzes and 'revelled' in the Wagner operas. He was also sketching and painting. He had met James Paterson, a member of the Scottish Academy, who gave him the freedom of his studio. One of his own earliest ventures in oils was a large copy of Romney's version of Lady Hamilton as a Bacchante.

Once King George V came on a visit to his Fleet, and Charles's sharp eyes noted his Sovereign closely. 'Of course he brought bad weather with him, as I am told he always does,' he wrote to his mother. 'Consequently we had to stand for hours in pouring rain waiting for him to inspect us. He *is* a queer looking man,' he added. 'Rather delicate with very light blue eyes—weak eyes—and extremely red lips, and a grating voice.' The King had, in fact, a resonant naval voice, much admired when, years later, Charles heard his Christmas broadcasts.

Charles did not escape the troubles apt to beset a midshipman's life. On 13 April 1918—an appropriate day—he was in charge of a picket-boat which rammed a pontoon landing-stage, and as a result he had a fortnight's leave stopped, and six of the best: but as there was a piano at hand, good company, and plenty of books, including Compton Mackenzie's *Sinister Street*, this did not unduly worry him.

Three months later, in July, he was sent to the *Voyager* for a month's destroyer course, which he found 'ripping', a contrast to the very different life of a battleship. The *Voyager* was new, fast, and had lively young officers. She was of a type built in large numbers towards the end of the war, incorporating its lessons. They were so successful that many had a long life, some surviving the ardours of a later conflict.

> We have got such a nice lot of officers, [he told his mother] they are a cheery lot but not the usual type of destroyer officer who is as a rule an absolute rotter, rowdy and vulgar. I sleep in the captain's sea cabin which is a minute place with a bunk and nothing else in it. There is no room.

In later years Charles would have been amused to re-read his earlier thoughts about 'destroyer officers', for it was not long before he became one himself.

He returned to the *Emperor of India* in time for the Armistice celebrations on 11 November, the destroyers all blowing their sirens together, and sending up rockets, searchlights swivelling about the sky, the battleships following suit, the noise all so ear-splitting that Charles had to go below, deafened. Within a few days he was composing a song, 'words by William Morris'. This, though he feared it might have been an 'unconscious crib', he was assured by a friend whose opinion he valued, was 'the real Charles Lambe'.

On 22 November 1918 censorship was removed, and he was able to give his mother an account of the surrender of the German Fleet, fifty miles off the Firth of Forth: first a light cruiser, 'a cocky little brute', then battle-cruisers, battleships, light cruisers, and des-troyers. 'I have *never* seen such a sight,' he wrote. 'They are *damned* fine ships though.' Next evening, on watch, he heard someone playing a cornet on board the battle-cruiser *Von Der Tann*. 'He played several tunes—the only one I recognized was "The Last Rose of Summer".' This was an odd note on which to end a crowning episode in what had been the most shattering war known to Western man.

III

The Armistice of the Allied Powers with Germany did not signify the end of active service for Mr. Midshipman Lambe: if anything, it intensified it, for he was sent to the Baltic in H.M.S. *Wryneck*, another newly built destroyer. Politics had scarcely begun to con-cern him, but his ship belonged to a force under the command of Admiral Sir Walter Cowan, which was to play a significant part in Baltic history. For the Bolshevist Revolution of 1917 had, as one of its more immediate effects, fragmented outlying parts of the former Russian Empire. By the summer of 1919, when the *Wryneck* was in Baltic waters, Finland had broken free, and three small states, Estonia, Latvia, and Lithuania, were in the throes of self-liberation. In the countries concerned, Nationalist forces were being opposed by roving Bolshevist armies, by German divisions under Count Rüdiger von der Goltz, who liked to describe himself as 'the last of the Generals', and by partisans of the Baltic Barons, those great landowning families who had enjoyed extraordinary powers and favours under the Tsars.

Cowan's orders were less precise than he could have wished, but in one way at least they were clear. 'Self-determination' was a slogan of the time, and Cowan was to allow no interference, on the part of the Bolshevist Navy based on Kronstadt, with the Nationalist forces of the nascent Baltic States. Intervention was not possible or desirable ashore, for Cowan had no troops, but he was eager to discourage, so far as he was able, any attempt on the part of von der Goltz to help the party of the Baltic Barons, which from time immemorial had been Teuton in sympathy.

Cowan succeeded brilliantly, and as a result became the first and only 'baronet of the Baltic', a title he chose himself. The three States duly became established, after a good deal of fighting, mainly on land. Although their independence lasted only until the onset of the Second World War, yet for twenty years it was as real as it was precious and it was primarily due to command of the sea exercised in the area by the Royal Navy.

Merely to reach Baltic waters involved the *Wryneck* in danger, for the seas were mine-strewn, and Cowan's losses were serious, mines being far more lethal than Russians. On 20 May 1919, from 'off the North German coast', which in a sketch-map Charles interpreted as being near Königsberg, he wrote to his mother that a day or so earlier he had

> had the first watch (8–12 p.m.) and we sighted floating mines, some of which we sank [by rifle fire] others we had to leave. It got dark about 10 p.m.—glassy colour. At half-past eleven one of the look-outs reported an object right ahead. We looked—saw a mine going under the bows!—altered course at once but we could not have made any difference as we were already on top of it. The mine must have scraped along the side—but it didn't go off.

When his stepfather read Charles's letter, he would have realized that Charles had had one of the narrowest escapes of his life.

By 23 May the ship was at Libau, a Latvian port where the people, half-starved as they then were, eagerly exchanged their amber and furs for ship's rations, soap, and cigarettes. Charles traded, as did most of his shipmates, and did so well for himself that he urged his mother to send him more supplies: he had already got a charming amber necklace for his sister Betty.

On 31 May, the third anniversary of the battle of Jutland, he had his first taste of action. It was with units of the Bolshevist Fleet. The ship was then at an island off Reval, well within the Gulf of Finland, ready to act against the Russians, who were thought to be trying to land men behind the Estonian Nationalist lines. Charles wrote:

Produced and bottled in Germany
abgefüllt in Bernkastel für:

ARTHUR HALLGARTEN GmbH

GEISENHEIM (RHEINGAU)

Niersteiner
Gutes Domtal

Qualitätswein — Rheinhessen

Amtliche Prüfungsnummer 4 907 243 111 80

"DOMGARTEN® — BRAND"

Shipped by
Hallgarten Domgarten Brand Company

. . . we suddenly got a signal to weigh instantly and everybody went to action stations—mine is on the bridge. When I got up on the bridge we were weighing our anchor and on looking round we saw that the destroyer which was on patrol—the *Walker*—was in action firing away like anything.

It was rather a misty day so at first we could not see the enemy but we all steamed out at full speed to her assistance. Shortly after getting under weigh there were two big splashes about 400 yards away from us and on looking up I saw an aeroplane trying to bomb us! Some destroyer fired a few rounds with her high angle anti-aircraft gun and it soon went away.

Meanwhile the *Walker* was blazing away ahead of us and by now we could see the enemy on the horizon. There was one battleship, one cruiser, one destroyer and a trawler and they were all running away like Hell! ! Unfortunately we could not chase them as they were the other side of the mine-fields.

The *Walker* had splashes all round her but she was only touched by a couple of bits of shrapnel which did no damage. Soon the Bolshies disappeared and the *Walker*, who had gone well to the eastward into their minefield, returned. Luckily she did not strike a mine.

The Bolshevists didn't fire at us at all as we were out of range to them—all except the battleship and she was busy dealing with the *Walker*.

I was intensely interested and more to my surprise than anyone else's I wasn't even nervous when the two splashes from the bombs dropped, though we thought for a minute or two that it was their shore batteries of 12-inch guns opening fire at us. I was far too interested to be nervous, I was merely disappointed.

The *Wryneck* had already put in at Helsinki, then generally known by its Swedish name of Helsingfors, to which she would return, Charles by that time equipped with a Rob-Roy canoe which he acquired at Reval. Cowan was negotiating with the Regent of Finland—the great Gustaf Mannerheim—for the use of Finnish bases by the British squadron, facilities which were gladly given.

Charles was impressed by Helsinki, which is indeed a fine place, especially when approached from the sea.

It is a most wonderful town, [he wrote home] quite the finest I have ever seen. The streets are very wide with trees down each side and trams and magnificent buildings all along it. There are apparently no slums and all the streets are very fine. . . . Prices were high, and no bargaining to be done! However, I got some books which can't be got in England and I was very pleased with myself.

In his first brief visit, Charles had discovered some essential Finnish characteristics: civic pride; love of architecture; high standard of living; above all, literacy, which extended a welcome to books in most languages.

He soon heard of a report, circulating in England that the *Wryneck* had struck a mine and sunk—as indeed she nearly had.

Some people say they saw it in the papers [so he told his mother]. It just shows *never* believe the papers . . . never believe anything until you get a letter from the Admiralty. Not that we are likely to be sunk, but this is just to warn you *never* to believe the papers in a case like that.

On 8 June, once again from Reval, where he had bought a German camera for £5 which was 'a wonder of workmanship', Charles reported:

A rather amusing incident took place this week. Our C. in C. out here made a signal to the Bolshevists saying that if any of them wished to surrender, their lives would be spared! The next day the Bolshevists replied by wireless something like this:
'Seamen-brethren, why are you in our waters? We suppose you are here to fight us but if I were you I should go home. Why fight when we have done you no wrong?
    Still, if you do want a fight we are quite prepared to give you a pretty stiff one.'
That was the general tone of the signal!! Rather sporting of them. They have far more 'go' in them than the Huns had.

Charles was thinking of the German big-ship navy in the later stages of the European war: the Bolshevists were thinking of their fellow-seamen in units like the *Wryneck*, not of potentates like Admiral Sir Walter Cowan. They themselves had got rid of their officers, often in murderous fashion; they hoped that the British would do the same—and then go home.

It was at Helsinki that Charles had an adventure in traditional midshipman style, best described in his own words.

We had such fun the other night, [he wrote on 26 June] when we were at Helsingfors, over the Hun consul there. He had a house on a rock close to where we were lying at anchor, and just opposite the British general's H.Q., and he had a habit of hoisting the German flag when the British one was hoisted, which considerably annoyed the British people.

Well, this Hun had hoisted his flag last Saturday and I had a brain wave and by hook or crook I was determined to stop it somehow. So last Saturday night I enlisted Dymott as second in command and he and I made an expedition ashore shortly after midnight. We went in one of our small canoes and crept inshore disguised in mufti and slouch hats!

We made the canoe fast and breathlessly climbed up through the woods—pine-woods which come right down to the water's edge—up on to the top of the rock where his flagstaff was, beside a little summerhouse. To our joy we found that his halyards—the rope that you hoist the flag with—were only hemp and not wire and so we speedily hauled them down and took them away, so that the fat Hun consul will have to climb up the flagstaff with a new rope and put it through the pulley at the top if he wants to hoist his ensign again. . . . The ensign itself was unfortunately locked up in the summerhouse, and to break the glass we thought would make too much noise, though it would have been a fine prize.

However, content with the halyards, I stuffed them inside my coat and we made off down back to the canoe. At that moment we heard the splash of oars in water and voices. So down we dropped and hid. Two women and two men, Germans, all came ashore in their boat and walked past us, about 10 yards away and went up and sat down on the rock under which our canoe was lying. They *must* have seen our canoe we thought and we didn't know what to do. It was now about 20 past midnight and these people shewed no signs of going to bed. One went up to the house and brought down a bottle and we lay about 30 yards off watching them, hardly daring to breathe and being terribly bitten by mosquitoes! We prayed for rain and at last it came but they only got up and came and sheltered under the trees among which we were hiding, about 15 yards away at most.

At last the rain stopped and up they went again and sat down on the rock laughing and talking and love-making. Now the nights are very short, the darkest part being about 11.30 p.m. and then it is really only twilight. So to our horror we realized about 1 o'clock, as we still waited for these people to go, that it was rapidly getting light! We waited another ½ hour & it was pretty nearly broad daylight. This made us desperate. So in full view of them—if they had turned round—we dashed round behind them, crawling, running & lying still alternately, & eventually we managed to get in sight of the canoe underneath the rock on which they were sitting. Then we didn't know what to do because we thought they were watching the canoe. . . . However at half past two we grew desperate & choosing a moment when their voices were more or less silent we walked quickly down to the canoe, jumped in, and paddled away as quietly as possible. On looking back, for we expected shouting and were surprised nobody shouted, we saw they were all lying down at full length in couples kissing and making love. So we got away without them even seeing us after 2½ hours ashore. . . . Unfortunately we left early in the morning so we couldn't watch through telescopes & enjoy the sight of the Huns' displeasure.

On 7 July Charles reported, in his last letter from the Baltic, that the *Wryneck* had spent two successive afternoons 'bombarding the coast where the Bolshevists are fighting the Estonians'. He did not think it had much effect, and he was surely right.

We managed to knock down a lot of pine trees and set them and also one wooden house on fire. The houses we were firing at were the Bolshevik billets or headquarters or something. We fired 50 shells both days, moving off when their fort woke up and dropped a couple of fat 11″ projectiles within about a mile. But really we were out of range of them except for ricochets. . . . They were only random shots because they couldn't have seen us as their kite balloon was not up. . . . I suppose the only effect it had was on their morale as we couldn't possibly have killed anyone.

He wrote from Bjorko, on the Finnish side of the Gulf, reporting the weather as 'boiling unbearably hot. The temperature of the sea—which is fresh water—is 65° and inshore by the sandy beaches it is as hot as toast'.

Away across the North Sea, the 'Huns' had scuttled their ships at Scapa. 'Unfortunately,' Charles commented, 'they will not have spoilt Scapa Flow as a harbour. We all hoped they would have blocked it sufficiently to have prevented us ever going there again! It really is extraordinary they didn't do it before.'

IV

Charles's next appointment was to H.M.S. *King George V*, a battle-ship with the Home Fleet. She was slightly older than the *Emperor of India*, and he found her gunroom 'horribly rowdy', though 'they are all good fellows I think'. The Navy was being reduced, and there were rumours that the ship would, by the autumn, have only a nucleus crew, which meant that his own future movements might be highly uncertain. Meanwhile, he was hoping to get some hunting from Weymouth—he had ridden since childhood, and enjoyed it. 'I think I shall wear my tweed coat and cap and an ordinary collar,' he confided, 'as I don't think I have a stock and in any case I've not the least idea how to tie it!'

He was soon engaged in serious and even crucial discussion with his mother who, intelligent reader as she was, had come across a book with an odd history. This was *The Gunroom*, by Charles Morgan. It had just been published, the author being then at Oxford. The story had been written three times, one version having been lost when Morgan's ship was sunk under him as he was returning to England on parole from Holland, where he had been interned after the Antwerp expedition of 1914.

It was a story which included gunroom bullying of the most brutal kind, and it derived from Morgan's own experiences in the pre-war Navy. It would have upset any mother with a son consider-ing a career at sea and it was a book which was so disapproved of by senior naval officers that they were reported to buy up all copies seen in bookshops, in order to destroy them. Charles soon saw the reason for his mother's alarms. It gave him the opportunity not only to allay them, but to express his current ideas about his profession. Referring to the book, he said:

> . . . it was written of before the war, and whatever the conditions were then, these circumstances are exceptional now. I have never come across anything like that. Of course one had to do the usual fagging and we had to keep the gunroom cleaned and polish the brasswork, but that does not hurt anyone. However, those conditions are not impossible. I believe that there is nothing in that book that is untrue, though all the worst cases are made out to be general ones. . . .

The war I think has done away with a vast amount of bullying, but nothing will ever do away with the Naval Officer's contempt of art. It is not required in his profession in fact it is a sign of individuality, of something out of the ordinary and so has to be squashed. All Naval Officers have to be stamped to a type, & there is no room or occasion for individuality. In fact if one is to get on high in the Service one has to squash all outside interests & one must do away with dreams, and it is terribly hard for anyone who loves art honestly as I do.

However once one gets a stripe and a cabin things change considerably, & the higher one gets the more pleasant is one's existence. But however high you get you are never your own master.

He ended reassuringly—and, as it happened, prophetically: 'Darling, do remember that I am not dissatisfied with my life at present. I have all in front of me.'

There were schemes being bruited, about this time, for junior officers of the Navy to transfer to the Royal Air Force, either for a number of years or permanently, and Charles gave much thought to the subject. He was attracted to flying, would shortly qualify as a free-balloon pilot, and a few years later possess his own light aircraft, but as he was aware of his mother's fears on account of his safety, he proceeded gently with his investigations, relying much on the advice of his stepfather, who now had had experience of both Services, and was in a good position to advise him. In the end, he decided to do nothing, and in a long undated letter from Invergordon, written late in 1919, he unburdened himself at length and to some purpose.

I am going to tell you all I feel [he wrote]. Firstly you mustn't think . . . that I am dissatisfied with my life. It is only because I entered the Navy with exactly the same enthusiasm as I would have become an engine driver, and, now I can think for myself, I wonder if I am in that profession in which I can do the best work for the world, and to which I am best suited.

Everyone is subject to dreams of their future when they are young and I dream of doing something to make men happier. I want to help in the fight between Beauty (and happiness) and Commercialism. The whole world is rushing blindly towards the wrong goal—money. It is all wrong, because money does not mean happiness. The ideal of course is that a man should take pleasure in his handicraft—that he should at any rate know what the word 'Beauty' means. But as long as he takes a pleasure in his craft he will be happy. It was done in days gone by and I am sure it could be done today.

And—of course—the first step is to revolutionize all the schools. Education should be the first thing that should be made a pleasure. Every child has the sense of Beauty, of Song, of his own strength, of the beauty of the world, and a thousand other senses born into it, and these should be developed instead of crushed.

It all sounds very socialistic and impossible but whether it is or not, if the world is going to be a happier place in the future than it is now it has got to be revolutionized on these lines.

And if there is one thing I simply cannot do it is to order a man about like a dog, simply because he has the misfortune to have been born lower than some one else—oneself. He is probably as fine a person as any of us but he has not had the chance to show it. All the finer side of his character has been crushed by the crowd following Commercialism. I hate the thought. So I always *ask* one of my juniors to do something, whether it is for me or for the Service.

I don't know whether this shows to you what my ideals are. I hope so. You will probably say it is all a mad dream, but nevertheless it is my ideal. I want to do something to help the rest of mankind to see that the road they are following at present is wrong and to try and show them the right road.

And so I wonder if the Navy affords me all the possibilities of working towards my ideal that other professions would? The average naval officer after he gets his second stripe settles down into a groove and stays there for the rest of his life. One in 100 are brilliant at their profession, but they are all stamped exactly the same. They are charming to meet, but utterly uninteresting. They cannot talk of any subject but of their profession or their hobby. They are splendid at a social dinner party but they are all the same. They are in the groove and they never get out. . . .

Personally I think the 'groove' terrifies me. I know I have got a certain amount of individuality and it is my refuge, and I guard it jealously and hate to think it will be stamped out of me as it inevitably will. . . . Then comes the question of what to do if one left.

My first objective would be a University. In fact I have a sort of feeling that it is the thought of going to a University that makes me write all this. I should be absolutely in my element. I have heard such wonderful tales of Oxford and Cambridge. But after that—I don't know. And in the meanwhile I am happy and contented in the Service. I should always enjoy myself. But I do want to do something worth doing.

There is very little chance of another war in my time and one feels that all one does will bear fruit in another's time. I want to do something big. I suppose all young people dream that they are going to make a name for themselves, and that is the cause of this letter.

The New Year, 1920, began with a test of Charles's fitness as well as his attachment to the Navy, for he was sent on a course to Whale Island, the Gunnery School, known for its spit-and-polish, strenuousness and iron discipline.

We leave the ship at 8.30. every morning, [he wrote] and from 9 till 12 we drill with only ten minutes stand easy. We then double down to the pier, wait for the boat which is always late & come on board for lunch for which we get 20 minutes. We then drill from 1 p.m. till 3.30. The afternoon drill consists of loading dummy guns (6 inch, with shells weighing 100 lbs.) so you feel pretty tired at the end.

One of the results of the course was that in the summer, when he was an acting sub-lieutenant serving in the destroyer *Torbay*, where he had what he described as comfortable quarters, he was 'detailed off as gunnery officer' and hoped he would be able to hit the target in future practices at sea.

Later still he was appointed to the minesweeper *Leamington* and sent to Ireland, which was then in the throes of the Civil War which eventually gave the country her independence. This was an interim appointment before Charles was posted to the cruiser *Raleigh*, which was completing. He was based on Queenstown, to which prisoners of the Irish Republican Army were sent before being taken by sea to Belfast. Queenstown was, so he found, a live enough place, often with fires smouldering from burning buildings.

Large lorry-loads of soldiers in steel helmets and with loaded rifles patrol the town at a tremendous speed [he told his mother]. Armoured cars follow them. Just to show you the state of affairs, a lorry-load of soldiers was careering round the town the other day and one man dropped his rifle. Before they could stop and pick it up a Sinn Feiner had snatched it and run off with it.

All the shops have bullet holes in the windows. The Finnigans (Sinn Feiners) are very short of arms and are, I think, on their last legs! In Cork one sees swarms of unshaven bareheaded monks walking round and all the passers by bow down low before them and doff their caps. It requires quite a lot of courage not to do the same!

I had to take charge of a harbour launch the other night to take General Strickland, who is commanding the troops there, to Cork. . . . He was shot at by six men with revolvers only about six weeks ago. They all missed him! We had a peaceful trip.

Queenstown itself is absolutely safe as long as you don't go for a walk in the country and run up against a battalion of the Irish Republican Army drilling in secret.

On 14 December 1920, from 'off the North Coast of Ireland', Charles wrote to his mother to describe a typical mission such as was undertaken by the *Leamington*.

We left Queenstown on Saturday and sailed for Galway. We arrived there Sunday morning and anchored in the roads out- side the harbour. Last night at about four o'clock we went alongside one of the quays and after a few minutes a large armoured car and two motor lorries drove up alongside the ship. Thirty Sinn Fein prisoners and an armed military guard embarked, and we are now on our way to Belfast, where we shall arrive about midnight tonight . . .

The prisoners are a most blackguardly looking crowd. One of them looks like a second Rasputin, very long black beard and horrid sly expression on his face. They are all fairly young. I suppose their ages range from about eighteen to thirty five. . . . They came on board with all their gear and we bundled them down into one of the store-rooms aft and took away the ladder. Two military sentries are on guard all the time at the top of the hatch, and so they haven't much chance of creating any trouble. Some of them began playing with the shafting to the steering- engine last night but I think that was through ignorance, as they were warned not to touch it afterwards and it hasn't occurred again. We shall probably spend tomorrow night in Belfast after coaling and landing these prisoners and then we return to Galway for another lot and so on until further orders. . . .

This is a wonderful coast round here. . . . Great big reddish coloured headlands and very bleak bare country. Yet the extraordinary part is that there are numbers of lonely little cottages all along the coast. It must be very lonely living here I should think, but a delightful place to come to in the summer. . . .

On 29 December Charles was at Smerwick Bay, County Kerry, and expecting to be ordered back to England. The ship had been supplying coal to coastguard stations, a change from transporting prisoners. He had had some sport with the 12th Lancers at Galway, where the regiment was then stationed, getting duck, snipe, and woodcock by shooting from boats.

His service with the minesweeper ended with a compliment from her captain, the incident being described as follows:

We were at anchor in a hell of a gale off Galway and I was keeping watch on the bridge during the night in case we should drag our anchors. Well we did drag, and so I worked the engines and succeeded in keeping her off the rocks while the skipper came up.

Afterwards in the mess he said: 'You did damned well this morning, sub. Put that in your pipe and smoke it!'

V

In January 1921, Charles was confirmed in the rank of sub-lieutenant and assigned to a job after his own heart. He was to be in charge of the gunroom of H.M.S. *Raleigh*. The ship was to fly the flag of Admiral Sir William Pakenham, Commander-in-Chief in North American and West Indian waters. Charles was to serve under a succession of celebrated admirals, but few were better known than Pakenham, who had fought with great distinction with the battle-cruiser force at Jutland.

Admiral Pakenham was known for his wit, and when, a few months later, Charles was his guest at dinner, he found that the popular notion was correct. 'A most amusing man,' he told his mother. 'Frightfully courteous with an exceedingly clever face. I believe he regards life as one leg-haul after another! He is however very pig-headed at times, and will not go to places at the best time of year; but some of his remarks and witticisms and his very pompous and yet courteous manner make up for it in amusement on board.'

1. *Charles Lambe as a sub-lieutenant*

2

3

4

2. *With his future wife, at Versaille[s]*

3. *With Kenneth Cohen, July 1931*

4. *On the polo field, in dark shirt*

The ship was a long time getting ready to sail, but in the summer she did so, and on 11 August Charles had his first sight of Bermuda 'after a wonderful trip across the Atlantic, the weather splendid and I have never seen anything like the colour and clearness of the water, the most intense blue I have ever seen.' He had resumed painting in oil, and had already tried a self-portrait.

The snotties, [so he told his mother] are simply a first-rate crowd and I am getting to like them all so much already. They are absolutely no trouble to me at all, as they are all so willing and keen about everything.

I am absolutely in my element here. I have never had such an interesting job as sub of the mess, and I simply love every minute of it. We have a very large amount of talent of every description. . . . There are two twin brothers who are absolutely indistinguishable at first sight, though I am beginning to know them apart at last, both very keen musicians, also a cellist and a flautist, not to speak of pianists. There is a fellow who draws *most* beautifully & also is very well read in Heraldry. . . . They are all frightfully good at games too—in fact they are altogether very exceptional and I am vastly proud of them.

Charles had one of his rare physical set-backs at Bermuda, a septic throat, due to change of climate, but it did not last. What annoyed him much more was the fact that the Admiral and his Staff took up their quarters on board at the end of August, and as a result he was obliged to give up his cabin, this, he said, 'in order that some bloated Paymaster . . . may have somewhere to lay his oily head'. His comments on the Staff were uncomplimentary.

The bitter part is, [he wrote about the Admiral's retinue] that his huge Staff are totally unnecessary. He has—for instance—brought a Fleet Wireless Officer who has nothing to do, as the Flag Lieutenant is a wireless expert as well. Altogether I've been feeling rather bolshie this last week. . . . I suppose it will all boil down but I was so looking forward to having somewhere to keep all my books and music and wherein to paint occasionally.

There is far too much talent in this ship. The officers tumble over one another and tread on each others toes, all because they dare not yet efface themselves from the scene of action whether it has anything to do with them or not. . . . The Captain has been suffering from gout too, which made it rather worse, as he has been chewing up the Officer of the Watch over the most trivial things. . . . Not that the officers aren't charming, but they are so conscientious and zealous that it becomes a farce and a pain to listen to the 'shop' they talk.

Once away from Bermuda, grievances were forgotten amid new scenes, new society, interests of every kind. First there was Canada, with golf and shooting included; then a brief return to Bermuda for a series of sailing races, the most important of which Charles won, in a whaler, much to the captain's pleasure and that of the petty-officer crew; then a passage through the Panama Canal and up to Vancouver.

It was in the Pacific that Charles came of age, 'and I'm glad to relate', he told his mother, 'that I don't feel any different!' That might be so, but he had now succeeded to a valuable family property which included the china-clay works, which were a staple source of revenue. His letters home almost invariably included decisions and suggestions as to how affairs should be administered, as indeed they had done for some years past.

> I *do* realize [he had written to his mother a little earlier] how extraordinarily lucky I am in every possible way, and I honestly think it is largely due to you. How you managed to bring up Bet and I as you did I don't know . . . and I am very proud of you, my darling.

His circumstances were such that, had he so wished, he could have idled for the rest of his life. As it was, immediate matters absorbed him.

His midshipmen were proving as good as he had hoped, but there was one set-back.

> I had to nerve myself to chastise one of the snotties the other day, [he wrote]. I had no idea it would cost me so much. I thought that provided I *knew* he deserved it I could do it without much of an effort but I went through a horrible few hours driving myself to do it, & trying to find some excuses for letting him off. The result was that I gave him a pretty good licking and ended by breaking his stick!
> The moment it was over the air felt a thousand times lighter and it has done him a world of good but I hope to goodness I don't have to do it often. I feel now that I should have done it

before while they were fresh to the ship. I think I was too lenient to begin with. However it has had a marvellous effect and I don't think the fellow hates me for it.

People who can get pleasure out of beating someone must be abnormal. I was very nearly sick at the thought of having to do it, and so would anyone be who had any decency. Up to recently I have always thought that when I was beaten and told it gave the other fellow as much pain as it gave me, that he was lying out of sheer bravado. But now I know it is true.

In January 1922, Charles was with his ship at San Francisco, where there was more polo, and where the great Pavlova was on a visit. 'Saw her do *Le Cygne*,' he commented, 'and very beautiful too.' The following month gave him the chance of a glimpse of Hollywood, the highlight of which was a meeting with Charlie Chaplin, who later attended an 'At Home' on board the *Raleigh*, and actually sang in the gunroom, delighting the young gentlemen with his fun. Charles himself actually took part in a little film-making himself—in *The Prisoner of Zenda*.

> When the producer, a rabid Sinn Feiner, was searching for someone to take the part of Rupert of Hentzau, the hero, in a long-distance view, [he told his mother] I offered my services and they were accepted. I was thrilled!
>
> The real star who was taking this—the leading role, was ill, and as the scene was to be at an unrecognizable distance from the camera, I was dressed up in a wonderful uniform. . . . spurs and all, and had to stand in the front door-way of a colossal castle and lower the draw-bridge, admit a man, speak to him, wave to his girl in the window opposite and then hoist up the bridge. Altogether it was great fun!

Less impressive than Charlie Chaplin was Elinor Glynn, a best-selling novelist at that time: 'a terribly painted woman of about sixty hoary winters', so he described her, 'and with a very blatant wig and thick mysterious veil'.

By March the ship was once again at Bermuda, the officers depressed by the Geddes report on the Navy with its forecast of severe cuts. This did indeed take place, resulting in much hardship and loss to the Service. By that time Charles himself had been made an acting lieutenant, and was looking forward to a course at Cambridge. His fear was that it would be stopped. If that happened, it would, he thought, be one of the disappointments of his life.

At Bermuda, a friendship began with Roma Horlick, a niece of the *Raleigh*'s commander, who was on a visit to the island. Charles told his mother:

> ... she is the most charming and cultured person I've met for ages. You don't know what it means to me after nine months of meeting people whose musical education does not go any further than Rachmaninoff's C sharp minor Prelude, to meet someone with whom I can speak of Debussy, or discuss Michaelangelo or anything under the sun.

He was also becoming great friends with Geoffrey Gowland, the elder of the twin midshipmen he had referred to in an earlier letter.

> It is such a wonderful thing, [he wrote] to have a boy's confidence and I feel so frightfully responsible because I can probably influence him more than anyone else he has ever met or will meet because he has given me his confidence at this, the impressionable age. I only hope I can do justice to the gift, and I think I can.

On 1 April 1922 he again referred to Roma in glowing terms. He told his mother he was longing for her to meet the girl as he knew she would like her—classic phrases from an eligible bachelor, guaranteed to strike a warning note at home. 'I know', he added, 'that if I was of a marriageable age or even a few years older I should have fallen head over heels in love with her.' He said he was going to New York, and that Roma would be there at the same time.

The result was not one cable, but two. The first said: 'YOUR LETTER APRIL FIRST WORRIES ME. BEG TAKE MY ADVICE. DO NOTHING RASH. MUM.' The second was a repetition; different words with exactly the same meaning. 'LETTER APRIL 1ST SOUNDS SERIOUS. BEG TAKE NO IRREVOCABLE STEP. MUM.' Charles replied at length on 14 April, which happened to be Good Friday.

> Your cable saying that my letter ... worried you came the day before yesterday and at first I could not think for the life of me what I could have said ... and then it suddenly struck me—though I could hardly credit it, that you might be worried about me and Roma! The idea made me roar with laughter but

I couldn't believe it and I was inclined to think that it was a practical joke on someone's part. . . . Of course, the more I think of it the more I roar with laughter. You utter darling! I thought you knew me well enough to know that my head rules my heart with a rod of iron.

I promise you I have no intention of getting married until I am at least twenty five! . . . Friendship is the most wonderful thing in the world and I have never met a girl and only once—possibly twice—a man with such a profound understanding, such a complete sympathy of every point, as has Roma. I did not know that a woman could have it in them to such an extent. She loves what I love, we both worship at the same shrines, we are both arrived at about the same stage of mental development. Can you wonder that we take pleasure in each other's company?

If you ask me, am I in love with her I should reply: 'Yes—deeply.' But I reply the same if you put the question to me about any of my friends. Ordinarily when one talks about being 'in love' one includes, under that heading, what I can only describe as 'passion'. But the love of friendship is infinitely more profound because it embodies respect, admiration, understanding, sympathy and all the intellectual and mental ties in the world but not 'passion'.

I hope this will make you see how groundless are your fears, how different is the case to what you have imagined from my misleading ill-expressed letters.

Charles duly visited New York, and at the end of April wrote still more fully about Roma.

I never could have believed it possible a few months ago, that I *could* have a girl friend that would rival any of my men friends, and yet Roma now is such . . . never have I met anyone whose outlook on life and all it contains was so sympathetic with mine.

And moreover I never believed it possible to talk frankly of religion and other such personal things with a girl—I always felt there would be a sort of barrier arising from the difference of sex but somehow I found myself able to talk to Roma as easily as I would have talked to any man. By this I don't mean there was *nothing* we did not discuss. There are some things one naturally cannot discuss under the circs. but I never thought that a girl would have the insight or understanding to talk about religion or art or anything else from such an intellectual standpoint.

The pair heard *Tristan and Isolde* together, Roma's first Wagner opera and Charles's third *Tristan*. Charles 'rose to such heights of ecstasy as I have never before reached, what with hearing good music again after such long starvation and what with being with such a sympathetic companion'.

Alas for romance! Within little more than two years he was reporting: 'I had a letter from Roma . . . the other day. She seems very happy and her baby is of course the fairest ever! But she used to write such an interesting letter, and now its all about babies and cooks and nurses and houses. . . . Why do people give up everything when they get married? I'd rather not get married.'

In May, Charles and his midshipmen were in camp on one of the islets off Bermuda. It was a spell of duty which helped him more than anything else to 'gain the confidence of the snots'.

> Although from a purely disciplinary point of view I am probably the worst sub that ever had a gunroom, [he confided to his mother] I feel that one can do so much more with them by appealing to the finer side of their natures than by instilling fear, which last seems to be what the Navy demands and of which I am incapable. By this I don't mean that there is *no* discipline in the gunroom. Far from it. But I have tried to make it the discipline of common decency and conscience rather than a discipline whose rigour depends entirely upon the awe one has for one's sub.

> In the *Emperor of India* one did the right thing out of fear of the consequences of doing the wrong. That is wrong discipline. Here I have tried—and I think partly succeeded with a few exceptions —to make the snots do the the right thing because it *is* the right thing, out of self respect and respect for the Community which is the Mess. If they have done wrong I have tried to make them feel ashamed rather than punish them.

Charles and a fellow lieutenant, Durand, had, in such spare time as they had, been designing scenery and dresses, stage-managing, and composing music for an operetta which was so successful on board that it was also performed ashore. 'Two of the scenes', wrote Charles, 'were loudly applauded the moment the curtain went up which was gratifying to me, sweating away behind the scenes.'

At the end of May the *Raleigh* signalized her first commission by a visit to Washington, where she was the first ship of her size to fly the white ensign within sight of the Capitol for more than a century. Much official ceremony and socialities were involved, the Admiral being received by the President and principal members of his administration.

This was not the only memorable event of the cruise, for its end was such. On 8 August, while in northerly waters, the ship was wrecked in the Straits of Belle Isle, on the Labrador coast, in very dramatic circumstances. Although the Admiral was not himself on board at the time and loss of life was small, no comparable disaster had happened to a flagship in peacetime since the collision of the *Victoria* and the *Camperdown* nearly thirty years earlier, when Admiral Sir George Tryon and many officers and men perished, the result of an injudicious tactical order.

Charles was able to give his mother an account of the circumstances as seen from the cruiser's bridge. He wrote three days after the event.

My only fear is that you may have been frightened by the newspapers over this affair. I hope you got my cable before you heard the news of the wreck of the *Raleigh*.

We only lost seven men out of the whole 800 which was miraculous.

I was officer of the watch.

Took on at 12.30 after lunch and it was blowing fairly hard. We were running up the west coast of Newfoundland. When we got to Belle Island Straits we kept head on across them so as to enter Forteau Bay. As we crossed the head of the Straits the weather thickened and we could not see very far. It was raining heavily. We passed an iceberg shortly afterwards and as we closed the coast ran into fog.

The Captain and navigator were on the bridge.

Suddenly the lookout reported land on the port bow, and one could just see the top of a ridge of hills. They seemed some way away. Then we saw land ahead and so reduced to 8 knots. Immediately after this I saw what I thought was breakers ahead and simultaneously the look-out reported 'Breakers right ahead'.

We went full speed astern but it was too late. I have never seen a more appalling sickening sight than that ledge of rocks with foam pouring over them—we seemed to wait hours for the crash and I remember the tinkling of all the bridge gear and the rattle that it made. It is still present in my ears. The stern swung round almost immediately so that we lay broadside on to the rocks with a heavy sea driving us on. All this in the eerie light of fog—I don't remember much of the next few minutes nor of the next half hour. The Captain—poor devil—was almost off his head. We worked our engines frantically and tried to drop the stern anchor to keep her stern off but it was no good. And then lying beam on to a heavy swell we bumped against the rocks all down the 600 feet of our starboard side. The crashes flung one across the bridge and we all feared that the mast would crash down on top of us. We clung to something solid for dear life. Then they lowered a cutter to take lines ashore. She was holed before she got into the water and then was nearly capsized by the surf. Many men jumped out of her and they were the ones who lost their lives. After the remainder got up on the flat ledge of rocks one of my snotties Hutton by name returned and though a bad swimmer and having no lifebelt swam out in the icy water and dragged one of the men back to the ship where he was hoisted inboard and saved.

I hardly dared to watch.

I remember after the engine rooms were abandoned having to stand on the bridge with nothing to do and just wait until I got an order to leave. I felt dreadfully cold and had an appalling shivering fit. Then someone brought me some tea and we all felt better.

They got several lines ashore and secured and the men went ashore on them hand over hand. Then they got some carley floats going and men were bundled into them and hauled ashore the rafts being hauled back for more afterwards. One could hardly see further than the high tide mark and the figures of men flat, dim and indistinct rushed about everywhere. Then I heard fire parties piped and wondered what was burning. Later it proved only to be some clothes in the galley.

Then we started firing a minute gun for help and to attract attention. The power failed and below everything was as black as night.

You have no idea how appalling it was each time the ship crashed her sides in against the rocks. She seemed as if she couldn't last much longer. Luckily we only had about 30 feet of water beneath us. The bows sank and she listed badly to port. We flooded the starboard side of the ship to try and keep her upright.

Then I got a message to abandon the bridge. When I got aft I found that there were only the officers and a few men left.

After procuring one or two little things I treasured from down in my cabin also a sweater, we embarked in a carley float up to our knees in water and by gad it was cold! We were hauled ashore over the surf and scrambled up the beach. There I found crowds of sailors drying round enormous fires. After dumping my wet clothes near a fire I went and helped to get every one else ashore. Worked for about an hour in the surf and got soaked through. By now it was dark and the fog still thick. The fires shot huge beams up into the fire [*sic* = sky?] and the surf pounded the rocks and all the time the horrible hollow-sounding roar of the old ship pounding her bottom out on the rocks.

Luckily there was a village near with several barns. The men slept in the hay and I went to a cottage with a large party where we dropped on the floor and slept after a small feed of wet biscuits.

Next morning we were down at the ship about 5 o'clock and worked all day till dark getting our gear ashore in carley rafts. I have managed to save all my things except some white uniform, a few old clothes, and many books, but I think I have been exceptionally lucky.

Now the ship's company has divided. Those required in the courtmartial and a few others are forming a salvage party. I naturally have to be courtmartialled because I was officer of the watch at the time.

The remainder are going home in a C.P.R. liner which is calling here on her way tomorrow. I only wish I was coming too but I have got to stay behind.

We work down at the ship every day, and hard work it is too. The Court of Inquiry begins on Wednesday 16th August and will probably be finished that week. . . . Am very well and happy.

Charles had a last sight of the wreck as he left the shores of the North American continent on 23 August.

The *Constance* [the cruiser in which he was taking passage] stood right in close and sounded the 'Alert' as we passed. The ship looked dreadful from seaward. One saw all her decks, apparently cleared of nearly everything except superstructure.

Oil fuel discoloured her everywhere and she looked a wreck pure and simple. From this angle her funnels seemed colossal. She was deserted save for one solitary figure, the sentry guarding her from the profane hands of wreckers. With a lump in my throat, I must confess, I had the honour of standing and saluting with all the *Constance*'s as we passed.

As a result of the courts martial, the Navigating Officer was severely reprimanded and the Captain was reprimanded and dismissed his ship. The latter sentence was sadly superfluous, considering her state.

Chapter Two

MATURITY

CHARLES had his wish, and in October 1922 went to Trinity College, Cambridge, for a course of general studies which lasted two terms. They were all too brief, eight packed weeks in each, and time was apt to race. A contemporary may here speak with feeling, for no term was long enough for what men wanted to do.

For the Cambridge period, there is a gap in Charles's letters. To write home was unnecessary, since he was never far from his people, and if he kept a diary or notes, as he sometimes did, they have disappeared.

In later years he used to say that Cambridge revolutionized his life, but, if he felt this to be true, the effect was inward, not apparent. That he was ripe for a university was obvious; but he was already mature in all the ways that matter, and what Cambridge could offer was enrichment, not awakening.

In a celebrated poem, Kipling signalized the Admiralty's step of 'piping the children off all the seas, from the Falklands to the Bight' enjoining Cambridge to be gentle with these men who were there to enjoy themselves as well as to learn, since they had given their youth to the defence of their country. The University certainly took them to its heart.

One of the many naval officers who went on the Cambridge course, Captain Eric Bush, had been at Dartmouth in 1914 and been sent to sea with the rest of the College, many of his fellow cadets being drowned soon afterwards when the cruisers *Aboukir*, *Hogue*, and *Cressy* were torpedoed, Bush himself winning the D.S.C. at the Dardanelles, the youngest recipient ever.

It was a happy idea sending us to Cambridge [he wrote in the notes to his anthology, *Flowers of the Sea*]. I think it civilized us

29

a bit after four years of war and in some queer way made us normal again. After all, we were very young when we went to sea and had had manhood thrust on us, as it were, not only prematurely but violently. All sailors have a rather different outlook from that of landsmen, and in our case circumstances had accentuated it. We must have been queer creatures. But Cambridge took us in her stride and taught us a lot.

Captain Bush spoke of the earlier arrivals in particular, and of the naval officer as a type. Charles Lambe was different. He was made for Cambridge, and if the University took others 'in her stride', he took the University in his. He got far more out of the experience than the average undergraduate straight from school, simply because he had much more to give. He was intellectually inclined, musical, artistic, good at sport, above all, he had the eagerness and quickness to learn and the unflagging vitality which characterized him throughout life.

Cambridge was an informal, light-hearted place of learning, but it is odd that while the Oxford of the time is amusingly, often brilliantly, reflected in some of the earlier stories of Evelyn Waugh, the chief work which at that particular stage derived from the sister University, Rosamond Lehmann's once best-selling *Dusty Answer*, came from a women's college. It was, therefore, unrepresentative, though authentic and moving within its framework, and Charles admired the author's work well enough to read her novels as they appeared.

As a rule, the naval officers kept to themselves; even their 'rags' were usually their own affair, boisterous in a nautical way. They mostly sat together in Hall, men among boys. It was natural enough, for there would have been far more in common between Charles, for instance, who had already seen more of the world than many undergraduates would see in their whole lives, besides experiencing action and shipwreck, and the younger dons. Not all officers felt that they 'belonged' either to the University or to the college to which they were attached, but this was certainly not the fault of the colleges. There were many exceptions, among them Charles Lambe.

Among his more lasting friendships was one with Boris Ord, then an organ-scholar at Corpus Christi College, and shortly to become a Fellow of Kings. As early as his Dartmouth days Charles had been attracted to the organ, and had played a certain amount. Now he learnt more.

Another Corpus man was Stewart Perowne, later to become an Orientalist, and to be the husband of Freya Stark. Perowne wrote of Charles at this time:

> I can see him now, in the ADC clubroom, wearing a navy blue blazer, and a red tie, talking with that wonderful mahogany voice of his. Somehow, he seemed to create an aura of awe round him, so that he was outside, not inside, any group he happened to be talking with. I say 'awe' advisedly, because I was afraid of Charles when I first met him: he had the glamour of having served with the Royal Navy at an age when I'd been a schoolboy; and then he had such authority, such integrity about him. He made me feel a superficial sham.

In the artistic line, one of the most promising men was Cecil Beaton, undecided at that time whether to concentrate on painting or photography. Charles and he both entered a competition for providing the décor for a production of Thackeray's *The Rose and the Ring*. Very charming and suitable they were, if distant memory is any guide.

One of his contemporaries at Trinity was Sir Steven Runciman, historian of Byzantium and the Crusades. Runciman was as brilliant, academically, as anyone of his time. His interests were wide. He was an individualist, and a great traveller. He and Charles soon made friends, and remained so all through Charles's life, meeting in many strange places abroad, though with long intervals. He and Boris Ord were closest to Charles at Cambridge. All three would achieve distinction in their professions, and if they, in their differing ways, enriched Charles, he undoubtedly opened their eyes to what might be discovered in the make-up of a naval officer.

II

Brilliant people are not always good examinees, but Charles did himself justice, and as regards written work, clear and flowing handwriting would have put the examiners in a good temper. He was given first-class certificates for his terms at Cambridge. There then followed technical courses which would result in an assessment of his capabilities as a lieutenant, concerned with gunnery, torpedoes and navigation.

The results must have pleased him, for he was awarded a first in each, by a handsome margin. He was such an all-round man that there was nothing much to choose in his showing between various subjects. Perhaps it is significant, in view of his later specialization, that one of his best results, in which he scored 141 marks out of a possible 150, was in Electricity and Mining, the tests being held in H.M.S. *Vernon*, the Torpedo School.

Charles was given additional seniority in his rank as lieutenant, a good sea appointment being foreshadowed, and it is noteworthy that, however much he valued and enjoyed his time at Cambridge, there had been no further serious doubts as to the suitability of his profession. He liked the Navy, and the Admiralty knew when they had an exceptional officer.

In 1923 he was sent to H.M.S. *Benbow*, which then flew the flag of Hugh Watson, Rear-Admiral, 4th Battle Squadron, Mediterranean Fleet. Charles knew the *Benbow* from the days of the Grand Fleet at Scapa, but he was fresh to the Mediterranean. This was the sea with which naval officers of succeeding generations became as familiar as with the greyer waters of the Channel, the North Sea, and the Atlantic. The Mediterranean was at once training ground, strategic centre, and source of refreshment. In time, Charles came to know it as well as anyone of his era.

His first acquaintance was characteristic. He wrote to his family on 22 August 1923 from Malta, describing an incident of his journey.

> While the train was waiting for the ferry to arrive and take us over to Messina we were drawn up only about 50 yards from the sea. I could not resist it and luckily I knew I had my bathing dress handy so I quickly got into it and had a delicious bathe. All the the rest of the people in the train kicked up a tremendous fuss. One old fat priest thought I was going to commit suicide I think!

Once in the ship, he found himself among at least five old friends or acquaintances, his only disappointment being that there were no fellow enthusiasts for polo—and, while he was at Malta, Charles was determined to play. His captain was James Somerville, afterwards, an Admiral of the Fleet, famous for his exploits in the Second World War. 'He seems a very charming man,' Charles reported, 'and I feel sure I shall like him immensely.'

Later, Charles took stock of his journey out from home. Rome had surpassed all his dreams, 'every building of that lovely rich creamy yellowy brown colour'. The Sistine Chapel and Michelangelo's statuary filled him with awe, as he knew would be the case. As for his destination, Malta, he grew increasingly attached to it over the years, with its superb setting, magnificent deep-water harbour, curious language, noble families, and its romantic history including the shipwreck of St. Paul, the conquest by the Normans under Count Robert of Sicily, the rule of the Knights of St. John, with the famous siege by the Turks and the defence under La Vallette, the brief occupation by Napoleon, and its cession to Great Britain in 1814 as one of the results of the protracted struggle with France.

Charles was so impressed with the experiences of his first year in the Mediterranean that he bought a finely bound quarto, made up of handmade paper, in which he carefully copied out items of interest, illustrating them mainly with his own photographs. His first excursion was to Alexandria, where the *Benbow* was joined by her sister ship, the *Iron Duke*, days being filled with sightseeing, including, inevitably, the Pyramids and the Sphinx. In the Cairo Museum, recent discoveries from the tomb of Tutankhamen had just been put on view, to the wonder of the world.

Back at Malta, life soon became less amusing. 'The less said about the winter the better,' he noted. Polo was hampered by wet weather, and there was general dissatisfaction because the paucity of the fuel allowance, in a time of stringent economy, meant that the battleships could rarely exercise, and the sailors had little to do.

Early in February 1924, Charles's mother and sister arrived for a visit, and although they themselves could not have been more welcome, he confided that 'from the day of their arrival there was nothing else for it but to abandon oneself to the clutches of Malta society'. There was some excitement as the result of the visit of Queen Marie of Rumania to Admiral and Lady Brock at Admiralty House.

> Quite unexpectedly, [he recorded] Lady B. presented me and I, covered with confusion, had no idea whether I should kiss her hand or what! It went off all right and apparently I was looked on with favour, as I was asked just afterwards to go picknicking with her. There was a terrible dilemma as it was the day of the final of the polo tournament but I pretended never to have got the signal and dashed ashore! One did not dare to refuse. The Queen was a wonderfully fine regal woman with that half-tragic expression born, I suppose of much responsibility.

Charles was to see a great deal of the Brocks. The Admiral, like Sir William Pakenham, had fought gallantly with the battle-cruisers at Jutland, and later became Beatty's Chief of Staff. More

recently, he had handled a serious crisis which had arisen in the
Eastern Mediterranean, the result of a clash between the Greeks
and the Turkish Nationalists under Mustapha Kemal, with
outstanding skill. He is described by Professor Arthur Marder, the
historian of that era, as being

> . . . unworldly, retiring, far more studious than most of his
> contemporaries and with wide interests. He was a great reader and
> thinker, and had sound judgement, an analytical brain, and great
> tact. He lacked one ace: despite his charm of manner, he was
> very impersonal, and so not a leader. He could never remember
> the names of staff officers, who were to him so many cogs in the
> machine.

That verdict concerned earlier days. Later, Sir Osmond Brock,
perhaps becoming less strained or recognizing a kindred spirit,
remembered at least one of his junior officers very well indeed, and
acted accordingly. Charles was marked down, probably at first
by Lady Brock, as a likely flag-lieutenant, though he did not himself
become aware of the fact for some time.

In March, Mrs. Lambe and Betty went home. 'Although I know
they enjoyed it, and so did I,' he recorded, 'one visit will probably
suffice them.' There, for once, he underestimated his mother's
capacity for travel and her pleasure in her son's society, and she
came in time to know Malta very well indeed.

Charles was soon off on the Spring Cruise, the object of the
strategical exercise being for the Atlantic Fleet to prevent Admiral
Brock's Fleet reaching the area of Pollensa Bay, on the north side
of Majorca, without being brought to action. The Atlantic Fleet
not only had a superior force but aircraft, whereas Brock was
without them. Brock succeeded in his object, proving, thought
Charles, 'the difficulty of aerial reconnaissance in this climate and
also the difficulty of light forces shadowing a battle fleet on a dark
night'. At the post-mortem, Charles thought that most of the
admirals spoke badly, 'trying the whole time to vindicate themselves'. Brock was different. He summed up much to the point,
advocating a 'go straight' strategy, because, he said, 'the enemy will
always give you credit for being cleverer than you are!'

Charles also liked Lady Brock and her children.

> I always admired her for not giving a damn for public opinion,
> [he wrote] and for doing what she liked and for keeping the
> naval wives in their places. As an illustration, once during a

5. *Riding from Buckingham Palace for a State Opening of Parliament, 1938*

6. *Edwina Mountbatten, the Duke of Gloucester, the Duke of Kent, Lord Louis Mountbatten, Charles Lambe*

7. *Captain Lambe H.M.S.* Illustrious *in a flash suit on operat*
service in the Far East, 1945

friend's leave I arranged to take him and his wife for a drive in
a flat country cart. Lady B. insisted on coming too, and despite
the protests of the C-in-C she started from the front door of
Admiralty House and drove out through Valetta at full length
on the cart. It was an amusing situation for me. . . .

Towards the end of March, Lord Beatty, who was then First
Sea Lord, as he had continued to be ever since he relinquished
command of the Grand Fleet in 1919, paid a visit to Malta in the
yacht *Bryony*. 'Beatty', so Charles wrote to his mother 'has been
playing polo and was really very good though obviously a little out
of practice.' He was not in his first youth either, being at that time
fifty-three. 'Lady Beatty is an odd-looking woman now,' he continued. 'Proper mutton dressed as lamb!—a sort of second Mrs.
Asquith to look at.'

In the early summer of 1924 Charles took a share in a yacht, the
Londeen ('I think I know a little more about sailing than Shelley
did!' he remarked) and in June he was off to the Holy Land and
Cyprus, busy making arrangements for visits of sailors from the
Fleet, and having to snatch time to see the principal sights. He was
again giving some thought to joining the flying branch of the Naval
Service, and consulted his stepfather, as he so often did. Although
he was dissatisfied at what he considered the 'stagnation' in the
Fleet, and at the 'professionalism of naval sport', he decided to
hold his hand, at least for the time.

In July, the *Benbow* visited Athens and Naples, both places
offering what was almost too much excitement to a mind wide
open to every new experience. In Athens 'the marble of which
everything is built is graduated in the most lovely colours, varying
from pale yellow to rust', he remarked. While his ship was at Naples
Charles became as engrossed by Vesuvius as that ever-eager
observer, Sir William Hamilton, had been in the eighteenth
century.

I don't think I have ever been so thunderstruck [he told his
mother]. I suppose it was largely due to not knowing what to
expect. But the sudden realization of this whirlwind of heat and
smoke coming out of the earth left me dumb. . . . There were so
many questions one wanted to ask and no hope of an answer;
it was such a magnificent sight and so defiant of research that
one wanted to worship it. Then suddenly a soft puff from the
great mouth, and a flicker of brighter light on the turning

4

smoke; then a rush and a roar and the whole thing would appear to go up. A golden rain of white-hot cinders would be shot hundreds of feet into the air; a great puff of smoke into the sky, and for a few seconds the whole of the surrounding crater would be lit by an eerie light.

Venice, to which the ship went next, was, thought Charles, all he had expected. 'I have never been to a place that grows on you so much,' he said. In those days there were gondolas in plenty, still built to individual order, as they had been for centuries. 'So much must have been written about them,' he said, 'that one hardly dares to mention them, but I know no more fascinating mode of travel.' He knew all about Titian and Tintoretto: the surprise was Carpaccio, of whom, until then, he had never heard. 'The old man must have had such a keen sense of humour,' he remarked, 'for even in his most serious pictures you will find some supremely comic incident.'

At Venice Charles heard of the death of Joseph Conrad, a writer he had long admired. 'I feel as if I had lost a personal friend,' he told his mother, and this was exactly how the event struck other contemporaries. 'It is tragic to think that the row of his books will not swell any longer.'

Admiral Watson was shortly moving to the *Iron Duke* and asked Charles if he would like to go with him. Charles declined, 'mainly', he explained, 'because I have never yet seen a commission through in any one ship, and too much chopping and changing is bad. . . There were awful rumours about my going with him as "flags", a job I'd hate because . . . I'd be "for social duties only" and would be without work as far as the Service is concerned.'

The threat of a flag-lieutenancy to an admiral he liked but by whom he was not inspired led Charles to consider whether he should specialize, and if so in what direction. In October 1924, he wrote a long letter on the subject to his stepfather who would, he knew, give useful advice. Navigation, in his view, was 'out of it. One has no men to deal with, and it does not help to fit one for higher command.' In view of how his future turned out, his remarks on Torpedo specialization are of interest. He liked the idea, so he said, but it offered, he thought, 'very little scope'. The electrical part, so he had heard, was shortly to be 'taken over by the En-gineers' and 'Torpedo Control is developed almost to its limits now'. Anti-submarine work seemed 'a deep groove into which one would slip and lose touch with everything else', and he had already

decided that naval flying was not what he wanted. That left
Gunnery, Signals and 'salt horse'—i.e. not to specialize. He liked
the idea of 'salt horse' as leading, perhaps, to the command of a
river-gunboat 'where one always has a chance of making one's
name', provided he had first done a staff course, which he hoped
to do as soon as possible. One of his doubts was whether, if he did *not*
specialize, the Admiralty would say: 'Here's a bloke with five
firsts who is too lazy to specialize. I imagine their attitude would be
that if one can specialize one should.'

Before an answer came, Charles had been to Florence and
savoured its treasures, thus completing his round of the greater
artistic centres of Italy. Nothing impressed him more than
Michelangelo's 'perfect Sacristy at San Lorenzo with the tombs of
the Medici family. It is the simplest and most melancholy little
building I have ever been in, its beauty severe and subdued with
nothing to mar the impression. . . . Even Americans are hushed
inside it, the atmosphere is so awe-inspiring.'

Stepfatherly counsel about his future left Charles still undecided.
'I'm not sufficiently keen on any one subject to make me want to
forsake all others,' he wrote. His aim was to get a command of his
own as soon as possible. 'If I was to do a two years commission in a
light cruiser in China, after that I should probably be just about
the right seniority for a War Staff course. Then—if possible—
command of a destroyer.'

On 31 October, still in a thoughtful frame of mind, Charles
wrote his mother one of the fullest letters he ever sent home.

It is very difficult for me to realize that you don't know everything about me. I suppose it is natural that I should take it for
granted that you do know everything, merely because my
earliest memories are of you.

. . . I am sure you look at me through rose-tinted specs. My
ideas on such things as religion, and such like, are probably,
almost certainly, different from yours. And if I am to tell you all
I think and believe on such subjects you must be prepared for
mild surprises.

Let's talk of religion now. You are a devout member of the
Church of England, and I believe you really are capable of
belief in all that the Church expects you to believe. If so I admire
you for it enormously. Such belief must require a great deal of
building up—I nearly said 'bolstering up'. I have tried, but I
can't believe the doctrines of the Church of England or of any

other Church for that matter. The more I read or hear of the
Bible (which I love for many reasons)—the more certain I am
that the teachings of the Church of England are not those of
Christ.

It seems to me this way.

Two thousand years ago the Jews thought, spoke and wrote
in metaphor, imagery or whatever you like to call it. The Church
today expects you to believe literally. They expect you to believe
in a literal Heaven and Hell, in condemnation and forgiveness,
and they expect you to believe literally the imagery of Christ's
teaching as set down by the Evangelists. It is as if we were to
take the rich metaphor of the Elizabethans literally. When
Shakespeare wrote:

> *Night's candles are burnt out, and*
> *jocund day*
> *Stands tiptoe on the misty mountain*
> *tops*

we realize that it is a very beautiful description of dawn—no
more and no less. But if the Church adopted *Romeo and Juliet*
in place of one of the Gospels I can easily imagine them trying
to explain such metaphor literally.

That Christ was one of the greatest men that ever lived I have
never questioned. That the religion he gave to the world is the
greatest and most wonderful religion I too believe. But that he
was the Son of God, mysteriously conceived by his mother,
nothing will ever make me believe it. It seems incredible that any
educated human being of the present day can believe otherwise
than that he was the son of Mary and Joseph—illegitimate as
we say now. And do you think that such a belief distracts from
his greatness, from the divinity that was in him? For divine he
certainly was, as we all are, only he far more so.

To me, it makes him far, far more human and understandable,
far more wonderful and great. The Christ of the Church of
England is a cold mysterious being, awe inspiring, to be feared.
But my conception of Christ as the illegitimate son of Joseph and
Mary, coming from the meanest, as he himself said, is a real
living man. In the same way as the figure of Michaelangelo is a
living figure to me.

Why label the figure of Christ 'Mysterious Son of God'—no
other religion does. Mahommet was a man like ourselves only far
greater, far more divine. So was Confucius and I believe Buddha

as well. And now that you have cleared your head of the narrowness and mysteriousness of the Church's interpretation of his birth, read the teachings of Christ, his wisdom and his philosophy.

It seems to boil down to this.

The wider the scope of one's imagination and the deeper the probing of one's thoughts, the more easily do you come to a brick wall. Certain things cannot be explained. They are the works of God. Deep down in oneself there is divinity. Your soul is divine; it is part of God himself. 'The Kingdom of God is within you.'

One's sole duty is to follow and obey the prompting of that divine spark. Whosoever he may be, I am sure no man, if he gives the question a moment's thought, can ever doubt what the *right* thing to do is. It is only when the inward vision becomes obscured by minor issues and all the complications of failings and sins against the promptings of the divine spark that it becomes increasingly difficult to see the right course clearly.

Every failing to live up to the prompting of that divinity within you is a sin and it makes it all the harder next time. At length a state will be reached where the knowledge of *right* is so obscured that a man may cease to be in touch with it altogether.

It is for this reason that Christ advocated prayer; for prayer is communication with the godhead that is in you. And if you are in close touch, how much easier is it to make the right deduction instantly!

Christ is probably the only man who has never failed to live up to the divine principles within him. Hence his strength and his wisdom.

In his attempts to summarize his views, Charles almost paraphrased some sentences he wrote in his diary a few years earlier, which have already been quoted.

It seems to me that Heaven is the state of dying with the knowledge that you have done your utmost to live up to your beliefs of right, and hell is the torture of regrets and remorse when one realizes how far short one has fallen of the mark, and realizes it too late.

Sins can only be got rid of—expiated that is—by confession either through another person or direct to one's own soul—and it is purely that confession that is curing people of every kind of mania and nerve disease today, only they call it Psychoanalysis: in the same way that love is a form of prayer.

That, darling Mum, is a rough outline of all that I feel about religion, but it is dreadfully incomplete. I only hope I haven't hurt your feelings, anyway do remember that letters are dreadfully ambiguous things and although I have tried hard to express my views, you may read a different interpretation to that intended. It is easy to do so.

III

The ward-room officers of the *Benbow* celebrated Charles's birthday on 20 December 1924 with a leg-pull, into the ramifications of which even the captain entered. By that time the ship had been ordered from Malta to Alexandria, part of a display of force by Navy and Army following the murder of Sir Lee Stack, Sirdar of the Egyptian Army. On the date in question, all was quiet in Egypt, and reparation had been promised. As a party of Charles's friends were celebrating in an appropriate way, a message was brought in which, so it appeared, was pretty disconcerting. Admiral Watson wanted him as flag-lieutenant after all! Charles was not long taken in (largely because the captain was a poor actor), but the joke had a sequel, for, by an extraordinary coincidence, he was in fact offered, that very evening, the flag-lieutenant's appointment on the staff of the Commander-in-Chief, a very different matter. The sickness of the current holder of the post had made a replacement necessary, and Sir Osmond Brock knew just the man!

The Admiral had influence in the Navy; his tenure in the Mediterranean had only six months more to run, and if, as seemed probable, he could see to it that Charles's next appointment was equally interesting, the future looked rosy. Charles cabled the news home, adding in a letter: 'think of the terrible awe-inspiring functions I shall have to organize! All my socks have holes in them and I shall have to keep my finger-nails clean. I sent a cable to Gieves to try and start them making me some respectable clothes.... Coo-er. Think of me! aiguillettes and all.'

The Commander-in-Chief flew his flag in H.M.S. *Queen Elizabeth*, which had been Beatty's flagship when he had been in charge of the Grand Fleet in the later stages of the First World War. To this famous vessel Charles now transferred. He was continuing his habit of never serving an entire commission in the same ship, but he liked his new quarters, was able to play almost as much polo as he wanted, and he at once took to the Brocks, and they to him.

> The C-in-C [so he told his mother] is the most delightful person imaginable to work with. He is very tolerant and has a keen sense of humour, but his chief attribute in my eyes is his cultured taste. One evening last week we were left alone together and I was a little nervous to start with. However we started talking books and I have seldom enjoyed an evening more. He reads everything that is published almost and has got many valuable books including first editions of Samuel Butler, Conrad and Stevenson. . . .
>
> Lady Brock wants to be remembered to you and tells me to tell you that she is looking after me! I have to do quite a lot of looking after her as a matter of fact. She is so casual that one is frequently having to make her do the things she should do in her position and not let her do always as she likes!

Warming to his theme, he reported on 13 January 1925 that his job was 'most delightful, although it is hardly that of a naval officer. Still it is amusing and I shall not have long enough at it to make me forget all my seamanship.'

Captain Somerville had been urging Charles to specialize in Torpedoes, and when the Commander-in-Chief added the weight of his opinion in the same direction, Charles made up his mind to take their advice. 'I could probably make more of it than of a salt-horse job,' he told his mother, 'although I hanker very much after the freedom of a salt-horse.' In the same letter he reported:

> I have more or less established myself by being very firm with Lady B. and I had occasion the other day to stop her making a signal, and I lectured her severely on the evils that are done by wives interfering in any way with the Service. She promised never to do it again!

In February 1925 the Brocks went on a short visit to Tunisia in the yacht *Bryony*, Charles with them. There was the chance of some sketching, though the weather was wild for that part of the world. In March, combined exercises with the Atlantic Fleet were held, the *Queen Elizabeth* afterwards anchoring off Majorca, visits being paid by Lord and Lady Beatty and by the First Lord of the Admiralty, William Bridgeman. One of the Brock children delighted Bridgeman by asking him when they could expect the visit of 'the Last Lord'.

Lady Brock, [so Charles told his mother at the end of March] wishes me to tell you that she has me thoroughly in hand. I am no longer allowed to put water on my hair as it causes baldness, neither am I allowed to part it in the usual place but to the right side only.

I find I have a reputation of being terrifying to all the young things in Malta! It pleases me to know this, as I like none of their flippant senseless manners and conversation and it is nice to be able to quell them frigidly.... How I hate those who need quelling!

By midsummer Charles was home, as he had expected. When they parted, Admiral Brock wrote a glowing confidential report on his flag-lieutenant. 'He is an exceptionally gifted officer,' he said: 'paints; very musical, and well read. He is full of keenness for the Service and is an officer who is likely to rise high in the Navy. I cannot praise him too highly.'

IV

Between the wars, Gunnery rather than Torpedo specialization was not only more popular, but provided a greater number of officers who eventually reached high rank. When he joined H.M.S. *Vernon* in 1925 for the long Torpedo course, Charles was one of only seven, but of them three eventually became admirals, and others achieved distinction.

The first establishment of its kind had dated from the 1870s when it was realized that electricity, when applied to submersible weapons such as mines and torpedoes, might revolutionize naval warfare. H.M.S. *Vernon*, where experts looked after electrical matters generally, had been moved ashore to Portsmouth in 1923, and it was there that Charles now worked. There he learnt not only the intricacies of his trade, but so much about the ways of electricity in general that it was a source of wonder to his family, who profited by it in the home. It was not long before its ramifications, when applied to naval affairs, grew so considerable as to require a branch of its own. It would not, as Charles had once supposed, become part of the already large province of the engineer.

Charles spent two years ashore, active in the hunting field and on the polo ground, keenly interested in the management of the Cornish clay-works and his property in that county, and pursuing his musical interests. As was his way, he did exceptionally well in his final Torpedo examinations, after which he was sent as Torpedo Officer to the destroyer-leader *Stuart*. Her captain at that time was 'Jock' Whitworth, later renowned as an admiral in the Second World War. The *Stuart* was in the Mediterranean, and on his way to join her, Charles met his future wife, who was then married to Victor Mylius, who had also at one time been in the Navy.

It was October 1927, [she wrote later] the day was hot, the train was slow as it wound its way along the coast towards Reggio Calabria. The Italian soprano in my carriage was restive and feeling the heat. She stood in the corridor spreading. Suddenly there were screams, drama, she thought she had been bitten by a passing dog, hysteria ensued.

Then came the soothing sound of a deep bass English voice, a young man with freckles, grey flannels and tweed jacket, such an amusing face and enormous charm, came to her rescue. But not a word did she understand, so I was called to translate. My life had always been in Italy and I felt half Italian so naturally I joined in. Later this young man and I talked of this and that, of music and literature, of cabbages and kings. I played the cello, he the piano. We both were reading D. H. Lawrence and both were bound for Malta, he to join a ship, me to join my husband of six months.

Charles found Malta itself little changed, but the Fleet was restive for Sir Roger Keyes, the Commander-in-Chief, who had had a spectacular war record, was at that time polo-mad. Good as Charles himself was at the game, he sympathized with the feeling on the subject.

People are very bitter out here about polo and rightly so [he wrote to his mother from Malta in November]. Keyes has done it a great deal of harm by such iniquitous favouritism as recalling a cruiser in the middle of a day's exercising and sending the barge for one of his team! The polo players in the flagship are never allowed to be prevented by duty from playing, and their work falls on the shoulders of others (who would probably play if they had the money). It is a great pity.

This was an admirably detached view, for Keyes soon made himself agreeable to Charles—the Admiral knew his stepfather well—and he was soon in demand both as a player and umpire. Nevertheless,

work came first, despite his versatility. 'Charles came often to our
house, with lions guarding the door,' wrote Mrs. Mylius. 'His life
was the Navy, and all that went with it. In those years there was no
thought of war and all was carefree. He had enormous zest for life,
everything, swimming, sailing, polo, entertaining friends, painting,
going to the opera.'

Charles's professional calibre was soon tested, for in December
the *Stuart*, with the rest of the 2nd Destroyer Flotilla were involved
in a complicated exercise.

> I had to umpire in a War Game which took every forenoon and
> ended up most hectically with a colossal imaginary torpedo
> attack, [he told his mother]. To my horror I was called upon
> to get up in front of the C. in. C, four other admirals and about
> 40 other officers and criticize the tactics employed and decide
> on the probable result. This with little or no experience on which
> to base one's opinions!
>
> I've never been so frightened in my life and still have no idea
> what I said. I heard afterwards however that I talked clearly,
> volubly and decisively and certainly nobody questioned the
> correctness of my opinions. Such is the power of bounce!

Before the year was out, Charles was making plans with a brother
officer, Lord Louis Mountbatten, at that time a Lieutenant-
Commander, for a 'young and well-balanced polo team'. He soon
became close friends with Mountbatten, and with Edwina, his
wife, 'very smart and charming to meet. I like them both immensely', he reported. Mountbatten and Charles between them
transformed the atmosphere of the *Stuart*, which had hitherto been
unattractive.

Mrs. Lambe and Betty paid their second visit to Malta in the
spring of 1928, and shortly after they left for home the destroyers
went on exercises to the Aegean, including a visit to Navarino,
which in 1827 had been the scene of the last major battle under sail,
when a force under Sir Edward Codrington consisting of British,
French, and Russian vessels, destroyed a Turkish–Egyptian fleet
and thus helped to secure the liberation of Greece.

At dusk, said Charles, 'the air was loud with crickets' songs and
heavy with the pungent smell of tamarisk and juniper bushes'.
Swimming in phosphorescence was an extraordinary experience.
'As your arms shot forward a trail of sparks flew from your finger
tips and at each stroke was created a new starry constellation in the
warm soft water.'

The worst of destroyers is the difficulty of getting over to a big ship, [he told his mother] as we are usually anchored miles from them and our motor boat is usually broken down. In fact compared with a big ship destroyers are a vile life in harbour, unless you happen to strike lucky with the right people. At sea, however, especially from my point of view, one could want nothing better, and at Malta it is so easy to get ashore that it doesn't matter.

On the way here we had a most exciting attack on the Battle Fleet at night . . . we got the target silhouetted against the setting sun 17 miles away and closed in with the failing light to 1600 yards without being spotted, getting round their screen. We fired 18 torpedoes, and got 7 hits. We lost 7 torpedoes too! But I think it has shaken the old battleships up a bit!

In the autumn, Charles got leave to visit Vienna—including the famous Spanish Riding School—with a party which included Mountbatten.

Travelling with Dicky, [he wrote to his mother about his friend, using the name by which he would refer to him in the future] is always full of incident. One can never tell who will suddenly discover his identity and start to treat him as if he was second only to the Prince of Wales.

Lord Louis was related to most of the reigning Houses of Europe, past and present, his sister was the Crown Princess and future Queen of Sweden, whom Charles had met at Malta. He was the constant companion, whenever Service conditions allowed, of the Prince of Wales, the future King Edward VIII, and one of the most popular men in Europe. Charles said of Mountbatten:

Really he is a much more considerable person in South Germany than in England, and consequently he was treated as a Prince at the hotel and we picked up the crumbs as if we were in his suite.

They gave us regal suites of rooms at normal prices—a sitting room with a grand piano and brocade walls, and a Union Jack was run up outside on our arrival. The only difficulty was to hide our amusement from the manager for fear of hurting his feelings. In this I think we succeeded, but he never really recovered from the initial shock of seeing one of us go out of a door before 'His Highness'.

As if by contrast to the sights and gaiety of Vienna, Charles had been reading that sad book, *The Well of Loneliness*.

It is so badly written, [he commented] that I thoroughly approve of its withdrawal. But why people will not admit that there are dozens and dozens of one's own acquaintance that are born more or less with perverted ideas and for whom I have every sympathy, I am damned if I know.

The poor devils suffer quite enough in themselves without the additional horror of being hounded out of decent society. They are mostly able and honourable people with a great deal more sense of morality than their persecutors.

However, it is assumed that they are unclean, however completely they suppress their tendencies, and so it will always remain, I suppose. I can't help feeling it is unjust. If only the psychologists would come forward and prove publicly that such things are more often in-born than acquired, perhaps people might be convinced. It must be much worse than being born with a deformed body, to have a deformed mind.

In December, Charles put in an official application to attend the War Staff Course, and, as a sensible and ambitious young officer would, pulled what strings he could. He thought his step-father 'could start a preliminary agitation'; Captain Somerville had also been enlisted; while Charles himself would write to Admiral Brock. The course would start in January 1930, and as the 2nd Flotilla was due home in September or October 1929, it would 'just give me nice time for my foreign service leave'.

The year 1929 began badly, with gossip, both in Malta and London, to the effect that Charles had been seeing too much of the wife of one of his greatest friends. He believed his mother was already poisoned against her, 'probably by Lady Brock, who ought to know better'. The truth was that he was devoted to both parties, but not in the least in love with the lady concerned. 'If only some of the dirty little over sexed minds who spread this gossip could know his [the husband's] attitude it would do them good. The trouble is that they know what they would do under the circumstances and cannot believe that other people could behave better.' He wished the gossips would publish what they said: 'I should much enjoy suing them for libel and I should enjoy seeing them pay heavily.' The upshot was, in fact, an apology, together with an explanation that one of the sources of the rumours thought she was doing Charles a good turn in saving him from a designing woman!

It was just as well matters settled themselves happily, for Mrs. Lambe was preparing for another visit to Malta with Betty, and Charles wished nothing to mar their enjoyment. His last injunction to Mrs. Lambe before she sailed was that she was not to sell her Georgian silver candlesticks to finance her visit!

Before his family arrived, Charles went on a lightning tour with the two Mountbattens to Morocco. This ended with a stirring return passage to Gibraltar in an ancient hired steamer, the *Sir George White*. The weather in the Straits was so tricky that at one stage Charles took the wheel 'sending everyone else, including the Captain, down below to stoke like hell!'

The visit of the Lambe ladies was as pleasant as usual. There were Fleet exercises soon after their departure, which would be the last before the *Stuart* sailed for home. In the course of these, disaster happened, luckily only to *materiel*, not *personnel*. Off Corfu, reported Charles:

> The Flotilla went minesweeping and unfortunately the divisional commander temporarily in charge took the whole party at 18 knots over a six fathom patch. As the sweeps were set to 60 feet (10 fathoms) they very naturally hit the bottom and we lost the best part of 8 sets of sweeping gear. This led to a Court of Enquiry and—as the technical expert—I had to attend and also to help in making out reports of the holocaust the day before.

The last event of the commission was an attempt of Sir Roger Keyes (abetted by Lord Louis) to contrive a Portsmouth appointment for Charles instead of the Staff Course, so that he would be more readily available for naval polo. Charles resisted. Had he succumbed, he would 'never be able to look Brock or Somerville in the face again'.

V

Charles was ashore for a little over a year and a half, during the course of which he reached, by seniority, the rank of lieutenant-commander. The Staff Course was interesting and strenuous, but allowed time for other pursuits. He and a musical friend, Stephen Roskill, later to become the Official Naval Historian of the Second World War, joined the Bach Choir, and Charles learnt to fly light aircraft, one of which he soon acquired, in addition to his Bentley.

Moreover, polo was so far from neglected that he played for the Navy in the Inter-regimental Tournament at Hurlingham in two successive years, 1931 and 1932.

Admiral John Godfrey, later to become Director of Naval Intelligence during the Second World War, recalls the seriousness with which, in spite of such diversions, Charles took the Staff Course itself. Godfrey was then a captain, and Charles a lieutenant, so that it was an acute prediction on Godfrey's part that Charles would one day become First Sea Lord. He remembers particularly how fearlessly Charles would stand up and state his views at the discussions which followed the various lectures, and how shrewd his comments could be.

There were occasional chances of trips abroad, one of the first of them being to Munich, where Charles worked hard to improve his German. A later visit was to the Villa Olivetta, on Lake Como, where he was the guest of Victor and Peta Mylius.

> The villa, [so he told his mother] stands right on the edge of the lake, with enormous mountains at its back. The garden stretches for about ¼ mile on either side, filled with water-falls, rock gardens and fine trees. Hibiscus, cannas and zinnias grow in masses, and the oleanders and tuberoses provide a heavy scent in the evening.

After the Staff Course, which was based on Greenwich, Charles went back to H.M.S. *Vernon*, attached to the department concerned with the development of torpedo control material and techniques. Early in 1931 his stepfather, at that time an Air Vice-Marshal, was given his K.C.B. shortly before retirement from the post of Air Officer Commanding Coastal Area. In one of the earliest letters Charles addressed to his mother as Lady Lambe, written on 16 February for her birthday next day, he said:

> You know well how much I love you but I am sure you have no idea how much I admire you. Nobody I have ever met anywhere is so consistently unselfish or puts others before yourself as you do. Moreover you do it in a most unobtrusive way. I suppose that is the essence of Christianity and you are the most truly Christian person I know, in the very best sense of the word.
> Don't let this humble praise go to your head!

The Lambe family had been settled for some years at Grove House, Semley, near Shaftesbury, not far from where Charles was born,

and with the Air Vice-Marshal's retirement, farming was in
prospect. But before matters could be fully worked out Charles
was at sea again. He had been appointed Squadron Torpedo
Officer in the cruiser *Hawkins*, flagship of Admiral Nasmith,
Commander-in-Chief, East Indies. His captain was Tom Phillips,
later, as Admiral Sir Tom Phillips, to lose his life when H.M.S.
Prince of Wales was sunk by Japanese aircraft in 1941. 'Am very
fit and well,' he wrote to his mother soon after he embarked, adding:
'It is lovely to be in a ship at sea again.' The pack of hounds which
he was escorting to Gibraltar would scarcely have agreed with him,
particularly in the Bay of Biscay.

By 22 October the *Hawkins* was at Malta, which Charles was
delighted to see again, and he even enjoyed the sometimes stifling
passage down the Red Sea, waking one day at day-break, when he
'never saw anything so lovely as the dawn over Arabia. Huge stars
hung like lamps just above the horizon, pellucid and liquid, and
the sky behind a kind of smoky pink'. At Aden there was polo, and
then, early in November, the cruiser reached Bombay.

This was Charles's first visit to the Far East, and his remarks
were uninhibited, as was his way in letters home. In later years he
grew to love the East, and to know and admire its people. His
first impressions were bleaker.

The people here are awful stiffs [he wrote to his mother from
Bombay on 16 November]. All very public school conscious and
vilely punctilious about such things as calling etiquette. It is all
such nonsense. The natives are terribly poor looking specimens.
Spindly legs and expressionless faces. They never seem to laugh
or look anything but miserable or to expect anything else!

Ten days later, the prospect had cheered considerably.

The Admiral arrived aboard the day before yesterday, [he
reported], and the first thing he had to deal with almost was a
request for leave from me! . . . I have had such a marvellous
offer! . . . We went the other day out to the local flying club and
had a fly—a young lieutenant called Buckley who had flown for
years in the Fleet Air Arm and in the King's Cup at home, and I.
The Club members are very enthusiastic, and at once placed
a Moth at our disposal to fly to Cawnpore (about 700 miles) . . . so
as to take part in an air race from Cawnpore to Lucknow (about
500 miles) and then to fly back.

A second machine is going from the Club, and we shall travel in company. . . . Apart from the fun of the flying we ought to see a lot of India in the 5 days and visit places that one will never have another chance of seeing. The Captain and Admiral are apparently both keen on our going as being good advertisement for the Navy.

The flight was completely successful, proceeding without any untoward adventure, though as a race it was not taken very seriously. Charles indeed had an opportunity of seeing varied country within a very short space of time, and enjoyed every moment of the trip.

VI

In December 1932 the *Hawkins* visited the Persian Gulf and in January and February of the following year she was at Ceylon. At Trincomalee, Admiral Nasmith had a visit from King Alphonso XIII of Spain, who was in exile. Charles had already met him, also his son Juan, who was serving as a midshipman in H.M.S. *Enterprise*. The King had recently been staying with the Mountbattens, so Charles could expect news. Their encounter was in fact rather embarrassing, for Alphonso came into the ward-room of the *Hawkins*, and 'in front of all the officers assembled to meet him, suddenly threw his arms round my neck and said: "Ah! My old friend!" I thought for one moment that I was going to be kissed!'

In March, at Madras, Charles had some remarks to make on the running of the ship which reflected on the limitations of the captain, but which other observers besides himself were to note.

Like all small men, [he told his mother] he is very sensitive and suspicious of being neglected and must in consequence have his finger in every pie. He will not trust anyone to do a job. He must do it himself, which means a lot of extra work for him and everyone else. Still, he is becoming more human gradually, I think.

Captain Phillips was, in fact, a centralizer, a trait which was strong throughout his career. But he could at least appreciate the quality of being able to delegate, when others showed it, for when Charles left the *Hawkins* he said, in the course of a warm tribute, that he 'has the gift of decentralization without loss of efficiency to a marked degree. I consider he should do very well in the higher ranks of the Service.'

After a stay at Madras, the *Hawkins* returned to Ceylon, then made an extended cruise in the Indian Ocean, with the prospect of some weeks in East Africa, during the course of which Charles hoped to climb Mount Kilimanjaro. In due course he attempted to do so, only to be foiled because of the severe sickness which overcame one of his party on the way up. He was making arrangements for a visit from his mother, this time by herself, as Betty had married and was beginning to have the cares of a young family, when there came a bombshell, and all his plans were changed. He was promoted Commander, his 'brass-hat' being given him at an exceptionally early age.

This promotion, [he wrote from Mombasa on 1 July 1933] is still, after 24 hours, so unexpected as to be unbelievable. I haven't done 3½ years as a Lieut. Cdr. yet, and the most junior Lieut. Cdr. to be promoted in recent years has always had at least 4–4½ years in the rank.

The possibility of it happening had honestly never crossed my mind and I was almost stunned last night when the Signal Officer rushed in and congratulated me. It would have been too cruel a practical joke to play on anyone and yet it seemed that was the only explanation.

I wonder how you will hear of it! Charles will probably spot it in the papers but if he doesn't I can imagine you jogging along at Semley without knowing for weeks that your son is a commander and the most junior promotion, probably, since the war.

It has been a bit difficult on board. Poor old Cecil Gairdner has only got one more chance and our No. 1, Eccles, who is my greatest friend on board is a struggling married man and beginning to wonder whether he will be passed over too. We were all hoping and waiting for his name to come through when mine came instead. So it has been a mixed period of consolations and congratulations.

This, of course, means home for me as soon as they can send a relief. . . .

By the end of August Charles had heard what his future movements would be. He would go to the *Vernon* for a short refresher course, and then to the Mediterranean as Squadron Torpedo Officer on the staff of the Destroyer Admiral. In his view, this was 'the best Torpedo job in the Navy'. Few would have disagreed— least of all his future Admiral. His name was Andrew Browne Cunningham, and he was the greatest sea commander of his era.

5

VII

By 1934 the spirit in the Mediterranean Fleet had been transformed, and the Navy, in its professional aspects, came a long way before polo. The change was effected by Sir William Wordsworth Fisher—known as 'the great Agrippa'—a big man in every sense of the word, and possibly the only British admiral of the present century capable of corresponding in Latin, as well as being at home in French and other European languages. He was an inspiring chief, and this was exactly the case with Cunningham—'A.B.C.' as he was called—who, though he had none of Fisher's range of intellectual interests, was the best handler of destroyers the Navy ever produced. A leader himself, he fired others by his example, and among those with whom Charles found he would be serving, to name but three, were Philip Vian, Geoffrey Oliver, and Mountbatten.

It was actually Charles who first introduced Mountbatten to Cunningham. This was in Paris, on his way out. The three men were to see a great deal of one another in the future. Each in his turn would, in course of time, become First Sea Lord. The Admiral and his wife were travelling out together: 'kindness itself', Charles described them 'and in very good spirits all the time'. He had no sooner got to Malta than he heard that the promotion of his friend Eccles had at last taken place. This relieved him of a long-standing worry.

Although there was a good deal in his letters home about polo and his ponies, Charles was to be much at sea, exercising in a strenuous way, for Cunningham had charge of over thirty destroyers, believed in work, and demanded the utmost efficiency. His flagship was the light cruiser *Coventry*, and it was to this ship that Charles had been appointed. She was, so he thought, just the right size for the job, and he found her ward-room a happy place. Others on the Staff were Commander Anthony Buzzard, and Lieut.-Commander D. O. Doble, who looked after Operations and Signals respectively. Doble was older than Charles. Buzzard, like Charles, had done the Staff Course, and the first thing Cunningham said to him was that the sooner he forgot everything he had learnt the better! The Admiral's experience of war was considerable, and he preferred practice to theory. Staff work bored him, but, as he was a prince among delegators, and trusted a man once he had proved him, he got exceptional service and devotion from those about him. Although he would never tolerate slackness, and sometimes expected the near impossible, his infectious gaiety usually carried all before it. Certainly he was a man after Charles's heart.

In mid January, Charles wrote from Bizerta, to tell his mother that the Fleet had had

... a great two days at sea on the way here. I couldn't have enjoyed my job more. The Admiral is a quick and active-minded man who makes decisions instantly, but who will always listen to what you have to say first. Just the type of man one enjoys working with.

Plans were soon in train for another visit to Malta by Lady Lambe, Mrs. Cunningham—as she then was—offering to put her up on arrival, or to help in any way. 'The more I see of the Admiral,' reported Charles, 'the more I like him. They are a very nice pair.' There were further exercises in March, including a visit to Gibraltar after a rendezvous with the Home Fleet west of the Rock.

We had an amazing five days in the Atlantic in about the worst sea I've ever seen, [Charles reported]. Actually I think this ship was about the right size for that sea and we did not suffer so badly as the battleships and destroyers. It was an absorbingly interesting exercise and I enjoyed every minute of it though it was hard going.

During May, Charles found a fellow enthusiast for organ music, Henry Cecil. They played 'two harmoniums simultaneously in church. He is a magnificent organist so we had a lot of fun together and the sailors played up well and sang loudly'. Edwina Mountbatten had arrived in Malta, and so had King Alphonso.

He was in very bad odour—so he said—because on his way through Rome, the Pope had organized a special Mass etc. for his birthday but he couldn't stop for it without missing our polo match, so he came on, much to the chagrin of all the dignitaries of the Roman Church!

Lady Lambe's summer visit was the usual success, though she was worried about a possible entanglement. 'You must not think any more about this marriage business,' wrote Charles in July from Cephalonia. 'You need never worry about my getting married to someone I don't know well enough to be quite certain, so don't think anything more about it, my darling.' This was indeed a counsel of perfection: what fond mama could help speculating about an attractive, brilliant and well-endowed son, who was already past the age when many of his friends had made their choice, for better or worse?

Autumn and winter brought more music. There was Squadron-Leader Jones of the R.A.F. who was a César Franck enthusiast and a fine pianist. He and Charles played much together, and he also made friends with the wife of one of the canons at the Cathedral, who was a violinist. He hoped as a result to be given the chance of playing the cathedral organ. In December he actually gave a lecture on music 'to a crowd of about 30 or 40 men of all sorts at a Toc H hostel. I think it went fairly well,' he reported. 'Anyway most of them were still awake at the end.'

This was the time of the Fascist heyday in Italy, and although Charles did not refer to the incident in letters home, he figured in an amusing scene with his Admiral, at a time when the *Coventry* was on a visit to Leghorn.

Among the official visitors was the local Fascist boss [wrote Lord Cunningham in his autobiography *A Sailor's Odyssey*]. He was received by a Royal Marine guard. The marines had the greatest difficulty in keeping straight faces as the black-shirted visitor strutted importantly round the ranks flapping his arm up and down in the Fascist salute. He was taken into my cabin and we conversed in bad French, Commander Charles Lambe acting as my interpreter. Suddenly, to my astonishment, just after I had put the question: 'How long have you been stationed at Leghorn?' our visitor leapt to his feet, hurried out of my cabin past the guard, who had not time to present arms, ran down the ladder, jumped into his boat and cast off. Lambe afterwards confessed that in error he had translated my question: 'You've been here long enough!'

At one time, early in January 1935, he shared a house with Mountbatten, whose wife and their two small children were shortly expected. 'I can't think what will happen,' he told his mother, 'as in addition to two bush babies there is now a bear in the house. It is a honey bear about 9 months old . . . about 18 ins high with tremendous claws and teeth. Edwina bought it as a baby in Singapore and will get the shock of her life when she gets back and sees it.'

Charles seemed likely to continue his custom of never serving a full commission in a single ship, for in February, when his mother was making preparations for yet another trip to Malta, and the Cunninghams had offered her their usual generous hospitality until she got settled in a flat of her own, the Admiral suddenly sent for him.

'Bad news,' [Charles reported him as saying] 'I've had a letter from the Second Sea Lord today saying you must leave the *Coventry* as they want you for a special job.'

So many surprising things have happened in the last few years that this did not surprise me very much but he went on to tell me what the job was and that *did* rather surprise me. Dudley Pound says that the *Vernon* is in the grip of an inferiority complex and that the Admiralty have decided to send a live wire there as Commander. The live wire is you and you are to go in April. If you cannot be spared they will have to send someone who is not a Torpedo man so there is no question but that you must go. I am very sorry etc., etc. . . . Finally he has given me 24 hours to think it over before he calls back but apparently there is no question of any alternative . . .

It is a great compliment I feel and so I'm naturally delighted despite being very sorry indeed to leave A.B.C. and the *Coventry*. Still chances like this don't often come in one's way and so nothing else must count. Actually I have asked the Admiral to ask the Admiralty if I may stay here till we come home in June. There are many Service reasons for this—and also I want to play in the Army–Navy match in May! . . .

It's a difficult job for anyone as junior as myself. The place is full of Senior Commanders and most of the others were once senior to me. Still, it's a wonderful job and I'm delighted at the idea, and so will you be I'm sure because it means two years (probably more) at home.

In the upshot, the Admiral decided to protest against Charles leaving, as a result of which the *Vernon* job itself might well have gone elsewhere: in any case he would request that Charles might stay in the ship until June, when she was due home for a refit.

Before the end of February, the news was firm that Charles would be allowed to stay in the *Coventry* until June, while Pound actually spoke of getting someone else for the *Vernon*. But his luck held. His mother enjoyed another visit to Malta, Charles went home with his ship, and he went to the *Vernon* soon afterwards.

VIII

The year Charles spent as Commander of H.M.S. *Vernon* brightened that establishment. His high spirits, versatility, optimism, and efficiency soon rid the place of any trace of that 'inferiority complex' the Second Sea Lord had mentioned, and it was able to compete on equal terms with its neighbour and friendly rival, the Gunnery School at Whale Island. The Captain of the *Vernon* was Algernon Willis, yet another officer with whom Charles worked closely who rose to the highest rank in the Navy. Cunningham had written of Charles: 'If this officer has any weak points in his character I have not discovered them. . . . A charming personality, but a strong one, not afraid of expressing his opinions in any company,' and it was not long before he was telling Mountbatten how much he missed him. Torpedo experts with Charles's gifts were not found on every admiral's staff. Willis, when his turn came, spoke of him as 'an officer of outstanding ability' who had 'done much for the Establishment' of which he had charge. 'Between us,' he added in a reminiscence noted down many years later, 'we managed to get the men to keep their hair reasonably short, which is a prerequisite of a smart seaman, for even 30 and more years ago the long hair vogue was beginning to creep in.'

At least one naval wife still remembers him gratefully for his consideration for his juniors; while successive holders of the same appointment had cause to thank him in that, though a bachelor of means, he occupied the Commander's official quarters, thus ensuring that there should be no precedent for the authorities to scale down their appropriation in this direction.

Among his other activities, and they were legion, Charles resumed singing with the Bach Choir, continued his flying, played polo a third time for the Navy in the Inter-Regimental Cup, and made a film. This was called *The Prize is Paris*, in which his future wife, Peta Mylius had a small part.

For this adventure the *Vernon*'s mess was converted into a baronial hall, the 'daughter of the house' being engaged to a socially eligible young man. When preparations for the wedding are well advanced, the bridegroom-to-be wins a newspaper competition, the prize being a week in Paris. He decides to go, but promptly gets mixed up in an espionage plot, and is kidnapped. His fiancée then flies a Tiger Moth over to France, and rescues her young man from the clutches of a most improbable set of thugs. All ends happily.

The cast was made up almost entirely of *Vernon* ward-room officers and their families, and it was Charles, in appropriate disguise, who piloted the aircraft. The film was much enjoyed, and it was actually reshown, twenty years later, when Charles, by that time a Flag Officer, was guest of honour at an annual gathering.

During his year at Portsmouth, much was happening in the world at large. Europe was approaching war, and Britain was slowly and belatedly rearming. King George V died on 20 January 1936 and there followed the brief reign of his successor.

Against all expectation, Charles suddenly found himself removed from Navy to Court, the exchange being due not to any desire of his own, but to the persuasion of Lord Louis Mountbatten. Always close to Edward VIII, both as Prince of Wales and King, it was Mountbatten's idea that his cousin should have about him someone not far from his own age who would represent the Navy at its best. In the autumn of 1936, Charles became an Equerry.

Chapter Three

AT THE COURT OF KINGS

KING GEORGE V, trained as a naval officer, and with
a highly developed sense of order and decorum, had been
the centre of a smooth-running Court, no detail of which
escaped his vigilance. His eldest son and successor, whose early
manhood had been spent as a soldier in France, and who had since
undertaken a succession of triumphant Commonwealth tours, in
the course of which he had come to realize something of the nature of the
modern democracy, was never happy in the thraldom of etiquette
and protocol. When he succeeded to the throne, it was his intention
to modernize the monarchy, and in the process to sweep away much
of the intricate machinery which had surrounded his predecessors.

An impulsive man, Edward moved far and fast: and he had not
at that time the advantage of a consort who would have given his
life some of that stability with which his mother, Queen Mary
had provided his father. When Charles joined the entourage of the
new King, matters were heading towards a crisis, part political,
part personal. Foreign affairs, and the very high rate of unemployment in Britain, were causing the greatest concern in Parliament,
while it was known abroad, and freely trumpeted, that the bachelor
King, the most eligible match in Europe, was deeply attached to
an American lady who had already been twice married, Mrs. Wallis
Simpson.

It was Charles's way, in the face of experiences of more than
usual interest and importance, to commit his impressions to paper.
It had been so in the case of the sinking of the *Raleigh* in 1922, and it
was so when he went to Court, though the record he kept was
brief, much delayed, and fragmentary. In a formal sense, his
mother was the first person he addressed from Buckingham Palace,
on 7 October, but a good deal had happened before that, which, at
the time, he kept to himself.

I cannot go to bed for my first night in Buckingham Palace without writing you a line to say how improbable it all seems! [he wrote to Lady Lambe.]

Having partially undressed, the whole situation seemed so fantastic that I have had to dress again and come and write to you. Two, three years ago how little did we think that I should find myself in so responsible a position! Though, in fact, it appears that there are very few duties, there are so many little ways in which it must be possible to help or hinder the King and the Navy and the Empire that I feel rather appalled at the whole business! But I am happy and quite confident that I can do it better than most naval officers.

Have just said goodnight to Charles [his stepfather]. He is the first person whom I have met today who hasn't plied me with questions, and is consequently a joy to talk to.

In this letter, Charles touched on a subject which pervaded all his Court experience, the intense *curiosity* about Royalty which is a characteristic of every age, and from which no country appears to be exempt. A Court is a centre, and the centre of that centre is a Sovereign, a man apart. That is one of the reasons for the fascination of the best Court memoirs, of which those of the Duc de Saint-Simon are the most illustrious. The Court which Saint-Simon described was the seat of power in France at the height of her glory; that of Edward VIII was a very different place, but it was of fascinating interest to most of those outside it, as well as to at least some of those within. It would continue so to be during the few remaining weeks of the King's reign.

According to Charles's notes, negotiations for his appointment began in June 1936, when he was presented to the King by Mountbatten. He was supposed not to know the reason for the interview, and mutual embarrassment resulted. Mrs. Simpson, who was also present, struck Charles as 'smart, slick and wise-cracking'. She kept the conversation going, Mountbatten meanwhile 'trying to show me off'. Presently the royal cousins removed themselves, and Charles was left alone with Mrs. Simpson. 'Realized this was the real test,' he noted, 'and played up to full capacity.'

Early in July, Mountbatten confessed he had over-propaganded. 'H.M. dug in his toes. Period of indecision. Mrs. S. the only method of control.' A little later, the King left for Belgium in the Admiralty yacht *Enchantress*. Mountbatten was to see him off, and was then to receive the royal command. Charles was woken by a telephone message at about 2 a.m. to say it was 'Yes'. Then came a tussle about allowances; not that this affected Charles personally, but he fought for his rights 'on grounds of consideration for successors' and with Mountbatten's help a reasonable compromise was reached.

Charles's first impressions of the Palace were unfavourable.

Atmosphere very 'unhappy' in naval sense [he noted]. A great deal of whispering and secrecy. One courtier always bleating, a centre of discontent. Everything an effort and done with a shrug of the shoulders. Another—*ancien régime*—outraged, pompous and ineffectual. Godfrey Thomas—forbearing, overworked and tired but always loyal and patient. Tommy Lascelles efficient and very helpful to me.

There was no welcome. I was an outsider like a guest in a Guards Mess. Tolerated but suspect. This suspicion was not confined to me. Everyone whispered. The Lord-in-Waiting superficial and rather facile—very selfish.

Arthur Erskine seemed outside the atmosphere of intrigue and was welcoming and kind.

From the first the organization seemed wrong. The nominal Executive Head was the Lord Chamberlain but inside the Palace there was no Chief of Staff. Consequently the good old atmosphere of competition for the King's Ear prevailed, as it must always have done in history. A really big understanding man could have made the system work by earning not only the loyalty of his own department but of all the many others who, while trying to co-operate, owed him no direct allegiance in a disciplinary sense.

Dined once or twice with Jack Aird who was very fully conscious of the above stress and asked how it struck the unprejudiced eye. . . .

Charles's account of his first actual encounter with the King, after he had entered his immediate service, was as graphic as the rest of his notes.

Had always supposed I was comparatively emancipated from the primitive magical concept of Kings, but the panic with which I anticipated this first contact since gazetting soon disproved that boast. Fear of unknown etiquette, awe, and the feeling that the flunkeys were watching made me very apprehensive indeed, and when the bell rang announcing his approach, panic nearly won.

The black Buick arrived at the King's door and out he got in the usual tight-waisted black coat with astrakhan collar, bowler hat and a windproof pipe clenched. Red dispatch boxes poured out behind.

He said: 'Hello, you've taken over have you,' shook hands, smiled rather nervously and paced into his little Chinese room. Phew!

Later he noted, about his first spell of duty:

I went out to dinner every evening, but not until the King had gone. It was almost impossible to find out what his movements were even inside the Palace. This was deliberate, of course, and meant no peace for anyone. For as much as an hour sometimes, the car would wait outside the Garden Entrance while a porter, & two footmen and I waited inside, sometimes talking feebly to try to relieve the monotony and gloom and sometimes studying the extravagant Arthurian and religious watercolours which adorned the passage or the tusks & savage weapons which hung on the walls. An inlaid cedarwood chest & a Victorian mahogany settee or replicas of the Pompeii Narcissus I looked at over and over again. It never seemed to occur to him that his lack of routine and impulsiveness entailed all this hanging about.

One of the King's ideas was that no directions should be given to the police about his movements to and fro. The embarrassment this caused led to Charles's first glimpse of the Duke of York, who, as King George VI, was to be his brother's successor. One day, just before the King was off on a journey the Duke came in to the Equerries' room to pick up his brother to go to the station. Charles had to tell the Duke that the King had countermanded his orders to have the traffic police clear a way, and the Duke burst out: 'Why *does* he do that? It's so stupid and only makes things much more difficult for everyone concerned.' 'That was my view too,' Charles commented, 'and I liked him at once for his outburst.'

It has been a very wearing week [Charles wrote to his close friend Stewart Perowne]. Lots of doubting moments: shall I beard him in his den? interrupt?—or shall I do whatever I think best and stand the racket. That sort of thing is tiring—so is Henry Harewood, though that is my fault because I can't talk racing . . .

I'm learning and learning slowly. It is rather painful sometimes & one gets fits of feeling that one will never learn. But I comfort myself by asking what Naval officer could do it better and I can find none.

Charles had his first view of Sandringham from the air. 'It was a most beautiful afternoon' he told his mother, 'and the place looked so marvellous despite the rather pitchpiney atmosphere of the house.' He amplified the account in a letter to Perowne.

It was brilliant sunshine with the sky that peculiarly clear blue that only comes after a heavy rain shower. There was no wind and the only sound was the rustle-rustle-plop of the acorns falling off the oaks. The shrubs and trees are so lovely.

Inside ... heavenly drawings of King Edward VII skating on the lake and pushing all his children in a sleigh. Amongst all the pictures is one small Lucas Cranach—quite superb—a hunting scene in a forest with hundreds of stags and horsemen and hounds.

A week later, he visited Norfolk again, with Sir Ulick Alexander.

Ulick and I drove down to Sandringham in the Humber, on 18 October, [he noted]. The conversation was rather strained. He didn't quite know what he could say to me or not so we kept off the subject of the King and the Court.

On arrival at about 7.30 there was a telephone message from the Prime Minister who wanted to get in touch with the King, who could not be found by phone. He had left the Fort [Belvedere] and wasn't expected at Sandringham till after midnight.

Next morning, after breakfast, Tommy Lascelles said: 'Isn't this Ipswich business frightful' [referring to the law case where Mrs. Simpson's divorce would be decided]. That was the first I knew. He then told me that it was on account of the divorce that the P.M. wanted to see the King.

That morning the King and Ulick went all round the gardens and planned many changes. In the afternoon we went out and saw the flax factory. . . . The King left after dinner.

Next day, 20 October, the King and Prime Minister had the discussion which Charles referred to as 'his famous interview with Baldwin'. This decided the King's future. 'I knew nothing of

what passed,' he recalled, 'but could not help feeling the anxiety
and stress which daily grew over everyone.'

The King returned to Sandringham half-way through dinner,
'obviously in great form', noted Charles.

Over the brandy I heard him say something about: 'Oh Charles
will know, we'll ask him' and then he called across the table
'Charles, what do they do in the Navy about—something or
other?'

It was the first time he had used my Christian name, and a
warm glow of satisfaction and flattery suffused my body.

Next day, duck shooting, a party of five, setting out at 5.30 a.m.
Two of the number, Charles noted, were 'really keen'. Another did
it 'because obviously it was the sort of thing that English gentlemen
do', and Sam Hoare [at that time First Lord of the Admiralty]
'because he wanted to show that even a politician can be a sportsman. I did it because it was my job.'

When Charles returned to Buckingham Palace, and continued
to live there, he found that one courtier showed 'chagrin'. He
'seemed to think that bedrooms should not be used, which seemed
rather unreasonable especially as mine was number 357 or
something'.

Preparations were afoot for the visit to the Fleet and Kinloch
came several times to see me. Most of the queries were thus
referred to me and I dealt with them, which seemed sensible
enough, though I only discovered afterwards what antagonism
this aroused in the Secretariat.

Later Charles confessed in a letter to Stewart Perowne that:
'the Naval visit is terrifying. I know some simple thing which I
ought to have foreseen will occur to mar the smooth working of the
visit. Luckily Dickie will be there but sometimes he makes things
more complex and therefore less smooth!'

Charles's notes continued:

One Friday night the King suddenly said: 'Would you like to
come to the Fort this weekend if you're doing nothing?' I said
I was shooting with Dickie but would get out of it. He said:
'Good. You can always shoot with Dickie, so come tomorrow
evening.'

I motored to the Fort, arriving about 6 p.m. In the sitting room there was Mrs. Simpson, Sybil Colefax, Mrs. Bonner and the King. I was frightfully embarrassed and had to devote all my energies to overcoming it.

The conversation was general and trivial and every now and again the King made some obscure remark and looked at Mrs. S. and laughed. He wanted to 'have secrets' with her like a child. Lady Colefax was nice, intelligent and sympathetic. I felt at ease with her. . . . Mrs. S. was smart, chic as ever and very talkative.

The octagonal room was delightful. Pickled pine walls, bookshelves let-in flush and 2 or 3 Canalettos. The hall was white above the stairs. The Munnings picture of the P. of W. was on the stairs and a lovely Stubbs of soldiers in the hall. My bedroom was very small & fitted like a yacht. White walls and ivy pattern chintz, a roaring fire & telephones etc., etc.

Half way through dinner Mr. Bonner arrived. The King wore a kilt and old Forsythe the pipe major did his round after dinner. Mrs. S. then said: 'Sir, *won't* you play us something on the pipes?' The others said: 'Oh, Sir, please yes' and we all said 'Please do.' Mrs. S. said 'He plays too beautifully, especially "Miss Otis regrets . . ." Do play us Miss Otis, Sir.'

The King said he'd go and try and disappeared from the room. The others all said: 'Don't you think that's a cute idea—the King playing Miss Otis on the pipes?' & we all said 'Yes, how cute it was' and I thought of the horror on old Forsythe's face.

Suddenly they started playing outside. They didn't come in. It *was* 'Miss Otis' or so they said. To me all tunes are almost identical on the pipes and equally unpleasant.

Anyway it was cute, & we all said so when the King came back.

Later the party went to the sitting room and Charles had to play the piano. Then they all sang—tunes from *Porgy* and so on—then gramophone, then more piano, so that Mr. Bonner could sing his song. Then more talk, Mrs. Bonner saying: 'We have a wonderful Roos-oh back home. Are *you* interested in Roos-oh? Say, Wallis, Commander Lambe is *very* interested in Roos-oh.' ('What would the Douanier Rousseau himself have thought, I wonder?' commented Charles.)

'Then bed. The King going up a separate staircase. The ladies curtseyed and we all went up together.'

Charles was to have ridden in the State Procession for the Opening of Parliament early in November but arrangements were altered. He sent Stewart Perowne an account of the ceremony, including a quick drawing, describing it as 'Heaven'.

Bitterly disappointed at being deprived of my ride after having spent most of the previous afternoon making friends with the Royal Horse. The ceremony in the Lords compensated.

As we assembled to await the King I was almost overcome at the sight of so many and such magnificent guardsmen. There was one on each side of the long staircase ... Every form of Herald and Stick and Great Officer of State was there & we processed at a funereal pace to the Robing Room. When robed the King emerged and we crawled down the Long Gallery into the House. Being ahead of the King, the House was almost dark as I entered.

The candelabra were dull pin-points & the stained glass glowed with colour despite the dull outside day. As the King entered, all the lights rose to full brilliance & once again I nearly swooned—such good theatre!

He took ample time and did it all with great dignity and authority—My only regret is that more people could not have been there to be as impressed as I was.

Charles's final experiences with Edward VIII as King were recorded in a long note covering various events, including those of the day following his first evening at Fort Belvedere, already described.

Breakfast in bed about 11.0.
When I came down about 11.30. Mr. and Mrs. Bonner were going out walking and asked me to go with them. The surroundings were lovely, wild and autumnal, and it was a bright cold showery day. The conversation was vapid and empty of all except superlatives and yet it never flagged. . . .

The King and Mrs. S. appeared for lunch and afterwards we were to walk again. We all strolled around the place. Lady C. was with me mostly. . . . Slipper got lost and had to be hunted for and the King showed considerable knowledge of rhododendrons.

The King and Mrs. S. entered the front door first, and he at once went on his knees to take off her galoshes. As the passage was thus blocked, the rest of us stood contemplating the spectacle, she, tickled to death and mildly remonstrative, he, earnest and intent, muttering slightly to himself but oblivious of us.

After tea, Mr. Bonner and I were shown the view from the tower. On a fine day you could see the Crystal Palace but even through glasses this was not today possible. In the turret was his museum. Bric a brac from all over the world. Shark's teeth, Princess Mary's Gift Box, 7 half crowns solid from the pocket of a dead British soldier and so on.

The evening was a repetition of the night before except that we all said goodbye and left at separate times in the morning . . .

* * *

On 11th November 1936, the King arrived at the Home Office in time to meet his mother. I handed him his wreath at the Cenotaph and was amazed at the naval guard of honour from Chatham who sang 'Oh God our help . . .' lustily by heart while the soldiers all fidgeted with little bits of paper.

About 5 o'clock I had to call for the King at Marlborough House.

Previously, discussing the route to the Legion Rally at the Albert Hall, I had undertaken to 'carry the can' if the King objected to having the Quadriga Arch open & the traffic stopped at Hyde Park Corner.

Now, as we drove from Marlborough House to the Field of Remembrance on a wet night, we were held up for fully 5 or 6 minutes in Parliament Square. Despite the crush in the stationary traffic jam, nobody recognized him as he puffed away at his pipe.

At the Abbey he walked round the grass plot. Only one man met him but the crowd soon recognized him despite the rain and the darkness. He planted a cross in memory of his father, doing it for all the world as if he meant it.

On the way back he said 'what time must we leave for the Albert Hall? I said 10 to 8 but he said: 'I think we should leave at a quarter to with all this traffic.' Was I to say I'd arranged a clear run or not, knowing how much he hated that sort of thing? Before I could make up my mind, it was too late and I was committed to hoping he wouldn't notice. Munster, the Lord-in-Waiting, was coming with us and he promised to talk gardening hard all the way down Constitution Hill. This worked a treat and he never remarked on the traffic being held up.

At the Rally he got a great reception, though I thought an unusual number of faces looked up at the Royal Box when the band struck up: 'Hallo! Hallo! Who's your lady friend?'

That night we left for Portland at 12.30 a.m. and my triumph of earlier in the evening was snatched from me as I got a proper raspberry for arranging that the car should drive on to the platform abreast the Royal train—which was an ordinary sleeper & dining car attached to the ordinary train.

'Why *must* they do this? Do they think I can't walk 20 yards like an ordinary person? Oh God! They've got barriers up to keep the crowd back. Who on earth arranged this?'

'I'm afraid it's my fault, Sir. I gave permission. It helps the railway people.'

'Well see it never happens again. Do they think I'm senile?'

*   *   *

Dickie was with us.

We sat up talking till 2.30 when the King said: 'Well, if we don't want to look our ages tomorrow we'd better go to bed.'

That night the royal saloons were unhitched at Westbury & worked down to Portland as a special & stabled in a siding there. When I got up, in the train, there was 2 feet of water all over the lines. Kinloch could not get near but sent a note saying all was well and the storm necessitated no alteration of programme.

It was a showery day. Many inspections had to be carried out below—a very tiring process looking at people so close to you. The rain pelted down as we arrived on the *Courageous*'s flight deck.

Lunched in the *Nelson* hurriedly.

One of Charles's friends, now Vice-Admiral Schofield, who was present at the lunch in the *Nelson*, vividly remembers the occasion, and how 'we were all dying to know what was happening', as indeed was the entire nation. 'Charles', so he recalls, 'deftly parried all enquiries with: "It's a good life as long as it lasts!"'

The King's energy was astounding [Charles continued]. He did not leave the Anti-Submarine School till about 5.15. which left a bare 2 hours rest before the evening dinner party at 7.30. Then a few of us went to the *Courageous* concert (ship's company). In the interval the King walked right down the centre gangway

6

amongst the men and asked the band at the back of the hall to play some well-known tune. They all sang and at the end a young Ordinary Seaman called for 3 cheers.

At the final curtain HM went on to the stage and made a splendid little speech. One felt very proud of him.

Then the *Nelson*—Wardroom, Gunroom and Warrant Officers' Mess. We left there about 1 a.m. & talked in the yacht till 2 a.m., Dickie, Sam Hoare, Chatfield and I.

Next morning he was very grumpy as we set off at 9.30, but the moment he came before the public he was his charming self.

A hurried lunch in the yacht and landing at Weymouth.

The train was stopped for him at Slough, & he drove to the Fort for the week-end.

*   *   *

The next week was the South Wales visit.

As before, we left Paddington shortly after midnight. Ernest Brown and Kingsley Wood, Ministers in Attendance, were on the train—also Alec Hardinge and myself.

After breakfast in a siding we disembarked into cars. The day was fine and everywhere his reception was wonderful, though E. Brown was inclined to arouse boos.

At the last unemployment centre, the King, E. Brown and I went into the cellar where men were repairing boots.

The King left E. Brown talking and, no sooner had he gone, than the whole party crowded round Mr. B. talking rather threateningly.

'I've a wife & 5 kiddies and all I gets is so and so—'ow d'you expect *me* to live?'

He let them have their say & then said 'Now look here you fellows—for the last 4 months I've been working till 3 & 4 in the morning on your behalf. Will you please believe I'm doing all I can?'

His booming voice had an instantaneous effect.

'Sorry Mr. Brown.' 'Sorry, Sir.' And we walked out.

Mr. B. certainly never lacked guts, & I admired him greatly on the trip.

The journalists—Hannen Swaffer amongst them—were shocking. If the King spoke to a man, they immediately rushed up.

'What did he say?'

'What did you answer?'

'What did he say to that?' and so on.

That was the origin of 'the King's message to South Wales' 'Something must be done'. The King never sent any message to South Wales, except to the Lords Lieutenant. He *did* talk to a man who had been unemployed for 5 years and, in the course of conversation with this one man, said: 'It's terrible, something must be done.'

* * *

That night we spent at a siding at Ross.

The King had a cold and wanted a hot bath. Since he refused to use the proper royal train this entailed telegraphing the station-master at Ross to buy a hip bath in the village which was filled with hot water in his sleeper.

A special telephone wire had been run for a mile or more so that he could talk to Mrs. Simpson that night.

Next day was much the same except the weather was poorer. Everywhere the people looked delighted and hopeful at his visit. They obviously loved and trusted him.

* * *

The next week was horrible. The atmosphere in the Palace was getting unbearable. Everyone looked ill and desperate and old and spoke in whispers. Up to then I knew no details.

One evening I went to see Dickie and he told me that the King had decided to marry. . . . The P.M. was constantly in and out, apparently in his usual humour.

All that week I had nightmares. I woke sometimes terrified, sometimes angry, and sometimes just unutterably miserable. There was nobody to speak to except Dickie. The subject just wasn't discussed in the Palace and one just had to wait and think.

Emotionally exhausted I went on Saturday afternoon to the film *Romeo & Juliet* and was profoundly moved.

Even nightmares end in time, and so did the King's crisis. Edward VIII made a last announcement to the public from Windsor Castle, after his abdication on 11 December 1936. He had reigned for 325 eventful days. He then left for the Continent. Charles had a similar idea. The King went to Austria; Charles flew north, to Copenhagen, to the oldest and one of the most refreshing kingdoms in Europe. He hoped he had 'left the whole business behind', but found it was not so easy. He continued to sleep badly, and, despite the kindness of friends, he returned to England after a week's leave, with a high temperature. Yet, as so often, his splendid constitution threw the sickness off, and he was soon fit for work. He had survived a phase of his life which in many respects was the worst he ever experienced.

II

Charles spent Christmas 1936 recovering, but he was quickly off on his travels again in royal service. Early in January 1937 he became sole attendant on the Duke of Windsor, as Edward VIII had now become. The Duke was the guest of Baron and Baroness Eugene de Rothschild at Enzesfeld, not far from Vienna. There he was able to enjoy some ski-ing, which he was beginning to take up. Lady Lambe was asked to find and forward her son's equipment as soon as possible. He had not used it for some time, but he had had far more experience than the Duke, who was still under instruction.

When Charles arrived at the Rothschild castle, he wrote to his mother to tell her that the Duke was 'in very good form'. Charles relieved Colonel Piers Legh, who had travelled out with his former sovereign from England. Baroness Rothschild took to Charles at once, and he found everything 'most comfortable'.

But—there was an enormous amount of work, some of it extremely tedious, for a great many people from all over the world took it into their heads to write the Duke personal letters. These had to be opened, sorted into personal mail, and into sane and crack-pots—and duly dealt with. The Duke spent much time on the telephone to Mrs. Simpson, who was in the south of France staying with American friends, and left the correspondence to his companion. The last few days of December had yielded an average of between seven and eight hundred missives daily. On 1 January, Charles reported: 'I don't think I have opened more than 300 or so today!' When he had time to look around him, he found 'hoar frost in all the trees and a thick fog: very cold'. He was tired when he wrote, and it was late, and it must indeed have been devotion which made him remember how eagerly his mother would be awaiting his first letter from the Duke's place of retreat.

The pair, when not ski-ing, were often in Vienna, and on 7 January the Duke, King Alfonso, the King of Spain's son Jaime, and Charles all lunched at the Hotel Imperial. Charles purloined a menu ('Germiny: .Suprême de sole sultane: Bœuf bouille flamande: Omelette Imperial') saying to his mother: 'I don't suppose I shall ever lunch with two ex-kings again, so keep it.' He added: 'All well here. H.R.H. is in good form and seems amazingly content and settled. We went ski-ing yesterday at Semmering—a place about 1½ hours by car from here. It was heavenly to be on snow again. Brilliant sun and a sky of Italian blue.'

A week later, the volume of letters seemed to be increasing. One day there were 1,000, but on 5 January 'only 800—from all parts'. He was dealing with them single-handed. 'The country round here is marvellous,' he reported. 'You might be in Canada when you get on the golf course. Wooded hills, valleys and streams. All the woods are carpeted with lily of the valley in spring. . . . The Duke is very well and surprisingly cheerful and has been most awfully nice to me. All the frost is gone and still no snow. We played golf in spring-like weather the last 2 days but both want to get some ski-ing if only there was snow.'

The Duke enjoyed his new-found freedom. Baroness de Rothschild in later letters to Charles, with whom she became great friends, hoped that reality would not bring the Duke up with too much of a jolt. Certainly at the moment it was Charles who was dealing with the paper-work which used to pursue the Duke everywhere when he was on the throne and which he found a strain. On one of the many jaunts to Vienna, the royal purchases were mainly pots of strawberry and cherry jam, a series of road maps of Austria, and a number of thermos flasks. Picnics were much in mind. The Duke could shop in German; so, by this time, could Charles, who was improving daily.

Charles summed up his impressions of Enzesfeld in a letter to Perowne, who was then at Malta, dated 17 January.

When I arrived here I was not only a stranger to my host and hostess, but virtually a stranger to my master. That, coupled with the knowledge that the whole world's glasses were focussed on Enzesfeld made it very disturbing, and I must confess to being rather miserable when I had time to think during the first few days.

But whatever else has happened, I feel that these 3 weeks have entitled me to call myself his friend. The old awe which had never yet left me in his presence has been conquered, and lately I have been able to talk as frankly as I wished without the attendant embarrassment of hitherto.

Who could have predicted this time last year that I should be here as his sole confidant?—that I should be playing about with him *à deux* in the snows of Austria? It seems all so ridiculously improbable still, though it *has* happened.

He has been surprisingly settled and well in mind and body. There is no looking back and apparently still not even a shadow of a question as to the rightness of his decision. He regards these few months till April as a period of 'mourning' or penance and his whole being exists only for that not so distant date.

To begin with I had to steel myself to the possible consequence of showing him the more serious adverse letters. But these, like everything else, leave him totally unmoved and I hope that this condition may long remain.

During the last 8 days we have spent 5 days on the Semmering, a mountain ridge 40 miles from here. Three of these days have been of such quality I could have cried from happiness. A rich wine-coloured sky, paling near the horizon and a brilliant hot sun transforming everything from the snow at one's feet to the most distant peak into jewels; still, rare, cold and incredibly clear air; a landscape made out of nothing but white and every shade of blue like a Vermeer picture, and a foreground of this symbolic figure attended by a fair-haired Bristow, his instructor.

These are the things I shall never forget—nor skating with him on a pond in the hills behind here, seeing him conduct a gramophone record, going into shops with him in Vienna where he is instantly recognized—and behind it all letters, letters, letters—thousands of them, written seriously, sneeringly, heart-brokenly, lovingly, honestly and dishonestly—the whole world profoundly moved and disturbed.

I go back glad to have helped a little, and having learnt a lot of very odd things.

Charles returned to a new 'master', for the man who had assumed his elder brother's burdens ordered the Lord Chamberlain to write to him to say he would be glad if Charles would continue to be a member of the Royal Household. This was a compliment which Charles valued highly. He had liked and admired his Sovereign ever since their first encounter; he respected the resolution with which he assumed signal and unsought responsibility, and the two became such friends that in the course of time the King would feel able to unburden himself to Charles, both personally and in writing, in a way which he found it hard to do with most other members of his staff.

III

Charles had not long returned to London from Austria when he decided to revisit the Mylius's at their Lake Como villa. He found Peta Mylius seriously ill. Charles hoped to persuade her of the benefits of a change, perhaps to England, when her health was better. His plea was successful. 'His kindness, patience and understanding were beyond belief,' she wrote later, 'and I began to think it was worth while to live.'

Charles found the beauty of Lake Como as breathtaking as ever.

It is difficult to believe that I have written the right date at the head of this letter [he wrote to Perowne on 22 February 1937]. I sit under an English midsummer sun looking at the snow capped mountains across the lake, with primroses, cowslips and carnations growing in the garden all around me.

This place is sheer heaven. Last night the brilliance of the few stars and the icy radiance of the mountain tops made the lights on the other side of the lake look pale and yellow. The darkness in the garden was warm and velvety. One needed no coat.

Charles had already had his first turn of duty with the new King and Queen. This had gone well. His letter continued that it had:

. . . ended up with a visit to the East End, where they got a really warm welcome. The King is tackling his job in an admirable spirit; working very hard, keeping very cheerful and refusing to let it get him down as it so easily might.

The filthy innuendos in the Press about his health are quite untrue and quite criminal. However, he laughs at them, which is the only sensible way of taking it. The other day he said: 'Of course you see what they are up to? They cannot accuse me of living with somebody else's wife so they are trying to prove I'm mad!

In a great measure, though with differences which were due to the outlook of a younger generation, the King restored the orderliness so insisted on by his father in everything which related to the Court. This eased the way of those in attendance, and Charles found duty far less of a strain than those imposed by his first autumn and winter.

One of the advantages of his job was that as attendance, or in Palace terms, 'Waits' were by rota, Equerries doing a fortnight of duty with at least a month and sometimes more before the next turn, there was much free time. After the Coronation ceremonies of May 1937 were over, Charles used his leisure for travel. He went so often to France and Italy, particularly to Venice and the Adriatic, that a clerk in the principal air-line office made him laugh by saying: 'Not *again!*'

In August, he was at Balmoral, almost alone with the Royal Family.

No guests. No parties [he wrote to his mother on the 5th]. Today a perfect morning—the King took me walking all over a new grouse moor he has leased. Marvellous air, soft and invigorating and we got very hot and both enjoyed it a lot.

This afternoon we have all been up to a loch in the hills and spent the afternoon damming a burn until we got a big pool and then bursting the dam, to the delight of the children. Afterwards we mucked about in a boat and the children caught three tiny trout.

Some time later, Charles recalled that on their morning walk the King said to him: 'I say, you've got on a pretty old pair of shoes, haven't you? They'll hardly keep out the wet.' Charles replied: 'Oh, they're quite good enough for mucking about here.' This made the King roar with laughter and whenever he saw him in later years he always said: 'Been doing any mucking about lately, Charles?'

His August letter home concluded:

It is lovely to be with such a happy and united family in such lovely surroundings—especially when, for a change, they have nothing to do but enjoy themselves. If only the weather stays good, one could not wish for a more perfect place or nicer people.

In the autumn, Charles paid a fleeting visit to New York, partly to savour the speed and power of the recently launched giant liner, *Queen Mary*, partly to see the effect of the ever-recurring architectural explosion which makes the city so visually exciting: he sent his mother a photograph of the Empire State Building, telling her he had had 'lunch on the top'. The leisure he had on board ship was put to use by jotting down his impressions of his brief time of service with King Edward VIII.

At Christmas he was at Sandringham.

> We've had a great party here [he wrote home on 30 December]. Wonderful presents and charades—in which even Queen Mary took part—in the evening.
>
> I had 3 grand days shooting ... and hope to shoot again tomorrow. We got over 400 pheasants each day except Tuesday which was a wet morning so we walked up woodcock in the afternoon getting about 15.
>
> My shooting is quite extraordinary. On the left side I can hit quite high pheasants and really am shooting quite well, but I can't hit a haystack to the right.
>
> Lastly, I have some great news for you. The King told me last night that I am to be promoted on Saturday. Hope you will be as pleased as I am! I was afraid I was going to lose a length on Dickie but all is now well!

Charles's promotion to captain at the age of 37, though early, was not exceptionally so considering his career, but it had to be the subject of special consideration by the Admiralty, since he had not held an executive sea-going appointment. In the event, he did not have many months to wait for that. He was the junior in a batch of fifteen, all of whom later distinguished themselves in war. The zone for promotion was from four to eight years seniority as commander, and Charles, together with Guy Grantham, another officer who later reached flag rank and held high commands, was the only promotion who had served for as little as four and a half years. For a time, he was the youngest officer of his rank in the Navy.

IV

The year 1938 was marked by international tension, the result of Hitler's demand for the expansion of the Reich at the expense of other countries. It was Charles's fate to be in attendance on the King at the time of the last great efforts by Great Britain and France to contain Hitler by means of appeasement. Although they failed, and led to the loss of independence by Czechoslovakia, that unhappy country eventually going the same way as Austria, which had already been absorbed, it seemed to many as if it might have secured peace, if not 'in our time' in Mr. Chamberlain's hopeful words, then at least for a space which would allow the Western democracies to equip themselves to face still worse threats.

Charles's idea, which was shared by many, was that Britain was being unrealistic, leaning on hollow props like the League of Nations, talking too much about ideals and principles without facing facts.

'Idealism,' [he wrote to Perowne on 21 February] 'what a menace it is!'

Principles have been a menace throughout history and have accounted for so much misery in the past (Divine Right, religion, wars of succession, revolution) that the Communist Party have given them up altogether—by which they mean that they are subordinated to the object which they are out to achieve . . .

We and France have *never* lived up to the League's ideals except when it was in our own interest. Everyone in Europe except the English knows that. No: but an ideal is not jettisoned because you admit that you can't attain it tomorrow.

A few weeks later, on 23 March, when he had been on special duty connected with a State visit by King Carol of Rumania, Charles escaped to listen to music, and he wrote a long letter about it to Perowne.

. . . I broke out with the Lady in Waiting and sneaked unobtrusively to St. Paul's [wrote Charles]. We were given stalls in the Chancel, otherwise we certainly should have had to stand— so great was the crowd for the Matthew Passion.

The escape was complete and more profound than ever. Senses are sharper, perception is keener and intuition has advanced at the expense of logic as the result. After such an experience values become keener, clearer, proportion more apparent and essentials more undiluted.

Goodness! How grateful one should be on such occasions; for one brief moment at least, I see what my life *ought* to be and how it *could* be if I wasn't a lazy, self-indulgent turd. In the same moment one realizes that it never *will* be what it *ought* and *could*, but for some obscure reason that does not seem to matter so much. To realize one's faults and shortcomings is to remove in great part their poison, even if they are not eradicated.

Presumably this approaches psychologically the mystical virtues of humility and confession—perhaps it is even the same thing in modern terminology. The true churchman is, however, always so insistent on the essential difference between philosophy and religion (whereas they differ only as two pilgrim paths to Mecca) or between psychological and mystical experiences.

What is the difference between an Epstein head—say Rima—and an African negro carving? Do they not both appeal by virtue of something above laws of reason and logic, the one by illogical processes in aesthetics, the other by equally illogical but more understandable magical processes?

In the summer, Charles once again spent much of his time travelling about between home and Europe. The King had appointed him a Commander of the Royal Victorian Order, and in September, the month when Hitler was almost on the point of war on behalf of the Sudeten Germans in Czechoslovakia, he was much with the King in London, the rest of the Royal Family being away at Balmoral. On the 19th, he wrote from Buckingham Palace to his mother:

It is extraordinary that once again in a crisis I should find myself . . . alone with anyone so high in the scheme of things.

At Enzesfeld, all was over and done with. There was only the music to face. But this week-end decisions were being taken and, of course, the telephone brought constant reports of each Cabinet decision.

We tried to avoid the topic as much as possible but it couldn't be done entirely and I was surprised to find how much our respective views had in common. More than that I cannot—obviously—say . . .

A little earlier, Charles had been at Royal Lodge, Windsor, which the King thought was 'almost better than Belvedere'. He had been taken a tour of the gardens.

We walked around all the hundreds of rare rhododendrons, [Charles noted] and fingered the dry terra-cotta undersides of the big paper leaves and the King knew all their long Latin names and I could only think of Eugina.

Then the telephone would ring and I would walk up and down the terrace stepping only on squares or lines, determined not to listen but wanting awfully to hear.

Then grouse for dinner and champagne and conversation

became much easier and for the first time all glamour and awe-
someness departed and he was just an ordinary person with a
very difficult job and . . . I felt for the first time that we could be
just ordinary with each other, which was nice . . .

Later the pair walked round the room looking at the Baxter
prints of Victoria and Albert and at the woolwork seats to the
chairs, some of which the King had worked himself. 'I said "I do
that too,"' reported Charles, 'and we talked about the relative
merits of mercerized silk and wool, and of how one got round
corners.'

Then somehow, [the account continued] we were talking about
the British Israelite movement and he told me how old Lady
Waterford on her death-bed had sent for his father and said if
only you will christen your eldest son David all will be well in
the world and he had said but it isn't a family name and she had
said no but won't it do for a Prince of Wales and so David was
tacked on to the end of a long list and he was always known as
that in the family. . . .
   On Sunday there was church, just the two of us and the organ
got stuck on its last note just before the sermon and the parson
had to wait till the bellows were switched off and the note wailed
away like a Christmas pig-balloon and the King looked round
very pleased.
   After lunch we walked for 1½ hours in the Great Park and these
terrible Cabinet deliberations still overshadowed all else. . . .
After tea he read or wrote letters and I read *In Hazard* and the
wireless relayed a Negro Service from the Church of God at
Washington which was rather like Henry Hall doing Akomfud-
zifoo with the Bach Choir, and outside the thought of war—
perhaps in a few day's time those birds outside would not be
heard singing.
   After dinner we sat opposite sides of the fire and he read the
Cabinet minutes and I read the book of Tobit and later some of
the incredibly beautiful poetry out of Ecclesiasticus which I didn't
know.
   Then talk started again about Italy and our Agreement and
how Boris of Bulgaria had given such a perfect impersonation of
M. Lebrun at Balmoral and of how when King Victor Emmanuel
met Musso at Rome after the famous Fascist March and asked
him to be Prime Minister, Musso had said yes on condition that

I may appoint your successor—so that's why the Duca D'Aosta has gone to Abyssinia as a 'try-out'.

Then he said it's funny—I couldn't have done this with any of the other three Equerries—you see, you and I are of the same generation, the others all think differently to us, which of course brought out all the spaniel in me and made me want to lick something.

The political gloom was destined to continue. 'The probability of war looms large,' wrote Charles, 'and at times I find myself near panic—not through fear for myself because funnily enough I don't feel very afraid—but fear of the horror and misery and distress and destruction.' Temporary relief of tension sometimes came in odd ways. 'The King', he noted, 'has just sent for me and given me a terrible-looking dead bug in a Cartier box which fell out of his spectacle case, and told me to find out what it is, or was.' (The answer is, alas, unrecorded.)

Ever since his Cambridge days, Charles had seen Steven Runciman whenever the chance offered. Steven was at this time in Prague, with his father, on a diplomatic mission for the Foreign Office which was foredoomed to failure. The King sent Lord Runciman a message of encouragement, and Charles heard from Steven how much this had helped to cheer a sombre situation. 'It arrived' [wrote Steven] 'when my father was feeling very low and worn out and H.M.'s message just gave him—and all the mission—a stimulating glow that is carrying them on over the next stage whatever that may be. I really can't exaggerate what it meant to him and them all.'

On 23 September the Admiralty rang Charles up to ask whether he was available for a sea-going job if the Reserve Fleet was mobilized. 'The King', he noted, 'has regretfully decided that I must go at once in such a case. So I may be off at a few hours' notice to God knows where—probably to some dug-out ship in one of the Home Ports to get ready for sea as soon as one can.'

Again by way of relief, there was a story circulating in the Palace, said to derive from an august source, of a lunatic who was left a fortune. The head of the asylum sent for him and asked him what he intended to do with the money. 'Well I know one thing I'm going to do,' said the patient, 'and that is—buy a new behind.' 'But why?' said the doctor. 'Because I'm not at all satisfied with the one I've got. Why, only last night I had a look in the mirror and I distinctly saw a hole in it.'

V

On 29 September a telegram from the Admiralty addressed to
Captain C. E. Lambe, C.V.O., R.N., notified Charles of his
appointment to H.M.S. *Curlew*, then at Sheerness. It was his first
command.

I got to the ship at Chatham at tea-time [Charles told his
mother on 18 October], expecting to find officers and men living
in barracks for a few days until the ship was fit to inhabit, but
to my astonishment I found we were moving into the lock that
evening and sailing next morning for Sheerness.

Everyone had stolen a march on everyone else and the ship
was ready for sea except for oiling and ammunition. So we
steamed down here early yesterday morning and picked up a
buoy and have been all working like blacks till this afternoon
when we have been told that we shall not leave here but will
probably put the ship back into reserve next week.

I have got 21 officers and nearly 500 men crowded into an
old 'C' class cruiser built for about 12 officers and 350 men. The
whole party have played up wonderfully. Our Master-at-Arms
joined with only a bowler hat and a large proportion are reserve
men but they have all been good and are in excellent heart. . . .

It was lovely handling this ship down the river and picking
up the buoy in a strong tide and moderate wind—I was a bit
too gay with this first pull and brought the ship up with the buoy
abreast the funnel but we managed to pick it up all right.

Privately, Charles's reactions were slightly different. 'The
officers are very old,' he noted, 'the senior Lieut.-Commander
having been one since 1924 and I don't think he likes me much
especially as he has been captain here before I came.' The officer
concerned had been in charge of the cruiser when she had been
under 'care and maintenance'; now he was himself under orders.

There are two more fairly old ones, [the notes continue] the
second being my 'term' at Osborne and Dartmouth, but I think
the Paymaster Commander is rather nice.

I have an enormous triangular cabin opening out on to the
quarter deck and also a sleeping cabin and bathroom. The
sofa and chairs are covered in one of those terrible drab sort of
pomegranate patterned cretonnes and the walls are green.

In London, Charles had been seeing something of Victor Stiebel, the famous dress designer, and his eye was very much 'in', as indeed it generally was, for the looks and qualities of material.

Perhaps it *is* rather nice being captain of a cruiser [he wrote to Peta Mylius]. The strangeness and the fright have worn off a bit and it's nice having a large comfortable cabin to myself and everybody very deferential which of course makes me wonderfully Queen Mary-like at once. I have more confidence since I spoke to all the sailors on the fo'c'sle yesterday and told them they must go on working all weekend until the emergency was officially proclaimed over and they were lucky to have only four days instead of four years thanks to Mr. Chamberlain and would they like me to write on their behalf to him to say thank you and they all shouted yes please very loudly and so I said all right and now carry on and be careful not to put flour in the magazine or ammunition in the provision room 'cos we were embarking both at once and they all laughed and didn't mind at all to go on all Sunday if need be.

But we stopped work at midday and I went ashore and George [his servant] and the car were there and I went over to see Noel Coward for tea and Zena Dare was there and two young men and it rained awfully hard.

They were all very depressed that the P.M. hadn't been firmer at Munich and said Fascism could have been broken for ever if he had and I didn't agree and then Noel Coward told some very funny stories and said my car was like the Odeon in Leicester Square and we came back, to find that I'm probably going to sea in the ship tomorrow to fire off a few guns which will be fun if it's a fine day.

On 10 October Charles wrote to his mother to say:

I've had a wonderful week. Last Monday we did a full power trial with the engine-room manned chiefly by reservists—officers and men. The average age of the four engineer officers was $53\frac{3}{4}$—not bad. Then this terrific gale. I had to anchor outside [Sheerness] and keep anchor watch for 24 hours and since then we have lost all our mobilization party and have started to put the ship back into reserve again.

It has been the greatest fun handling the ship under way but the isolated life cooped up in glory on board has been rather terrible.

'Outwardly splendid but inwardly rather small,' he told Peta Mylius he had felt, 'and I am now feeling tremendous all through. . . . I feel a very old and experienced sea captain already and moreover I am the head man here at Sheerness of 1 other cruiser, 5 destroyers, 3 minesweepers and some drifters and this ship flies a special flag (like an admiral's) in consequence.' He expected to finish before the end of October, so he told his mother:

. . . and go back and finish my previous job with the King—if he wants me. That means being on duty for the first half of next month—opening of Parliament etc., and I hope a little shooting at Sandringham.

The last incident at Sheerness was when Peta Mylius brought her small son Andrew down to visit the *Curlew*—he was then aged three—together with a friend and her little boy. 'The two small boys were wonderful on board,' reported Charles, 'and very smart in sailor suits.'

Charles's life as a regular courtier was, as he expected, drawing to a close, though he would, in the future, be given appointments which would continue to bring him into touch with the Royal Family. A member of the Court of Queen Victoria was once asked about attitudes to their jobs which most courtiers went through. She is said to have replied that they were 'Be-dazzlement, Republicanism and Acceptance'. There is no suggestion that Charles went through the second of these stages, but the first and last are indicated clearly enough in his letters and memoranda.

. *H.M.S.* Illustrious *under attack by Japanese aircraft, Palembang, Sumatra, 29 January 1945*

. (*over page*) *3rd Aircraft Carrier Squadron, 1949, H.M.S.* Vengeance *leading*

. (*over page*) *As Commander in Chief, Far Eastern Station, arriving at Hanoi, 1953*

9

10

Chapter Four

THE WAR AT SEA

I N January 1939 Charles was given command of H.M.S. *Dunedin*, a cruiser slightly larger and a year younger than the *Curlew*, but, like the *Curlew*, a veteran laid down during the First World War. She was, however, reasonably well armed, and steady in a seaway. As for his ship's company, although at first sight he thought his officers seemed 'an unprepossessing lot' they improved with acquaintance, and he found the men first-class. The *Dunedin* became a happy ship, and remained so all the time Charles had charge of her.

During the earlier months of the year he was based on Portsmouth. He soon found himself a small house, and imported an Italian cook, so that he could entertain ashore when this proved possible, and incidentally improve his Italian. There was a further reason. He thought it very possible that his cook would one day have expert supervision, for there was the prospect that he would marry. He had been in love for some time with Peta Mylius, whose marriage had broken up. He tried to persuade her to become his wife, but for a long time she refused, as she feared she would always be too frail to make a success of marriage with such an active man. But at last she consented, and returned to Italy to wait. That country had been her home since childhood, though her roots were in Shropshire, and her father, Sir Walter Corbet, came of one of the very few families who could trace a direct male descent back beyond the Norman Conquest. Sir Walter had died when she was a child, and the only brother she remembered had been killed in the First World War. Her mother died when she was still in her teens, and she had married young and unhappily. Except in a material sense, life had been hard for her.

Peta found in Charles a true complement. They thought much alike about people and places; both were musicians; and their taste in pictures accorded to such a degree that they discovered, for instance, that they had both bought works by Christopher Wood, the brilliant painter who died tragically young in 1930. But their way was at first anything but smooth. It would not be possible for them to marry until late in 1940, and Peta's wait abroad was saddened by the fact for a long time her health did not improve.

Throughout the early months of 1939 international tension increased, and Britain, her armed services in particular, grew accustomed to the prospect and then to the near certainty of war. The difference between the First and the Second World Wars, to those who could remember both, was that while Germany started both and enjoyed both while things were going her own way, no one of sensibility in either Britain or France regarded war with anything but dismay. They had nothing to gain by it, not even the pleasure of revenge.

Charles's intention was to make the *Dunedin* as efficient as possible, and he succeeded. The first serious test of his seamanship came during rough weather towards the end of February, after the submarine *Sunfish* had run aground in Sandown Bay, Isle of Wight.

> Four days at sea [Charles wrote to his mother], and one 24 hours working on the stranded *Sunfish*. My boats got the wires across to her from the tug and did very well. The first wire pulled the bollards out of her because the ass of a tug tried to tow her off broadside on, but the boats got another line in, in the afternoon, by which time the tide was too low so we had to wait till midnight till high water before the second and successful attempt.
>
> She was badly damaged by the surf—the whole hull was strained everywhere. So it was a very tiring and rather anxious time especially the night anchored close off a lee shore in a southerly gale.

Lady Lambe, whose health had been poor, made a trip to Cannes. It was the last time she was able to go abroad, and the change did her good. By the summer, when war seemed increasingly certain, Charles's address changed to 'c/o G.P.O.', for the *Dunedin* was liable to be sent anywhere at short notice. In the last letter he wrote home from Portsmouth, he said: 'Things look very black but, if war comes, don't go assuming that we shall all be killed at once! The Navy is the safest place so don't worry about me!'

Charles now had two personal anxieties, his ailing mother, and his future wife. In August, he telephoned from Portsmouth to

Peta in Italy to tell her that general mobilization had taken place, and that she should return to England at once.

> In Italy [she noted later], there was no thought of war at that time and my Italian friends did not want to let me go, saying 'stay here, you will be safe with us'. As it was I took the last train across France with three small children in my care. We reached my house in Scotland which had belonged to my mother and later was to become the favourite home of Charles and our children.
>
> War was declared next day, and shortly afterwards my small house was filled with evacuees, children from Edinburgh.

The place concerned was Knockhill House, Newport, Fife, on the estate of the Stewarts of St. Fort, to which family Peta's mother had belonged. In course of time, it became Charles's own increasingly beloved retreat.

In the opening months of the war the *Dunedin* was on the Northern Patrol, her mission being to search for and intercept any merchantmen trying to use the northern sea route either to or from Germany. In such high latitudes it was cold and rough, and when at sea, Charles could never relax. 'The men are splendid,' he told his mother. 'The majority of them, reservists, have given up everything without a murmur, many have sacrificed one-man businesses built up over long years. It makes me realize how lucky we are.'

On 3 September, when Britain became formally at war, Charles wrote in his Night Order Book:

> Stationed astern of *Aurora*.
> It is possible that the nucleus of the German Fleet—probably 3 or 4 capital ships and 4 cruisers—may be met tomorrow after 1700.
> Call me as usual and as unusual and at 0400.

That was one possibility of encounter which was not to be realized, but there were others. Early in October the *Dunedin* intercepted an enemy merchant ship which, obeying strict orders from Berlin, scuttled herself as the cruiser approached. 'I had a large party of prisoners,' he told his mother 'mostly Chinese, aboard for several days. Everyone was saved. It all felt very unreal having these men under guard on board—just like a badly made cinema film, but life is like that now.'

Charles wrote an account of his time on the Northern Patrol soon after he had left the *Dunedin*, and so that he should not forget it. It gives a graphic idea of conditions from the Captain's point of view.

Up here in winter it gets dark at half past four and the long night drags on through seventeen interminable hours.

My sea-cabin is a small tin box just below the bridge. The thick greenish glass of both the scuttles is coated with salt and the spray rattles against the metal sides like a handful of rice thrown hard against a drum. At night it sounds like machine-gun bullets but then everything is more ominous at night when you can't see. There is a sort of ventilator above my bunk through which the wind howls and moans so loudly that it has to be stuffed with a woollen sock. The toothbrush slides round the rim of the washbasin glass with every roll of the ship and my oilskin and coats sway silently from the coat-hook in unison.

This morning we sent in a Norwegian under armed guard. Yesterday and the day before, when the weather was good and calm for boarding, we sighted nothing. That always seems to happen. But last night, during the middle watch, a swell came up from the westward and by five thirty the wind had started to freshen from the same quarter and the purple line on the barograph in the chart-house had started another sickening fall. The weather and the slender pen of that evil little instrument, placid beneath its glass case, seem to be the arbiters of our destinies out here on patrol. It's not the Germans but the weather that is our constant enemy on this job, and all the discomfort, the exhaustion and added anxiety that bad weather brings seem somehow symbolized by that purple line on the barograph chart, the outward and visible sign of the approaching storm.

There were still two more hours to daylight when the speaking-tube by my ear woke me.

'Captain sir?'

'Yes?' Subconsciously all night half of you is on edge, alert for the emergency which may at any time spring. It is impossible, in that instant of waking, altogether to remove from your voice the traces of that permanent anxiety which lies like an undigested meal heavy upon your chest.

'We've sighted a light bearing 283. It looks like a ship on an opposite course.'

'All right, I'll be up. Alter course as necessary to close.'

At night, there's a single dim blue bulb burning in my cabin
like a wagon-lit. This gives enough light with which to tumble
into seaboots and oilskin without blinding the eyes for the outside dark. The way to the bridge is automatic. Some of No. 2
gun's crew are sheltering at the foot of the ladder singing 'Down
Mexico Way'. Is it too rough to lower the boat? The water is
slopping in to the waist pretty often and sheets of spray hide
No. 3 gun-deck as the ship turns, but perhaps we can make a
good enough lee.

On the bridge the lookouts are stamping their heavy seaboots
on the wet corticene. It is bitterly cold and there are rain squalls
about. If we have to board, it'll be rough by the time we get the
boat back. Pray God she's one of the ships we are to let pass
without boarding. It's so difficult to see what the weather is
really like in this darkness. If we wait till daylight to board, the
sea will certainly have risen. It must be now or not at all.

The guns and the searchlight are trained on and ready. The
boarding boat's crew and the armed guard are ready too by their
boat. The Commander comes on the bridge with forced cheerfulness and stands beating his gloved hands against his oilskin
for warmth. The agony that precedes decision makes me
irritable and anxious and the most trivial thing could make me
lose my temper.

'All right, Chief Yeoman. Call her up.'

The signal lamp flashes, slowly, deliberately until the ship
answers and hesitantly spells out her own name. No, there is no
escape, we must board her if we can. This means dropping our
boat a few lengths ahead of her under our own lee. Now im-
patience rules. Since it must be done, let it be done quick, else
the weather will be too bad to get the boat back. We are just
coming into position and if we can't slip now it means going
right round again. Why isn't the boat ready aft? You can't stop
with submarines about. They must be ready now. At last. Half
speed astern both. Lower away aft. Can anyone see if the boat is
clear of the ship. All right, half speed ahead both. Let's get away
out of it, quick.

The next half hour seems interminable. Can anyone see the
boat? Is she alongside yet? The wind and sea are getting up fast.
If they aren't quick we are bound to damage the boat, perhaps
even the men, while hoisting her. Maybe I was a fool to risk it,
but the alternative is to escort the ship in ourselves and that means
leaving the patrol for so long. I can't think why the German

submarines have not followed a neutral ship like this through the patrol in the night and picked us off when we stopped her. This morning would not be quite so easy for them in this drizzle and darkness, but on some of those brilliant freezing nights when the Aurora catches great loops of light up into the zenith we must have been an easy target. At last our boat signals she is leaving the Norwegian. Clear Lower Deck. Now for it. All hands man the cutter's falls.

The boat buries her nose into the sea as the bow-men fight the heavy blocks with numbed hands, trying to hook on. Others try to fend her off as she crashes against the ship's side. In the half light she sometimes disappears under a sheet of spray. At last the order 'Hoist away', and two hundred throats break out into two wordless phrases of 'In a Persian Garden' to the beat of a drum. This is always so since the first day we had the drum to mark the rhythm of the hoist. The irony appeals. The heavy boat swings violently clear of the water, the motion of the ship adding to the momentum till the crew gains control as she nears the davit head.

Half speed ahead both. Thank God that's over without mishap.

Now, this afternoon, there can be no boarding in this weather. We are already down to ten knots and the ship is bumping into an occasional sea. Oh God, I suppose it's going to be another of those bloody nights when there is no peace of mind down here on my bunk nor any rest for the body leaning over the after side of the bridge watching the heavy seas breaking into the waists, and imagining things to be worse than they really are in the darkness. It's no use trying to go to sleep now even, while it's still daylight. Every lurch wakes you with foreboding of damage done, ever since that sudden sea lifted the motorboat out of its crutches and broke it in two like a cedar-wood pencil. It is cold and damp in here and the electric heater smells of burning japan black. Beads of cold dew-sweat form on the white enamel of the outer bulkheads. My tea is brought in; sandwiches and chocolate biscuits on a round black tin tray. The milk has gone all curdled from being frozen. Still, it's better than tinned and will probably last out till we get in. 'Till we get in.' That means mails, a bath and warmth and, above all, the lifting of this weight of anxiety, this undigested lump of apprehension, and quiet and rest and companionship and peace for a while. Oh God, how long can it go on for? Where shall we be this time next year?

There is a knock and the signalman brings in a submarine report. The position is some way from us but not far from our next-door neighbour on the patrol. What happens if she gets torpedoed? Do we go over and help and get torpedoed too, like the *Hogue*, *Cressy* and *Aboukir* in the last war? Or do we let our friends drown and keep well clear in safety? Christ, what a problem.

In the lee outside my cabin the sailors chatter and argue and laugh and sing above the noise of the sea and the wind. Their's not to reason why. That's up to the skipper. After all, he gets paid for it.

'Captain sir?'

'Yes?' God, what's happened now?

'Ship in sight bearing 237. Looks like a tanker.'

'All right, I'll be up.'

In November 1939, Charles had the chance of actually firing at an enemy for the first time for over twenty years. The Germans sent aircraft over regularly to reconnoitre the base at Scapa.

We let off guns quite often now [he wrote to his mother on the 9th]. So far, my ship has always been the first to give the alarm and open fire so I'm very proud, even if our antiquated arrangements don't put the bursts very near. But perhaps one day we'll be lucky and hit the brute.

Once he was able to arrange for a brief visit by his mother and sister to a Scottish port, when the *Dunedin* put in for a few days. He had been warned that he would shortly sail for an overseas station, and he took the fleeting chance to see her, and his sister, Betty, as he had so often done at Malta.

Just after Christmas, he had a letter from Admiral Sir Max Horton, who was then his Commander-in-Chief, which warmed his heart.

I am very sorry indeed to miss seeing you and your ship's company before leaving the Northern Patrol, [wrote the Admiral] especially as *Dunedin* under your command has been such a great success in everything you have been required to do.

I fully appreciate the severe conditions so splendidly stuck out by the small cruisers. Whilst all meet heavy weather, some of them make less of it than others, and the standard you have set in cheerfulness and determination has been of great value to me and the whole Northern Patrol.

The *Dunedin* was ordered to Portsmouth, whence she was to sail for the West Indies. Peta, though still seriously ill, was taken by her nurse to see him off. 'I remember to this day,' she wrote later, 'being pushed on a porter's barrow at Waterloo Station wearing a white fur coat and woollen stockings and clasping the Picasso picture of a harlequin and his dog which was to hang in Charles's cabin.'

II

In a letter to his mother dated 5 January 1940 Charles indicated that, however weighty his future responsibilities and however uncertain the future, he had no intention of letting even the war mar his enjoyment of what made life worth living. He asked her to send 'my large oil paint-box and easel if you can find it; all the Beethoven and Mozart and Bach music you can find; light clothing; *Tristram Shandy*; polo breeches, boots and cap, and a sea fishing rod and large reel that I had in the *Hawkins*'.

Before a warmer climate was reached, the *Dunedin* had a tough time. 'We had a filthy passage,' he wrote home on 19 February. 'Bad weather continuously, ending up with the worst gale I have ever seen at sea. The waves were colossal and almost frightening and I was on the bridge for 26 hours on end. My whole face got raw from continually being battered by salt spray, but we came through all right and all is now well.' His first area of operations was around Bermuda, and, in addition to conditions being far more tolerable than the far north, he soon had plenty of excitement, and responsibility.

I am now almost an admiral, [he wrote on 15 March] and have control of quite a lot of ships so I'm endlessly busy and have spent far less time in harbour than we used to at home! But the weather is glorious and we are all wearing shorts and open necked shirts and have had more excitement than I could have believed possible.

First of all, by a pure fluke, I met a German merchant ship who at once burst into flame and was scuttled. My fellows were wonderful and fought the fire on board till she was ablaze everywhere, but we couldn't save her.

Then within a week we met another at dead of night. She too set herself on fire but, with experience gained from last time, my party kept it from spreading and by going alongside this

burning ship and playing every hose we had, we managed to
subdue the fire before daylight. It was the most exciting night I
have ever spent and as day dawned our hopes of saving her rose.
It took 5 days to tow her to a British Port—fighting the fire the
whole time, but now we have got her in and she should be saved
and soon be working again to bring your food. You have no
idea what guts and determination my chaps showed. They
worked till they literally dropped exhausted and the bravery
shown in diving under water in the dark strange engine room to
close the flooding valves was past praise. She is a lovely brand
new ship and we are all incredibly proud of having captured her
despite the Germans' attempts to scuttle. This is the only case
so far as I know where a determined attempt to sink the ship has
been thwarted, so my shares are very high!

Charles did not exaggerate the value of his capture, which got
him an official Mention in Despatches and brought decorations
for some of the *Dunedin*'s boarding party. The prize concerned was
the German merchantman *Hannover*, which was intercepted off
San Domingo and, with the help of the Canadian destroyer
Assiniboine, was towed to Jamaica after a long struggle. She was
indeed a fine new ship, later converted into an auxiliary aircraft-
carrier. She was renamed *Audacity* and played a great part, while
she survived, in the battle of the Atlantic.

Presently came news of the Norwegian campaign, in the course
of which several of Charles's close friends were killed, Captain
Warburton-Lee among them; then the lightning events which
were to lead to the fall of France.

The situation looks gloomy [Charles wrote home on 28 May], but
it is not the first time that things have looked disastrous for this
country and I am sure that an Englishman knows better than
any other race how to face adversity and endure it until it is
turned to triumph. . . . Here where the sea is blue and the sun is
shining we only wish we could do something more active to help.

Very soon Charles had the chance he wished for. The collapse of
France had left the French fleet scattered, and among the more
valuable units were three in his own area. The cruiser *Jeanne d'Arc*
was at Guadeloupe, while at Martinique was the cruiser *Emile
Bertin* with a large quantity of bullion on board, and the aircraft
carrier *Béarn*. The *Béarn* was a big and important ship, the only

carrier the French possessed, and she was loaded with American aircraft bought on joint Anglo-French account.

Charles, in co-operation with the Captain of the *Fiji*, which was also in the area, and later with the help of the Governor of Trinidad, had the difficult task of trying to ensure that the French men-of-war did not sail for Europe, or even North Africa, thus running the risk of adding themselves to the forces at the disposal of the Germans, and of trying to release the *Béarn*'s load of aircraft for British use. His knowledge of French was invaluable during negotiations at Martinique, but the result was unsatisfactory in that there was no hope of moving the French admiral to disobey Pétain's government in any respect. But at least ships, gold and aircraft remained in the West Indies.

> Since the French tragedy [wrote Charles to Peta] there have been so many problems to be settled that all my energies have been canalized in one direction, and I have been unable to think of anything else. Our present existence is completely from hand to mouth rushing here and there for complicated discussions in my complicated and inaccurate French, which though unsuited for fine shades of diplomacy has been of the utmost value.

On 1 July he reported:

> Since I last wrote I have failed in my mission, despite working day and night and I feel very depressed and desperately tired. It has been exhaustion only exceeded by those weeks at Enzesfeld. The mental strain of trying to persuade someone who is foxy and stubborn to do something, and to talk all the time in a foreign language has been very heavy. But I already feel better.

The next important matters were personal. Peta and Andrew arrived in Bermuda in August, after a difficult passage from England, Peta wonderfully improved in health by the sunshine. The Duke and Duchess of Windsor were also at the island. They were on their way to Nassau in the Bahamas, of which the Duke had been appointed Governor.

> Of course, [Charles told his mother] I got very involved. Both were very different to when I saw them last. Much mellower and calmer and very nice. Peta and I were asked to Admiralty House

to meet them and then stayed on to supper there. The Windsors also came on board the *Dunedin* for tea and Peta came and helped me out. So you see we've been very busy and very happy.

The Duke would have been able to sympathize with Charles's situation from personal experience, for Charles was waiting for Peta's decree to be made absolute. This was now a matter of weeks.

Peta had spent the month of May 1940 in an oast house near Aldeburgh on the Suffolk coast, with her nurse and young son. It had at one time been shared by Benjamin Britten and Lennox Berkeley, both of whom later became close friends of the Lambes. After East Anglia, Bermuda seemed to Peta a dramatic contrast:

It was the enchanted Isle, [she noted later], playground of the rich, away from the war and the blackout. Beaches made of coral sand, lilies in the fields, tamarisks growing to the edge of the sea, red cardinals and cat birds landing at your feet without fear. Night flowering cyrius and hot moonlight nights.

Having had a glimpse of Charles, Peta was suddenly left alone, for the *Dunedin* was ordered back to England. She and her child, though safe, were far away from everyone that mattered to them, and in an island which, if enchanted, seemed only half real.

Soon after they parted, Charles wrote from sea that he had evidence of how real a difference he had made to the lives of some of his men, and he wrote to Peta that

. . . suddenly I felt inordinately proud—felt that if I could make people feel like that, then that was the justification for everything and fulfilment of all. Indeed the more I thought the more it became clear that the only thing that is left now is to make other people less unhappy than they are and I saw how any power to do that comes from my relationship with you and how splendidly and joyfully I can go on doing it provided you always believe in me and that we can remain true to one another.

Niceness is all.

Peta cabled: 'Don't be sad be strong am very proud', ending with her love.

III

Charles had been summoned to the Admiralty, to the corridors of power. He was appointed Assistant Director of Plans, a staff

Division which at that stage of the war was of such importance as to absorb three captains, appropriate commanders and numerous subordinates. Command of a cruiser had been an onerous, responsible, and war-like job, but it was one for which every senior executive officer had been trained. Few were qualified to work successfully in the War Cabinet offices, which was where Charles now found himself. He was well and truly at the centre of affairs, and at a time when the country stood alone, subjected nightly to the attentions of the Luftwaffe. It was a remarkable place to which Charles had returned, and he found it so.

In the last week of September 1940 he wrote to Peta:

> I travelled by night to London and kept waking like a child, not knowing where I was and thinking something must be wrong with the ship that it should sway so strangely. Everybody everywhere was in uniform, otherwise all much as before. At Euston it was a cold, brilliant still September morning, with very blue sky overhead and mist on the housetops.
>
> The taxi man explained the détours around the delay action bombs and a big fire was burning somewhere near. Windows in this area had all been shattered that night and the streets were filled with broken glass. Shopfronts were gone and window displays were open to the street and NOBODY TOOK ANY NOTICE. The traffic was less than usual and passed several shattered buildings, the dust from the explosion lying like a pall on the neighbouring houses. Men were working around them, but apart from this, life seemed absolutely normal. Old china shops still displayed fragile porcelain in their windows. . . .
>
> Gradually it dawns on you that all the Germans have so far achieved is insignificant compared to the vastness of the place, and I felt a great relief in finding it all far less damaged and disorganized than I feared. The news bulletins had been true.

One of Charles's first lunches away from his work was at Buckingham Palace. The King told him that 'the Queen was actually looking out of the window into the quadrangle when three bombs dropped, but the glass did not break!' Everyone from royalty downwards agreed that 'London by night was lousy' and for a time Charles slept on a luggage rack in a basement at Athenaeum Court.

Peta had an adventurous journey back to England, leaving Andrew behind her. She got a seat in a flying-boat for Lisbon, with

£10 hidden in her shoe. Everyone in Portugal thought she was mad to be heading for England—all the same, when at last she did find a place on a plane, an Eton boy offered her £150 for it! She landed at Poole, and as her passport had been issued in Italy she was grilled for two hours while lights were shone in her face, one interrogator asking, in perfect Italian, for minute details of places near which she had lived. A spy would probably have got through far more easily, but Peta did so at last, and she was married by special licence on 2 November.

Chapter Five

THE CORRIDORS OF POWER

THE beginning of the Lambes' life together was anything but peaceful. At first they lived in two rooms in Curzon Street over the Mirabelle. There were air raids every night, the restaurant band doing its best to drown the sound of falling bombs. The night of the biggest attack on the City of London Charles watched from the roof. 'I sat in the basement,' wrote Peta, 'covered in antiphlogistin and wheezing so loud with asthma it nearly drowned the sound of the guns.'

'Time meant nothing,' [she continued] possessions meant nothing. We seemed to change flats many times, always living in two rooms. We ate our meagre rations off the best Sèvres china, there was no point in keeping it shut away if tomorrow we might all be dead.

For three years we stayed in London. Charles always rode to the Admiralty on a bicycle after first having put our rubbish in a refuse bin across the road. Certain images stay clear in my mind, like the day a large white mongrel dog followed me all down the Edgware Road and at last its beseeching eyes persuaded me to take it in a taxi to the vegetarian restaurant where I was meeting Charles for lunch. Meeting friends in the Ritz bar in the evening: seeing a friend whose husband had been killed sitting every night in the Ritz, crying all the time, and staring at people with unseeing eyes.

Many interesting people lunched or dined in our flat: George Barnes came; William Plomer; Ian Fleming; Admiral Godfrey; Eric Miéville; Arthur Salter; Ian Jacob and many others. I had the strange feeling of living in a vacuum, for although surrounded by people one never knew what anyone did nor could one ask.

Charles knew all right, and he was so well aware of the importance of what he was doing that he began to keep a pencilled diary, in a book of bound-up Western Union cablegram forms. This was against regulations, but as these were disobeyed even by the Chief of the Imperial General Staff, the offence was venial, and the result is at least a footnote to history. He began on 17 March 1941 with the words: 'The difficulty about starting a diary is that it is always too late. So much has already passed unrecorded that it seems hopeless to begin now. Never mind, it's worth trying.' The effort lasted the better part of a year, during which time the whole aspect of the war was transformed. Britain stood alone until, in the summer of 1941, Hitler attacked Russia. Six months later, the final alignment was completed by the Japanese attack on the Americans at Pearl Harbour, followed by Hitler's declaration of war on the United States, the second of his two monumental acts of self-destruction.

Much of what Charles wrote was ephemera, and he noted down speculations and rumours, many of which were soon seen to be false, but certain impressions of people and events have, perhaps, some lasting value as recording how they appeared at the most critical time in British history since the era of Napoleon.

In the very first day's entry there was a typical piece of natural observation, interpolated among a lot of strategical memoranda. 'There is a belt of purple crocuses the whole length of the Park abreast Park Lane. The colour is intense and rich like a Roman Catholic funeral but it seems bright and gay against the khaki camouflage of our daily life.'

The way the war was run seemed to Charles fundamentally wrong. 'Too much of our strategy is dictated by personal considerations. It makes me sick the way nothing we do is related to a planned strategy. All our operations are sparks produced by the clash of personalities; meanwhile time, labour, material and even lives are wasted and nothing gets done except paper work.' Rationing was a case in point.

Talking of the way in which rationing is never apparently introduced until an article is really short i.e.—jam—down to 8 ozs a month suddenly—Oliver Stanley says if we had rationed everything at the start of the war—as everyone expected—the position would be much better. Apparently Winston thought such action would be a slur on the Navy's power to protect trade and, as 1st Lord, he fought tooth and nail and successfully to get rationing postponed for 3 or 4 months. Appeals to people to cut down their consumption only resulted in the case of sugar to a 25% *increase* in consumption.

This was a sad political blunder.

On 2 April, Charles depicted a very different statesman.

Churchill—the 'former naval person'—is a most astonishing man. For months past there has been an agitation proceeding to get some committee established to co-ordinate target programmes, imports, productive capacity etc. Now with a stroke of the pen he has done the whole thing himself. He has laid down the figure below which our war effort suffers, below which our food imports must not fall, what the division is to be, and where the cuts are to be made. He has revised priorities, told the Army to reorganize on a different principle more economical in manpower, hotted up the proportion of armoured units, cancelled the long-term heavy shipbuilding programme, all between a couple of brandies apparently.

These are decisions which have long been wanted, which even the most powerful committee would have funked taking and required endless study in many separate directions. Perhaps they are not all right and yet it is better to have some wrong than to have no decisions at all—in other words, indecision.

His knowledge of technical matters apart from politics, strategy and history, combined with his personality and readiness to shoulder responsibility and his intuitive flair for a situation mark him out as an outstanding man whatever his faults.

What he found most frustrating in his own work was endless argument over details and mere procedure. Shouldn't this wording be altered slightly otherwise it might give the impression that . . . ? . . . and so on and so on.

'Careful and clear drafting is essential in all paper work. There must be only one meaning. But really, given the minimum of good will and co-operation, nothing else should matter. As it is, everyone is touchy, greedy of power, and ready to take instant offence.'

Nothing could long keep Charles away from one of his greatest sources of distraction and refreshment—music. On 3 April he noted:

l. to r. Sir Hubert Graves (Ambassador), President Bgyen Van Tam (Prime Minister), C. E. Lambe, Oliquat (Minister of Defence)

Last night a discussion on Bach with P. She says he is always the same and not adult. To me he seems to live in a higher world than any other composer. His approach is scientific not political. . . . Romanticism, lyricism and all other earthly emotional qualities are discarded in favour of mathematical symbolism. It is the old division of form against colour, intellect against emotion, the west against the east, science against politics, male against female—they are all the same. P. maintained that because of this very sub-division her point that Bach was incomplete—un-adult—was proved. Perhaps that's right. Maybe it's only another form of escape.

Later that month Charles had two days' leave, which was the most he ever got in the exigencies of the time.

Nearly always [wrote Peta] we went to our favourite farmhouse in Cornwall near the Lizard and here we could relax and for a few precious hours, forget about the war by going for long walks and finding marvellous wild flowers, and being healed by the sheer beauty of nature. Once we walked for miles trying to find D. H. Lawrence's house, another time I rode a donkey down a long valley to the sea, and found Ronald Duncan living an idyllic life in a small cottage.

In the evenings C. read aloud (one of his most precious gifts) and by June 1944 he had read me the whole of Trollope, what a writer! Never have I known characters come to life in such a way. I felt they were all my friends and real live people. Only in Proust had this ever happened to me before.

Another time we went to that enchanting village in Wales created by Clough Williams Ellis, where the houses are painted bright colours as in Italy, built in a valley overlooking the sea. There Charles painted my portrait and we climbed up Snowdon.

Later on in the war, Peta worked, whenever she could find time, in Heywood Hill's bookshop in Curzon Street and at one point 'with enormous pleasure and trepidation', she was in charge for a whole week. Books had always been one of the passions she shared with Charles, who was never without them.

He had recently come on two passages which pleased him. The first was from Hegel: 'The only thing you ever learn from history is that nobody ever learns anything from history.' The second was from R. G. Collingwood's *Autobiography*. 'I saw that the relation

8

between theory and practice was one of intimate and mutual independence, thought depending upon what the thinker learned by experience in action, action depending upon how he thought of himself and the world.'

On 19 April, Charles recorded his first glimpse of Churchill in person, at close quarters.

> The other night, [he wrote] we were summoned to meet the P.M. after dinner ... Rendez-vous was the underground Cabinet War Room. It was like a nightmare without emotion. The news from Greece and Jugoslavia and Libya was bad and the P.M. came in ten minutes late very depressed. He was puffy and very pink and white—pig-like. Dressed in a grey siren suit, one hand clasping a cigar, the other, beautifully manicured, tapping the table impatiently, bearing a large four banded ring on the fourth finger. He was very depressed and desperately tired—in a sort of coma almost. His speech was rather slobbery and very slow. ...
>
> It was a terribly depressing interview. The general atmosphere of sycophancy and the old man's lack of grasp and understanding apparently, made me leave to walk home convinced for the first time that we could not win the war.

It was the time of the British withdrawal from Greece. The battle for Crete was about to come, to be followed by one of the greatest tests of nerve which any British naval commander of the Second World War had to face: the decision, once Crete was lost, to save as many troops as possible in ships which, without air cover, would face the whole might of the victorious Luftwaffe.

The man upon whom the trial fell was Sir Andrew Cunningham, one of Charles's heroes. He did not falter in his task, but the strain on his ships and men was appalling, and the operations left the Mediterranean Fleet, which had been trained to such a splendid pitch of discipline, in ruins.

Among those whose ships were sunk off Crete was Lord Louis Mountbatten. Charles had had only one brief glimpse of him since war began, when he had dined on board the *Kelly* at Scapa. Mountbatten himself had survived, but most of the flotilla he commanded had been sunk, and it was not the least of Cunningham's gifts of leadership that he made Mountbatten feel that the sacrifice had been worth while. He then sent him home to report personally to the Prime Minister.

The result was recorded by Charles after a lunch he had with the two Mountbattens.

The result was recorded by Charles after a lunch he had with the two Mountbattens.

Dickie told me he told the P.M. he had brought back a message from ABC which was endorsed by the whole Fleet, that whatever else they were asked to undertake they should not again be required to operate without air cover as in Crete. The PM's reaction was to put both his hands on Dickie's shoulders and say: 'My boy, I can't tell you how glad I am to see you back safely.' He entirely evaded the issue. Max Beaverbrook was there and complimented D. on putting over on the PM what all at home had thought but which nobody had had the guts to say to him.

In view of the protracted and savage way in which Beaverbrook and his newspapers denigrated Mountbatten later in his career, this was an unexpected opening to their relationship.

When the two were alone together one day at the Admiralty, Charles asked Mountbatten what Cunningham's *real* thoughts could have been when he was showing such a brave face to the world, and above all to his own men. It was exactly the sort of question which any admirer of A.B.C. would have asked. The answer was so typical of the man that Charles noted it down on the back of an official memorandum.

Dickie asked ABC if he could see him alone before he left Alexandria.

ABC's nephew-in-law, Starkie, was killed in the *Juno*, and this, together with the awful sight of the badly wounded in H.M.S. *Maine* (operations throughout 24 hours) had rather shaken him, Dickie thought.

D. asked him what his real feelings were. He said: 'I don't want this repeated but I feel like going out in a destroyer into the thickest of the bombing and getting killed or else like resigning.' Despite this, Dickie says ABC always appears cheerful and the whole Fleet ... would do anything for him. They have the utmost confidence in him.

II

After the invasion of Russia in June 1941, Charles got hold of a pleasing story of a conversation a Swedish Minister in London

had had, some time earlier, with Maisky, the Russian Ambassador.
It took place when the terrible Stalinist purges were in progress.

Swedish Minister: Well, Maisky, nobody in this country seems to
think much of the Russian Army!
Maisky: No. I wonder why they don't.
S.M.: Well, perhaps it may be something to do with the number
of changes you have in your higher command.
M.: I don't see why that should make people here sceptical of
our army—after all, Hore Belisha has been doing the same
thing here. Of course, you can't quite compare England and
Russia. We have no Bournemouths or Cheltenhams and so we
have to make other arrangements. Anyway, you must not
judge a machine by its spare parts.

Charles, who had been greatly heartened by the extraordinary
turn of events in the war, knew something of his own future as
early as July 1941. He would shortly become Deputy Director of
Plans, and would later on be given charge of the whole of Plans
Division. Late in November came sad news of the sinking of the
Dunedin with heavy loss of life. She fell to a U-boat in the South
Atlantic whilst on a lone patrol. Next month, soon after the
entry of America into the war, Charles was chosen to cross to the
States with the first British Staff Delegation, thus fulfilling a dream
Peta had had, in which she saw him standing with Churchill on
the quarter-deck of a battleship.

Admiral of the Fleet Sir Dudley Pound, the First Sea Lord,
headed the naval mission, Lambe being the only other executive
officer of captain's rank. Pound was not expansive, and during
the course of the voyage sent for Charles for only one brief
conversation. 'I get the impression that he doesn't like me,'
Charles noted, 'almost that he's afraid of me. Perhaps I talk too
much and too fast and too loud.'

He particularly noted the bearing of the sailors doing the work
of the ship, which was the *Duke of York*.

60% of the ship's company have never been to sea before. The
proportion of RNR's and RNVR officers is very high. They
are a shapeless lot somehow and there is none of the active
service sailor's swing about the ship. There seem to be no sailors
who have swagger or are sex conscious. They are all worried
little chaps doing a bigger job than they can cope with—

civilians dressed up in fact. The lovely atmosphere of innocence combined with acute sophistication seems to be lacking entirely.

On 18 December Charles was in the Map Room, with the Prime Minister and the First Sea Lord.

Discussion on American Pacific Fleet. Beaverbrook wants to make the gesture of reinforcing it. First Sea Lord against it because even if we did so, the force would still be inferior to the Japs. P.M. agreed and said the great thing to avoid if you have to cross a 12 foot ditch is not to use a 9 foot plank stretched to 10 foot. 1st S.L. said yes especially if the plank comes from a more important ditch.

Then the PM fell to talking of the poor shape of this ship's company. They are not ready for fighting. Discipline and manners are lax. He'd never seen such a thing. This I think is true. The PM proposed a Map Room for the White House. Dudley Pound said no for security reasons—even the President wasn't too tight though he did keep the secret of the Libyan offensive.

1st S.L. stood up to Winston better than I expected.

Charles for once did not make necessary allowances for the *Duke of York*. The ship, not long commissioned, was still in the process of 'working up'. Two years later, she played the principal part in the sinking of the battle-cruiser *Scharnhorst* in northern waters.

Next day, 20 December, was Charles's birthday. Peta had given him a book on Sickert, one of his favourite painters. The day after, he noted, was Stalin's, and he observed a characteristic piece of Churchillian fun.

The PM sent good wishes. He said to Beaverbrook: 'Well, Max, I suppose you have sent birthday greetings to your boy friend.' Max B. flew off the handle and said he didn't mind what anyone else thought *he*, the Beaver, was convinced that we must support Russia etc., etc.

'Yes, yes, I know' said the PM, 'but I only asked if you had sent greetings to Stalin.'

On the whole, it was, thought Charles, a boring trip.

The PM is bad tempered despite 2 eggs and bacon, a slice of cold roast beef and a bottle of Sauterne for breakfast.

The cinema starts at 10.30 most nights. As the clocks have
been put back an hour every day it means 11.30 really. These
great men do not seem to care how long they keep men—who
probably have middle watches etc.—waiting. Tonight we had
Blood and Sand in colour. A very beautiful opening of a boy
swimming the river at night and fighting the bulls in the stock-
yard with a blanket in the moonlight. Never realized before how
Spanish dancing is founded on the bullfight.

When the party reached America, Charles soon concluded
that 'W.S.C. must have done marvels with Roosevelt' since the
principal point of strategy, that Germany should be regarded as
Public Enemy No. 1 was agreed, and in consequence the main
drive against Japan would have to be postponed. He was not
impressed with the methods—or lack of them—that the Americans
showed in committee work, and was startled by the rivalry
between Navy and Army. Admiral Turner, U.S.N., with whom
he had mainly to deal at first, he found 'a tight-laced dyspeptic
nonconformist, quite cordial but ready to be very critical and even
rude'. Turner did not improve with acquaintance. 'Long and
hard arguments ending up with Turner producing a new priority
paper and more or less saying he was going to bitch our Xmas
evening arrangements unless we agreed. We refused to accept
this and got it altered.'

A Boxing Day entry included a Christmas story.

An American told Arthur Salter that it was Sir John Dill's
birthday yesterday. A.S. said: 'Oh, so that's whose birthday
we're celebrating!' The American said: 'Well, who else's
should it be? . . . Oh I see!' Beaverbrook, who was present,
said: 'Really, Salter, I don't think that is the sort of joke to
make on a day like this.'

The same day Charles recorded a success which went unrecog-
nized:

We were told to draft a signal home giving policy direction as
regards reinforcements, moves of forces and priority of operations. I wrote it out and Dykes [Military Director of Plans]
took it to the White House. Hollis read it out and the PM said:
'Good. Very good. Go on.' At the end he said 'A very good
signal' but Joe Hollis had not the courage to disclaim author-
ship—he has had such bottles lately.

Charles himself had become known by reputation to President Roosevelt through a signal he had made in the *Dunedin* when the ship had been operating in American waters. An American naval officer had signalled to ask where Charles proposed to go next. Charles replied that he couldn't say, adding, 'but by tomorrow we'll be miles outside the Chastity Belt'. This had been reported to Roosevelt, who had been much amused. 'I got a good laugh in reading of this incident,' wrote the President to his informant, Captain Randall, U.S.N.R., 'and I very much appreciate your thoughtfulness in letting me know there are still a few people left who like a little humor injected into the task at hand, however trying it may be.'

Charles was in the Senate when Churchill gave an address to which he knew Peta would also be listening in England. 'The Chamber rather like a coloured print of the Great Exhibition,' he told her: 'steel girders and glass roof rather faded yellow walls, light wood doors with dark wood carving, desks and—spittoons.'

Before the end of the year there were rumours that Charles might have to stay on in the States after the rest of the party had returned. He did not relish the prospect and much resented Pound's not consulting or even informing him about the matter. 'He is almost as silent as stepfather Charles,' he wrote to Peta, 'and speaks about as slowly!' On the other hand there seemed a chance that he would be able to get Andrew Mylius from Bermuda to the States and so home. He saw no risk, after the involvement of Russia and the U.S.A., of a German invasion of Britain; and it would, he knew, be a tonic to Peta if she and her son could be reunited. A little later on, he managed this.

Dined with the Halifaxes [Charles wrote on New Year's Eve]. Halifax was amusing about the PM's French. At an Allied meeting he once said, 'Eh bien, mon général, le bon Dieu nous à beaucoup blessé'—'béni, Winston, béni' said Mrs. W. C. On another occasion he said: 'Je vous assure, M. le Ministre, que nous avons de la chance d'être sur nous seul—what *is* the French for 'on our own'?'

An entry by Charles on Pacific strategy, under the same date, was both shrewd and prophetic.

The wider aspect of the wisdom of forming 2 mediocre fleets in the Indian Ocean and in the Pacific neither of which is greatly superior to the Japs, is questioned. The more I think of this the more I feel that one big Pacific Fleet forcing a big action on the Japs by capturing island bases is probably the right solution if it is practicable. It is only by a severe threat which they are forced to face that we can regain naval control of the Pacific and so check this rapid Jap advance.

By 10 January the great ones were away from Washington and Charles had more leisure to observe his colleagues and opposite numbers. One who came under scrutiny was Admiral King, professional head of the U.S. Navy. Charles found him

an outstanding man and a fascinating personality. He has brains and that aloof sort of contempt which comes from superior conviction. . . . Beautiful hands which he uses to good effect, and great intolerance. A fascinating but frightening man.

Churchill left for home altogether on 19 January and Charles went to stay with William Hayter and his wife and small child. They lived in 'a little modern Georgian box' which rocked at night to the sounds made by 'a grand English nurse brought from China who only took on to get home and now learns heavily to typewrite in an effort to achieve emancipation'. Years later, Sir William Hayter recalled that 'when Charles first arrived in the United States we hardly knew each other, though we had many mutual friends, and he took some time to decide whether we were the kind of people he liked. As soon as he decided we were, he proposed himself and was the most delightful guest imaginable.'

To the Halifaxes stage box [wrote Charles on 4 February] to a Presidential Command performance of 'The Watch on the Rhine'. The house filled with G men and the departure of the President afterwards accompanied by about 50 motor cycles and three 1920 open cars with G men with Tommy Guns on the running boards covering the crowds was all very pre-1914 Balkan somehow.

Another evening he met Ann Bridge—Lady O'Malley—who, he thought, was like his half-sister Dolly. 'Quite overpowering' was Charles's impression. 'She almost forced me to write an article for her to put into the *Woman's Weekly*—circulation 4,000,000 etc.' It is possible that what he wrote about his life in the *Dunedin* was the result of his conversation with this persuasive 'best-seller'.

Charles's diary entries ended on 11 February with some remarks on general conditions, as he saw them, among the American Naval staff.

Apparently they still have the sort of petty—1914, Jacky Fisher—type of jealousy present. King was Chief of Staff, Atlantic Fleet, last war and saw all the sourness that built up around Sims when he got control of all US ships in British waters. He is determined the same thing will not happen again.

Between their two services, jealousy is worse. The Army distrusts the Navy and the Navy despises the Army. . . . The Navy seems really to blame, the soldiers being genuinely ready to co-operate—but the Navy wants to keep control of all it has got and is simply not playing.

It is the same at Presidential level. There is no system to ensure that all concerned are acquainted with some Presidential decision. . . . Against all this, I heard a most encouraging account of the showing made by the junior officers and enlisted men at Pearl Harbour. It is said that they could not have fought better—especially considering the conditions. The Americans have always fought well at sea—it is not that. It is the way they are being led which frightens me now. The hard relentless atmosphere of this war is a thing they cannot understand. . . . Perhaps King does.

King did; and although the Navy-Army jealousy was to persist throughout the years of struggle, the Americans, who had much to learn, and who were reluctant to believe that the British, despite their searing experiences of war, could teach them anything, came in the end to realize that their allies might after all have something useful to pass on. Then they learnt fast.

III

Charles was given charge of Plans Division as soon as he returned to London in March 1942, and from then until the summer of 1944 he was in the most responsible Admiralty post to be held by anyone of his rank. 'As I had realized would happen years before,' wrote Admiral Cunningham in his autobiography, 'his outstanding ability had placed him in one of the key positions in the naval and defence staff.' Much of his work was done in the Cabinet offices but with his acute sense of what people were feeling, and what motivated them, he made it his business, whenever he could, to visit workers in the factories and to try to make them, by means of informal talks, more aware of the importance of what they were doing in the national effort. In the First World War, with vast British armies continuously engaged with the Germans just across the Channel, realization had been easier. At least until the invasion of Normandy in 1944, he felt that for far too many people the actual fighting was too remote for them to be able to appreciate how vital it was for them to work with purpose.

Peta sometimes went with him on these duties, and was impressed at the way he held his audience, speaking from on top of a box or packing-case. 'His approach to their problems of monotony, and not knowing what they were making was quite extraordinary,' she wrote later. 'He described the actual use of each individual's very dull job and how it was connected with the life of the sailors, who were living in terrible conditions, and how very often it could quite literally be a matter of life and death that this particular job had been done well. This immensely boosted their morale and raised the standard of production.'

In January 1943 Charles took part in the high-level conference at Casablanca. This was convened after the successful Anglo-American landings in North Africa, and when it had at last become possible to plan assaults on what Mr. Churchill called 'the soft under-belly of the Axis'—Sicily and Italy.

Charles wrote on 16 January to Peta describing his journey out, and his immediate surroundings:

> . . . a comfy trip, and we arrived in heavenly sunshine and balmy air—only 8 hours. There is mimosa and begonia and bougainvillea and hibiscus and poinsettia and oranges and lemons and olive trees and we are about a mile above the sea in a villa which is half Adam half Casa Nina and Bill Elliot and I are sharing a room and the sitting room has a surrealist decoration over the mantelpiece signed Hans Aarpe 1930 and a rude bronze statuette of Soixante-Neuf below and lots of rather bawdy French books. . . . Working hard under most pleasant conditions.
>
> There are linnets singing outside the window and I've seen Sardinian warblers, blackcaps and willow wrens and the frogs croak down at the bottom of the hill at night.

Lord Louis Mountbatten was among the great ones at the Conference. He was now Chief of Combined Operations, with acting flag-rank and a seat on the Chiefs of Staff Committee, bringing youth and fire to an otherwise rather elderly assembly.

Dickie, Bill Elliot, Guy Stewart and I rushed off one day and flew to Marrakesh, [Charles wrote to Peta] a very famous Arab town, the seat of the Sultans. It was a perfect clear calm sunny day and brilliant hot sun with the snow-capped Atlas mountains behind this pink city amid cocoanut palms and olives.

Then a rush round the bazaars with the party—all in uniform—Dickie visiting the most expensive shop, turning it inside out—finding the most expensive object—ordering four of it—and getting something absolutely lousy. That always gives me a kick. I've done it with him in nearly all the capitals in Europe and it still makes me laugh.

I only bought some French post-cards for our album and nobody could understand why except Bill Elliot. Guy Stewart even asked Bill afterwards what *could* I see in such things!

There was a good deal of argument at the Conference between the British and American Chiefs of Staff as to whether Sicily should be the next immediate objective, or a move against Germany across the Channel. At one of the meetings, so Admiral Schofield relates in his book on *British Sea Power*:

…when argument and counter-argument had reached a deadlock, Mr. Churchill entered the long conference room, and, sensing at once the sultry atmosphere prevailing, said as he took his seat at the head of the table: 'So, gentlemen, you are only little brooms, you can sweep away pebbles; but I am a big broom, I can sweep away boulders.'

The tension was immediately removed, everybody laughed, and the Prime Minister proceeded to carry out his threat.

One day, [continues Admiral Schofield] after a mid-day conference on the sun-drenched roof of the Anfa Hotel with the Director of Plans, Captain Charles Lambe, and myself, the First Sea Lord decided to invite Admiral King to take a stroll down the beach with him during the dog watches with a view to talking him into agreeing to increase the number of US destroyers allocated to escort duty in the Atlantic.
Lambe and I waited impatiently for their return. Admiral Pound saw us as he approached, smiled, but shook his head.

'Every time I raised the matter,' he told us, 'King stooped down and carefully selecting a flat pebble from the beach, he sent it skimming over the water, and that was the only answer I got.'

Pound was by then a sick man, and in his last year of life. King would see the war out. But there was respect between them, and when it came to the point, King was sometimes more reasonable than he was on this occasion. Charles saw the American admiral briefly again when he was sent to Washington on official business in May, just after an event which made him deeply happy: the birth of his son James. He had been at work in the Admiralty when Peta rang to say that the child might arrive that day. Charles could not concentrate thereafter so decided to take the tube to Baker Street, walk to the London Clinic, where Peta was to have her confinement. The journey took half an hour. When Charles arrived he was told he was the father of a son. One of his first presents to the child was a wonderful *tiny* hot-water bottle.

The family were now united, though for a short time, for preparations were in hand for another top level meeting, at Quebec, which was due to take place in August. On this occasion, Charles was given splendid quarters at the Château Frontenac, 'the Chinese suite which is at the top of a front turret, panelled green with Chinese furniture and lacquer beds with basket work . . . very comfortable and a lovely sitting room with a red, a dark blue and a grey armchair'—one for each of the Services, he noted.

'I had one afternoon off' [Charles wrote to Peta]. We drove about 25 miles north, across great rivers through country rather like lower Switzerland along a terrible dirt road across covered bridges to a sawmill in the forest where the road ended. Then we walked up through fir trees and rocks and moss and ferns to a chain of lakes. No birds sang at all. I remember the silence of these Canadian forests from last time. It is very eerie. Wild red raspberries grow in a profusion like blackberries in England.

One of Charles fullest letters to Peta, written on this Canadian visit, was begun in a train on 10 August, and gave her another glimpse of Churchill who, according to one of Charles's fellow Directors of Plans, had already once 'sacked the lot of them'.

I am lying in the bottom bunk of a double sleeper which Bill [Elliot] and I shared last night, [he wrote], and the train is waddling along the bank of the St. Lawrence through country just like Finland—fir trees, wooden and wire fences enclosing potatoes and poor crops and rocks and lakes and wooden houses and churches covered in grey shingles. The mist is down on the hill tops and it is lovely to be in daylight again and to have escaped from the atmosphere of the ship—an artificial existence insulated, by layers of luxury, from life.

The crossing was uneventful and in moderate weather. We ate too much and drank too much and there was too much rain to let us get much fresh air. I was very sleepy and lay on my bed a lot and with the clocks going back every day it all seemed very long.

The Directors of Plans were sent for by the Great Man one morning—nominally to explain a plan to him. He lay in bed in an open necked night-shirt and a gold and black dressing gown, cigar, cigar-holder and a bed table with special Sorbo rubber pads for his elbows.

We talked for 10 or 15 minutes until he interrupted and, starting quite quietly, we were treated to sixty minutes of staggering rhetoric culminating in his views on how the war should be waged and expanding in particular on an operation of his own conception for which he wished us to plan.

Next day we were invited to lunch. I sat between him and Mrs. Churchill which seemed a funny arrangement. A daughter, and Tommy Thompson [Commander Thompson, Churchill's Aide] completed the party. Lobster mayonnaise, braised ham and Cumberland sauce, peaches in syrup and ice cream, excellent Liebfraumilch and 2 glasses of brandy.

Towards the end we got him speaking of his ideas of a post-war world, of Russia and Communism (Harry Pollitt was mentioned and I could not avoid one or two provocative remarks), of the leading American personalities and of his early experiences in the Boer War and the Cuban War. It was all said so wonderful that it is difficult not to be blinded by the magic of his words but behind it all there was no real hope for the future: 'You can't change human nature' etc.—all the old tags and never a shadow of suspicion that it was the *system* which wanted changing, *not* human nature.

The party is colossal. Wingate and his wife and Gibson—the airman who led the dam busting and has the VC, two DSO's and two DFC's. Wingate—you remember—led that long range penetration into Japanese-held Burma the other day. He is shy, silent, with a well-shaped head, studious and rebellious—a second Lawrence in fact. He seemed very surprised when I referred to modern painting at dinner last night and we had a very nice time discussing the connection between great periods of painting and periods of economic stability. We agreed that the 19th century was such an epoch—that the modern French School represented the first prophecies of the coming revolution and that we are now in a period of transition and confusion which prohibits great art but out of which the new era and the new art will be laboriously born.

The evening I said goodbye to you on the phone, Wingate was dining at No. 10 and the PM suddenly said 'You had better come too', so he did—at 2 hours notice—and his wife was travelling down from Scotland to meet him and her train was stopped and she was removed and replaced on the big man's train and whisked off with us with clothes for a week in London! She was married 7 years ago at sixteen and is slight and dark.

The letter ended with an expression of Charles's pleasure at having Elliot with him, because there were so many things they could enjoy and laugh about together, most of which Air Chief Marshal Sir William Elliot still remembers vividly. He also sent a message to Andrew Mylius which must have gone straight to that boy's heart, since it showed that his stepfather recalled enough about steam trains to know what would entertain. 'Tell Andrew', he said, 'that I have just seen a freight train go by with a little red caboose on the end, and give him my love. Our engine is enormous and is a 4–8–4 and has a cow-catcher.'

Charles's principal excursion from Quebec was to Ottawa, and he was able to write to Peta on 25 August from Government House, where he was staying with Lord Athlone, the Governor-General, and Princess Alice. 'I had to write to you on this grand notepaper,' he began, though in fact it was inferior by Buckingham Palace standards.

Bill Elliot and I flew up here for the night and very comfortable and restful one too. . . . Princess Alice looks younger I think. Very alert and birdlike and very kind. A wonderful Lady in Waiting . . . unbelievably ugly and so affected (with shyness originally) that she speaks for whole very long sentences with her eyes shut. Bedrooms very comfy and like Buckingham Palace—indeed so is all the interior of the house. Marvellous photographs of previous Governors General and their ladies. Lady Byng of Vimy looking like Sarah Bernhardt, Lady Bessborough trying to look like Edwina etc. Champagne and salmon and peaches at dinner. Many footmen and several ADC's—one is Admiral Chatfield's son who is unfit, the other a rather attractive ½ French ½ Irish Canadian airman.

The flight up here was grand. The first bit along the St. Lawrence then across glorious wooded country with hills and richly farmed valleys and huge rivers and secret hidden lakes and a few of the maples just beginning to go red. Malcolm Macdonald was on the plane with us. I think he is a *very* nice person and would love to know him well.

Outside my window are acres of lawn and beautiful trees, formal beds of red cannas, stone urns and a fine herbaceous border. Breakfast in bed, punctuated by Bill rushing in and out ringing up the Chief of the Canadian Air Staff to fix an aeroplane for our return this morning. Bill got very regal even before we left Quebec. Having packed in a hurry, he walked airily out of the room saying: 'Have we got everything Charles?' quite oblivious of me carrying *all* the luggage behind him—and *then* he left his pyjamas behind.

We are back in Quebec now. A lovely flight down the St. Lawrence in bright sunlight this morning. Just going to do a little more shopping—Bill is buying mink!

In September 1943, very soon after Charles returned from Canada, Admiral Cunningham replaced Pound, who had not long to live, as First Sea Lord. To Charles, and indeed to the Navy as a whole, it was the best possible choice. Charles found he could speak his mind on strategic matters, which were his business, with all the old respectful freedom he had used in former days with 'ABC'. Pound had valued him, or he would not have stayed in his post so long, but he did not encourage that give and take with subordinates which is often so valuable.

It was with Cunningham as head of the naval staff that Charles travelled to the last high level conference he was to attend. This was held in Cairo in November 1943. One of his companions was Ian Fleming, who was then working in the Naval Intelligence Division, and the party were held up so long in Cornwall waiting to set off that there was time to visit old friends, including people in the firm which for so long had managed the family clay works. When he wrote to Peta, on 20 November 1943, he was in the air.

We are flying about 6000 feet over the Mareth Line ... and you can see bomb craters and zig-zag trenches and the tracks of endless vehicles in the barren biscuit-coloured desert. . . . It is not yet 9 in the morning and the air is like silk though a heat haze is just beginning to rise.

We left Biskra at daylight—called in the dark with all the cocks in the oasis crowing and no other sound. Huge limpid stars hanging like lamps over the date palms and the pomegranates and the citrus trees. Five minutes in an RAF lorry and we were in the desert, stretching flat and limitless across the whole half circle of the southern horizon. To the north, a semi-circle of rose brown mountains, sharply modelled like the sides of a toy fort.

Beneath the brilliant light of Venus the sky was paling and as we stood waiting for the aeroplane to be ready, a prismatic radiance appeared. I have seldom seen anything so lovely as that sunrise—the sense of illimitable space and silence was profound and unbroken until we were all tumbled into our aircraft again and the engine started up.

Last night it was stormy when we arrived. After a hot bath at a good hotel Bill Elliot and I walked around. The sun came brilliantly out at a very low elevation and the minarets and towers were brilliantly lit against a black sky, surcharged with a double rainbow. It was all very dramatic like the light in a picture by Vlamink, and the oriental smell of spices and coffee and dung pervaded all.

We were of course followed everywhere by Arab children, slender, graceful and smiling with eyelashes that rivalled James's, who offered to show us the Garden of Allah, the Minaret or the Quartier Reservé.

Later in the same letter, Charles remarked on a prophecy of H. G. Wells's about a world controlled by a Freemasonry of the Air.

This trip, [he continued] makes me realize how nearly this has come about during the war. Amongst the crews of our aircraft are Poles, Canadians, New Zealanders and Englishmen. We have met Americans, Australians and Dutch who all belong. Only the French seem to be absent.

There is something intensely moving about these people.
They are young but 'serieux', daring but not scatter-brained,
gay but not flippant. They have a swagger of their own—the
way they wear their caps tucked into their shoulder straps,
scarves around their necks etc. They are tough but sensitive.
Indeed it is astonishing to see the delicacy and charm of their
movements amidst a background of lion-tawny sand.

Oh! The Beaton photographs that there were at 'Marble
Arch'. A hot dry wind was blowing and a river of sand flowed
past your ankles. Macadam runways and tents—nothing else
but the wreckage of war, half buried in the sand-waves. A
brilliant sun and dark blue sky overhead shading to saffron over
the horizon. All the tents had been blown down yesterday: the
wind never stops, they say. Your tea cup grates as you put it on
its saucer.

Everywhere lithe and youthful figures in shirts and the sort
of shorts you like! Bleached hair and tanned skin and the other
side of the dunes, the turquoise sea.

*   *   *

Now I am sitting in my shirt sleeves 10,000 feet over Cyrenaica
and down there must be about where people like Hugh Winship
were killed and disappeared. The half dried shallow salt lakes
reflect the glare of the sun from miles and miles away. There
are a few more tracks but otherwise the landscape is still the
colour of a lion's skin but broken by veining like the cracks on
old varnished wood. Who could have foreseen 20 years ago the
strategic importance that this thrice conquered desert would
assume?

Due in soon now. As the sun set we were still flying over this
endless uncharted desert and it changed its colour as the light
faded until it looked like an elephant's hide as the sun dipped.
Now it is dark and there are many stars and we are beginning
to lose height and our journey will soon be over.

It would have pleased Charles if he had had *Rasselas* with him,
with Johnson's eighteenth-century 'contemplation of flying' in the
sixth chapter.

How it must amuse the pendent spectator to see the moving
scene of land and ocean, cities and deserts! To survey with
9

equal security the marts of trade, and the fields of battle; mountains infested by barbarians, and fruitful regions gladdened by plenty and lulled by peace.

This was exactly what he himself was doing. A day or two later, on 27 November he wrote again from Cairo—much more cheerfully and colourfully than he ever did from America.

I am sitting in the sun in a dew-spangled garden before breakfast. There is a crimson and a brick-red bougainvillea over my head and the ordinary puce-coloured one grows in profusion amongst the jasmine on the far side of the small lawn.

Through a screen of eucalyptus, acacia and feathery desert pines, the Great Pyramid towers over the desert; only $\frac{1}{4}$ mile away; it looks enormous and human figures on the top look remote. There was a dove on the lawn when I first looked out this morning and many little grey wagtails are chattering about now with big Egyptian kites soaring high overhead. . . .

We are very comfortable and only 200 yards from our work which has not been as heavy as usual although there has been no spare time till now.

Mountbatten was with the other big-wigs, as at Casablanca and Quebec. At the meetings in Washington in May it had been agreed in principle that all Allied forces in the South East Asia theatre of war should be under unified command, and at Quebec the appointment of Mountbatten as Supreme Allied Commander was approved, his area of responsibility to include India, Burma, Ceylon, Siam, Malaya, and Sumatra.

Dickie is in great form, [Charles reported] never still for a moment, and has been doing very well I think. My master [Cunningham] has been very wonderful and stimulating to work for, and we are to go and spend an evening with his niece—a sort of cousin of mine on the Bramwell side—one day next week.

Charles was home from his last Conference in December, and in the New Year Honours list for 1944 he was given proof of how much his work as Director of Plans was valued. He was made a Companion of the Bath. It was also intimated to him that he might soon expect an appointment at sea. Great developments of the war were about to unfold. Preparations for the cross-Channel invasion of the continent of Europe were in full swing, and a powerful fleet was being assembled for moves against Japan. Charles, from his rank and experience, could look for an important post, and he was given one. At the end of May he was appointed Flag Captain and Chief Staff Officer to Rear-Admiral Aircraft Carriers, Eastern Fleet, Clement Moody.

The news was not unwelcome, for few officers on the active list relish the prospect of unending attention to staff duties in time of war. Charles had been trained for command, and was likely to gain added distinction on operational service. Cunningham understood his case as thoroughly as any admiral of his era, for staff duties were his own idea of Hell. Of such duties, Charles had indeed had his share. They had given him extraordinary experiences. He had made endless contacts, from the Prime Minister downwards, and he had attracted at least two lasting friends. One of these was Elliot; the other was Sir George Mallaby, who from the very different world of head-mastership of a famous school, found himself Secretary of the Joint Planning Staff.

Mallaby greatly admired both Elliot and Charles Lambe. He saw in them two people who could rise above even the high attainments which their posts required, to 'give manhood a supplementary and exciting significance'. Of Charles he wrote:

I should find it hard to be critical about him. He was, I think, conscious of his superiority, but I never felt there was any suspicion of vanity or conceit. He had, I fancy, an affectionate nature. He could be cold and severe with what seemed to him inferior work or vulgar manners. His intellectual powers were considerable, and his mastery of his profession complete. In political and social matters he was a liberal thinker, sometimes, I thought, almost too ready to be attracted to left-wing opinions.

For his part, Elliot set down his impressions and recollections of Charles many years later, as a tribute deriving from that 'affectionate nature' which he certainly shared with his friend.

He took everything as it came, [he wrote] people, work, situations, crises, problems, disasters, defeats, victories, with a confident imperturbable equanimity. The demands on the Planners seemed, to me at least, to be depressingly exacting at times. But never to Charles. He rose to every occasion, rode the crest of every challenge that came his way—indeed he went out of his way to seek them.

He never seemed tired and in fact gave the impression of being stronger than he was. The explanation is, I think, that he truly enjoyed and was stimulated by the nature of the work and the great issues it involved. This is one of the reasons why he was such a compelling companion to work with. He infected one with his courage. And there were many other qualities. He was quick to see and make a point, and, if need be, to concede one. He was easy in debate, made the more pleasant by his deep rich voice. In the written word he was rightly concerned more with the substance than the style.

Charles was essentially a man, the 'picture' of a man. Yet there was a charming feminine strain in him. He was both catholic and cultivated in his tastes, and self-sufficient in his enjoyment of them. He played the piano as happily as he did polo. He flew and he sailed. He knew and liked all manner of men and women. Entirely free of any form of snobbery, he was comfortable in every kind of company. He was sophisticated and yet surprisingly simple. He preferred the public to the saloon bar—and the simpler the better, such as that of the dock-side pub at Greenock into which he couldn't wait to plunge me the moment we set foot on land from the *Queen Mary* on our way home from the Quebec Conference. This earthy taste was in marked contradiction to the elegant comfort and civilized society which surrounded him and Peta in their home.

He had a love and understanding of music, and an appreciation of painting. 'I'm surprised you haven't given birth to a baby grand' was the mordant quip of one of his fellow officers after the birth of his son James.

His position in life placed him among the ranks of the privileged, but his politics were those of the under-privileged. It was part of the duties of the Directors of plans to advise and keep a watching brief on behalf of the Chiefs of Staff on the military value to the Allies of the various guerilla and resistance movements round the world. One day in the summer of 1943 Charles burst into one of our meetings and exuberantly announced: 'Do you know that I've just found out the fellow we ought to be backing in the Balkans!' 'I bet he's a Communist' I said. I was right—but so was Charles, and in more ways than one as time proved. It was Tito.

IV

Charles left Britain, actually Glasgow, on the 5th June, the day before the invasion of France, and a few days before the first flying bombs came over. Owing to his previous job he had known when these were to be unleashed and consequently insisted that Peta and James should live in Scotland. His mother died of a heart attack before he left England.

Charles described a fleeting look at Salisbury, babe in company, which was made on the way back from a final visit to the parental home.

It was warm and sunny, [he wrote] so we all walked out into the town and Peta went into the Cathedral, and James and I sat in the Close and looked at all those beautiful houses. I think that the people of Salisbury thought it was a very funny sight to see a Captain in uniform and a baby sitting alone in the Cathedral Close on a public seat!

On that happy glimpse ended a notable series of letters. They had begun in a childish hand when Charles was little more than a baby, on visits away, or from Horris Hill. When they ended he was Captain Charles Lambe, C.B., C.V.O., R.N., and destined for flag rank.

Chapter Six

H.M.S. *ILLUSTRIOUS*

THE *Illustrious* was a large and famous ship. Since the loss of the *Ark Royal* in 1941 she was probably the best-known aircraft carrier in the Royal Navy. Her aircraft had played the principal part in Admiral Cunningham's destruction of Italian ships in the harbour of Taranto in October 1940. She herself had been the main target of attack by the Luftwaffe in the Mediterranean a few months later, and had only been saved from destruction by the strength of her armoured flight deck, which had in fact been pierced, and by heroic work in repairing her under further bombing attacks at Malta. She had been sent to the United States for repair, and there she had been put under the command of Mountbatten; but before he could take her to sea he had been summoned to England by Churchill to take over Combined Operations from Sir Roger Keyes. The *Illustrious* had been in operations off Madagascar, and had been in support of landings at Salerno in 1943. She was indeed a proud ship, and the Admiralty's description of her heraldry was: '*Field*: blue. *Badge*: In front of a trumpet erect two trumpets in saltire gold.' Under Charles she was to add to her battle honours.

He took passage in H.M.S. *Indomitable*, a ship of the same class, leaving the United Kingdom on 12 June 1944, six days after the Normandy invasion, and arriving off Colombo on 7 July. There he reported to the Commander-in-Chief, Eastern Fleet, Admiral Sir James Somerville, a friend of long standing. His very first mission was to be diplomatic. He was asked by Somerville to go to Kandy at the earliest opportunity to try to persuade Mountbatten to reorganize his planning arrangements on different lines. Friction was developing between the Commands, and the Admiral, knowing of the friendship between Charles and the Supreme

Commander, had hoped Charles would be an acceptable emissary, as indeed he was.

On 8 July he joined the *Illustrious*. Next he went, as requested, to Kandy, where he had a long talk with Mountbatten. The prospects of agreement between the Commands at first seemed hopeful, and Charles and Mountbatten, after an evening's dinner discussion, had an early morning ride together before Charles returned to his ship. In the upshot, difficulties were not resolved until after Somerville had left the Far East in August to head the British Admiralty Delegation in Washington, to be relieved first by Sir Bruce Fraser and later by Sir Arthur Power.

Charles was now plunged once again into war at first hand, and under entirely different conditions from anything he had experienced in the first year of the conflict. Then, he had had charge of an obsolete cruiser of under 5,000 tons, armed with six-inch guns and torpedoes. The *Illustrious* was nearly five times the size of the *Dunedin*, a comparatively new ship of a type which had already replaced the battleship as the principal arm of the Fleet, her aggressive weapons, aircraft—Barracudas, Corsairs and Avengers.

Charles kept full notes covering his year in the *Illustrious*, embellished with photographs taken of or from the ship. His assurance, from the moment he assumed command, was reflected in his almost invariable lack of comment on what was intricate and ever-changing operational fact. His only real self-doubt occurred much later, when he wondered whether he had not made a serious error of judgement under the threat of a cyclone. He had always been considered professional in the fullest sense of the word, and with every reason. What was now additionally valuable was that he had had considerable experience of flying. He was, indeed, as well equipped as any captain of a Fleet carrier could be who had not had actual service as a pilot with the Fleet Air Arm. For years, he had specialized in the torpedo as a weapon. Now, he became a dedicated naval airman, and—to his great pride and satisfaction—he was accepted as such by those who flew.

The position in the Indian Ocean theatre of war when Charles joined the Fleet was that, as the Japanese threat to India on the Manipur front had failed, the 14th Army was presented with the chance, which it took, to throw the enemy across the Chindwin river. This put Mandalay within range. Mountbatten decided that its capture should be attempted without delay, and an advance continued south to Rangoon. At this point the Eastern Fleet's offensive task became apparent. Poor roads and an insufficient railway system made air supply of the Army essential if it was to keep up momentum, and for this an air supply base in the Arakan Peninsula was necessary. This in turn called for the capture of the Akyab airfields, which involved an amphibious assault, combined with an offensive thrust on land. To ensure success, it was necessary to have complete maritime control not only over the Bay of Bengal but over the sea area bounded by the Andaman and Nicobar Islands, the Tenasserin and Kra coasts, and the northern end of Sumatra, including the island of Sabang. That was the task which had to be accomplished before the larger units in the Eastern Fleet could join with the Americans at sea for the final moves in the battle of the Pacific and against the Japanese home islands.

Within a fortnight of his arrival on 22 July Charles sailed on his first operation, and with a force the size of which would have recalled earlier days in the Mediterranean. Rear-Admiral Moody flew his flag in the *Illustrious*, and she had another Fleet carrier, the *Victorious*, in company. There were three battleships, the Commander-in-Chief's flagship, *Queen Elizabeth*, the *Valiant* and the French *Richelieu*; a battle-cruiser, the *Renown*, wearing the flag of the second in command; seven cruisers including the *Cumberland* and the Dutch *Tromp*; and ten destroyers. The object was to bombard Sabang, the carriers to provide cover and to shoot up enemy aircraft on the airfields. All went well, the *Queen Elizabeth* firing her main armament against an enemy target for the first time since the Dardanelles nearly thirty years before. One of Charles's pilots ditched, but was rescued by the cruiser *Nigeria*. Two Japanese aircraft were destroyed in the air, in one case the pilot, Sub.-Lt. A. H. Brown, going in so close that his propeller hit the enemy. 'These two successes put everybody's tails up,' noted Charles. 'It is just over a year since an enemy aircraft was shot down by this ship's fighters.' Two more successes followed before the Fleet returned to Trincomalee, that harbour on Ceylon's east coast which Nelson once described as the finest he had ever seen.

The *Illustrious* was due for a refit, and on 30 July Rear-Admiral Moody transferred his flag to the *Indomitable*. Charles's orders were to proceed to Addu Atoll, one of the various island bases created during the war, thence to Diego Suarez and so to Durban and Cape Town, reached on 11 August. There the aircraft were disembarked. The ship then returned to Durban, and from 15 August to 10 October shore leave was given. Charles could visit friends, sketch, enjoy socialities and music ashore.

By 12 October the *Illustrious* was once more operational and under way for Cape Town. 'It was lovely to feel the ship coming alive again after so long as an Augean stable for stallions,' he noted. Next day, he berthed at Cape Town after an 'argument with the pilot, who got very rattled and wanted to use full speed etc.' Once again shore leave could be given, and Charles had the chance to climb Table Mountain, where he made some sketches and was nearly arrested by a security zealot who could not believe that this strange man—dressed for the day in country clothes—could possibly be the captain of the big carrier below in the harbour. On 17 October, just before he sailed to join the Fleet, Charles flew over the ship in a Swordfish, so that he could inspect her flying-on arrangements from the business angle. He thought they could be improved, and made plans accordingly.

A week later, he had a report of a cyclone just west of the Chagos Archipelago, noting: 'There is only 1 cyclone per 10 years in these waters in October.' He decided to steer at fairly high speed—21 knots—on a course which, he hoped, would put him due south of the centre after which he should be able to pass to eastward of its progress. On 26 October sea and wind freshened. The barometer fell rapidly—then steadied—then, shortly before midnight, took a big plunge. Charles considered that the ship was probably closing the centre: 'the seas were going too big to allow the destroyer escorts to run fast before them, and our port engine lost pressure. There was nothing for it but to accept being in the dangerous quadrant and heave to and hope for the best.'

All was well, and the centre of the storm evidently turned away. At one stage Charles felt 'great apprehension', which he duly recorded. This was rare with him. 'I was the cause of all this and would be responsible for the loss of aircraft, not to speak of damage to the destroyers. Perhaps I should be court-martialled! If only I had not turned the night before!' Later, when the ship was making 12 knots and the seas were moderating, he found there had in fact been no damage: 'not even to the accommodation ladders. So perhaps I won't be court-martialled after all! The moral of all this undoubtedly is that once you suspect there is a cyclone near, heave to and take accurate observations over a period. It's no use acting precipitately on insufficient evidence like I did the other night.'

Trincomalee was reached on 1 November and there the Admiral rejoined. The Barracuda squadron were due to go home, and Charles would operate henceforward with Corsairs and

Avengers. Moody objected to the men falling in for entering harbour in shorts without shirt. 'This made me very angry,' noted Charles. His temper was not eased when a staff officer came on board and ordered 49 maintenance ratings and 12 air gunners from the Barracuda squadron to stay behind in Ceylon instead of proceeding to England. 'This made me furious,' Charles noted, 'and I refused to give the order. With Moody's backing, went ashore, saw Admiral Rawlings and got the order reversed after stormy scene. Much gratitude from the men concerned.'

They were not the only grateful men in the *Illustrious*: another was Norman Hanson, who led one of the squadrons, and who had got into serious trouble, low-flying, while in South Africa, an incident which had involved the naval Commander-in-Chief and the General Officer Commanding South African Forces, over whose home Hanson had unwisely done some aerobatics. Immediately Charles heard of the matter he told Hanson 'not to worry' and suggested he approach the General who, when he heard what the likely penalties would be, said he would not press the charge. When Hanson reported back on board: 'The captain talked to me as only he could talk,' he recalled later. 'His sincerity and obvious affection for his "boys" moved me far more deeply than any Admiral's "blast" could ever have done.' This recalls a remark made by a seaman who once served in Collingwood's flagship a century and a half earlier: 'A man who could not be happy under him, could have been happy nowhere; a look of displeasure from him was as bad as a dozen at the gangway from another man.'

II

On 10 December Rear-Admiral Moody left the Fleet, and later wrote the briefest official report about Charles he ever had: 'In every way outstanding. I foresee a brilliant future before him.' Three days later Rear-Admiral Sir Philip Vian arrived at Trincomalee to take command of the carriers, flying his flag in the *Indomitable*. This was the first chance Charles had had to become acquainted with one of the most formidable tactical commanders the Royal Navy possessed, with battle experience in destroyers, cruisers and carriers, and with an outstanding triumph recently behind him as Eastern Task Force Commander at the assault on Normandy. Vian's standards were the highest, and his mentor was Cunningham, under whose direction he had fought some of his fiercest actions. He soon made himself known to Lambe, and was at sea with the *Illustrious* on 14 December, 'flying on board and ashore' as Charles noted. 'He had only been in Colombo for about 24 hours', Charles added, 'when he ordered *Indomitable* and *Illustrious* to be ready for an operation on 17 December.' The force included three cruisers, and had not been a day at sea when Charles noted approvingly: 'Philip Vian is splendid at keeping people on their toes.' He was no bad hand himself. He was always ordering surprise exercises, particularly for the engine-room and damage control parties.

On Charles's birthday, 20 December, the force was off the entrance to the Malacca Straits, flying a number of sorties in the hope of damaging an oil refinery, but without much luck owing to bad weather. The *Illustrious* earned 'a nice signal from Philip Vian' for a good land-on, and the airmen did a strafe on the airfield at Sabang but found little evidence of activity. On the way home, noted Charles: 'The Admiral twisted the party inside out in the dark. Quite exciting.'

On 11 December the *Illustrious* had a visit from Mountbatten who, so Charles wrote to Peta, was in splendid form and most amusing, as was another visitor, Ian Fleming. On 16 January 1945, after an intensive period of exercising, Charles sailed from Trincomalee to Fremantle, Australia, with what was now to be termed the British Pacific Fleet. Three days before, ominously the 13th, and just after a congratulatory signal on a good morning's work from Vian, who said it was the ship's 'Day of Days', the *Illustrious* had two misfortunes which caused Charles 'apprehension, worry and sadness'. One of his aircraft crashed into a barrier, caught fire immediately, the pilot dying from burns and shock, and another airman turned too steeply at low speed and dived his Corsair into the sea, leaving no trace. 'Deep down inside I am temporarily shocked,' Charles wrote to Peta, 'and it will take time to get right again. Perhaps if I had seen more death this war I should be hardened. Anyway I *must* get hardened somehow or else I shall crack myself in a bad emergency and then you would not be proud of me any more though I know you would always understand better than I would myself.'

The progress of the Fleet to Australia was to be marked by a final operation, a big air attack on the oil refinery at Palembang in southern Sumatra. Bad weather delayed it, but it took place finally on 24 and 29 January and was an outstanding and heartening success. On the first strike the *Illustrious* had four operational losses, and Hanson ditched owing to someone else's bad flying. 'A most efficient man and a very lovable character,' noted Charles, 'his loss in an unnecessary accident would have had appalling repercussions on morale.' When Hanson was reported safe, Charles asked to see him at once on the compass platform from which he was navigating the ship. 'He was obviously very moved,' Hanson noted later. 'He took my right hand between both his hands and could only say "Hans! My dear Hans!" before turning away.'

One of the saddest losses was Brown, a hero of the *Illustrious's* first operation under Charles, who dived into the ground while strafing Lembak airfield. One pilot, Sutton, was seen to bale out and land safely far inland. But Charles always worried about the fate of survivors landing on Japanese held territory, for it was far too often shocking, judged by customs of war in other parts of the world.

The enemy claimed many aircraft shot down, and that their 'Special Attack Corps chased the Carriers, but they escaped'. Actually the nearest shave the *Illustrious* had was from her own side. 'I had to reverse my rudder rapidly to avoid *Indefatigable*,' noted Charles, 'who was doing 28 knots through the Carrier formation whilst we were turning into wind.'

Next day, 27 January, which was Peta's birthday, Charles oiled at sea from a tanker, always a tricky operation. 'I've never had a more exhausting day,' he noted. 'We were settled down comfortably astern of the tanker. Her speed seemed to vary constantly and the strain of avoiding the Scylla of a bump and the Charybdis of parting the hose was terrific. I was at full concentration from 06.45 until 18.15. . . . I hope Peta had a better day than I did.'

Next day, Sunday, he was 'very on edge'. He spoke to the ship's company about possible suicide bombers. The second big day, 29 January, during which the Palembang oil refinery was severely damaged, was described by Charles in one of his most vivid letters to Peta.

You will have heard from the news how we renewed the attack, [he wrote] but oh there are so many details I want to give you. It was by far the most exciting day I have ever had and the first time I have been under air attack this war.

There was an atmosphere of great tension and apprehension throughout the ship the night before and the dawn broke grey and squally with patches of torrential rain but we had to go ahead and we got our boys away all right. . . .

Then that terrible period of suspense that I hate so but they all came back except two, one of whom was one of my squadron commanders. His loss was particularly tragic. He had led his squadron down below the balloon barrage the time before with great gallantry and this time he was under the impression that he had got a promise that the balloons would be removed for him beforehand but due to a balls-up, this was not done. He went down through them again and one wing was torn off by a balloon cable. The second also met the same fate but the job was done well and truly and the other half of the enormous refinery will also be of no use to the Japs for months and months, if ever.

Many aircraft with holes in them, and astonishing adventures being recounted by sweaty, grimy but happy faces.

Then the Jap attack on us came. It was a futile attack and no aircraft got away and no damage was done but at least 3 out of the 6 chose *us* as their target! I can't describe the sensation of watching these evil looking twin-engined aircraft coming very low nearer and nearer in a hail of shell-fire. It had a sort of mesmerizing effect on me. I could not believe that any one could survive but only one did get too close before he crashed in flames too and then we had an accident at that crucial moment—nothing to do with the Japs—but there was a nasty explosion and a number of my chaps killed and wounded and me very deaf with my right ear drum split (discovered afterwards) 'cos the explosion came from very close to me and not a scratch on me otherwise, so that made me feel very splendid and cool and calm and I at once felt very much happier to think that I had at last shared some small part of the dangers which my boys always run even though it was accidental. And it is an enormous relief to know that I don't get in a panic in the face of danger but that I feel calmer and calmer which is all very surprising.

I suppose the operation is about the biggest that has ever been undertaken by aircraft from the RN and it has been a great triumph. They had to fly over mountains over 6000 feet high, over miles of enemy territory and meet stiff flak defences as well as enemy fighters.

The day after it all, Philip Vian sent this signal to me: 'The determination of your Squadrons to hit the enemy to the full at whatever cost has involved *Illustrious* in important losses which we all deplore. I hope it may be satisfactory to you to know that I have no doubt that it is upon the gallantry and resolution of such men as these that the great successes achieved at Palembang chiefly depended.'

I do believe that my boys bore the brunt of the whole thing and contributed more than their share. Their spirit was absolutely magnificent and this praise from P.V. has been very well deserved. When it first came I showed the signal without comment to one of the bomber pilots who happened to be near by. He was an art student at Croydon. He read it and his eyes filled with tears and he could not say anything.

Charles noted some additional details in his *Illustrious* notebook. When the nearest enemy aircraft came in, he was pushed inside cover by the Commander (Flying) who was standing nearby. Afterwards, when he had the deck cleared for landing on two Corsairs, he

... was amazed ... to see several corpses on the flight deck and two Avengers riddled with holes. Then there were people lying on the compass platform being bandaged, and blood everywhere, and the screen of the outer bridge was wrecked and glass everywhere but we got the two Corsair boys on, and then I learnt that we had also been hit starboard side low down under the island and then I knew it was the gunfire of the Fleet that had done it, firing at the aircraft which passed overhead. It was not till after that that I realized that we had 11 killed and 8 dangerously wounded and 14 moderately wounded.

A week or so later, Charles himself was presented by the Surgeon Commander with an official 'Certificate for Wounds and Hurts' saying that 'he was on the Compass Platform when a shell exploded outside and just below at the position of No. 4 Oerlikon Gun' as a result of which he sustained a 'Traumatic rupture of the right Tympanic Membrane with mild concussional deafness'. The doctor's view was that the trouble would right itself within a week or so.

At Lambe's particular request, Admiral Vian allowed him to fly a search, which would have been followed up by an attempt at rescue of airmen he knew had landed, and who might have reached one of the Sumatran lakes. A Walrus amphibious aircraft was kept ready for the purpose, but no sign was seen. 'I felt', wrote Vian in his war memoir, *Action This Day*, 'that we were overstepping the limits of reasonable risk to the rescuers. It remained ever a problem where to draw the line.' Nevertheless, Vian himself was capable of equal concern. On the evening of 29 January he altered the course of the entire Fleet to ensure the rescue of a Seafire survivor in a dinghy who had been spotted by an air patrol.

The Fleet reached Fremantle on 4 February, all but one of the *Illustrious*'s badly wounded men being saved, a triumph, as Charles noted, for the sick-bay staff.

On the way from Fremantle to Sydney, Admiral Vian came on board the *Illustrious*. He:

> ... spoke to all Air Crews and Air officers in the wardroom about Palembang: [noted Charles.] He spoke very gently, rather hesitantly but quite frankly and said Palembang was out of action for a very long time. .... He had wanted to do a third strike but we had insufficient oil fuel. Then he spoke very nicely to the ship's company on the broadcaster saying how sorry he was about the unnecessary casualties and that he was taking steps to see that it never happened again.
>
> He has great charm of manner and I find him a stimulating person to work for.

This was the same phrase which Charles had used about Cunningham at Cairo, and Vian could scarcely have been paid a greater compliment.

III

At Sydney the *Illustrious* was found to have serious defects. She became the first ship to enter the new graving dock, where she had her centre propeller removed, after which her best speed would be 24 knots. She sailed on 6 March for the Pacific theatre of operations, with two destroyer escorts, and reached Manus, in the Admiralty Islands, on 13 March. It was an appropriate day on which to endure, as Charles duly noted, 'heavy rain squalls: very sticky heat. Everybody in *King George V* [the Fleet flagship] very depressed. No settled future for us. Manus was bloody, climate awful etc. Dined with Philip Vian who said today's was the first "weekly practice programme" he had carried out this

war and it was the last straw.' Two factors were depressing the
Fleet: the first was uncertainty as to whether the American
Admiral Nimitz would be allowed to request 'Task Force 57', as
the Fleet was now called, to operate with him. The second was the
inadequacy of the British Fleet Train of supply and amenity ships,
at least compared with that of the Americans.

The arrival of the *Illustrious* changed the Fleet's luck. On 15
March, whilst on an exercise at sea, orders were received that
'Task Force 57' could proceed to the immediate theatre of
operations. 'Evidently Ernie King has failed to stop us taking
part,' noted Charles with satisfaction. Three days later, the ships
sailed for Ulithi in the western Caroline Islands preparatory to
joining in the assault on Okinawa with the American main force.
The role of the carriers would be to neutralize Japanese airfields
by means of continuous attacks.

On 26 March, during the aftermath of a strike, a fighter
bomber came back to the *Illustrious* with a bomb the pilot could
not release. 'It came off as he landed,' Charles noted, 'and
rocketed up the deck, damaging an Avenger in the deck part
forward, but did not explode!' Charles saw the first Japanese
'suicide' attack on Easter Sunday, 1 April, when a Kamikaze
crashed on to the flight-deck of the *Indefatigable*, whose ship's
company had the fires out and were again operating within a very
short time. Next day, seas were heavy and two men were washed
overboard, only one of whom was recovered alive.

By 3 April the *Illustrious*, which had had an exceptionally hard
war, was beginning to show signs of bad strain, which was
worrying her shipwrights. There were other troubles too. 'Wrote
to Philip Vian about our older pilots,' noted Charles, 'who are all
getting a bit teased out. But we must keep going a little longer.'

The ship had a trying day on 6 April, two incidents in which
were described by Charles as follows.

I was watching a single aircraft on the starboard side
approaching across the Fleet when I heard Lewis gun fire, then
all close range weapons started . . . I looked out on the port
bow and saw an aircraft diving straight at us—at the island,
the bridge, at me. I said 'Hard a port' and looked away. There
was a whizz as it missed the front of the bridge and a heavy
thump and an enormous cloud of spray as he plunged in 50
yards clear abreast the starboard funnel side.

Nobody else on the bridge even saw it coming. It was about

9 seconds from the time he dived out of the clouds until he went into the sea but, in that time, he was hit and hit hard and it was only that which saved us, I'm sure. His starboard wing wrecked the 272 aerial lantern—a piece of wing was found there, and the whole flight deck was covered in debris. A cylinder complete, a piece of the Jap's skull, masses of bits of twisted metal, a red and white striped dinghy on the *port* after aerials and one of our Corsairs had its tail over the port after dip and another was turned 180 degrees—both with fuselages warped by the blast. This happened at about 17.17.

Seven minutes later, another aircraft appeared head on diving out of the clouds on roughly the same relative bearing. Off went the guns and this time, 'A' group got off one salvo across the deck. The aircraft pulled up and turned as if to crash on *Victorious*—and was then seen to be a Seafire. Cease fire was ordered but it was too late; it was hit repeatedly, a wing came off and it fell in the sea about 2 cables ahead—no sign of life. This was a most tragic affair but one I cannot regret. With only a few seconds between disaster and safety, you cannot afford to hesitate. . . . We had no casualties and only superficial damage.

Next day, Charles sent a message to Vian reporting the serious structural defects of the ship, the shipwrights agreeing that she was not in a condition to withstand any serious underwater damage. The answer came quickly. On 9 April Vian made a signal that on 12 April *Formidable* would take the *Illustrious*'s place in the Fleet. Charles's position was then about 60 miles from Formosa and about 30 from Kumi Island, which could be seen in the clear weather.

On 14 April, on one of his final days in the Okinawa theatre, Charles noted: 'During the operation we have embarked 3,549 tons of oil fuel at sea and 88,363 gallons of Avgas aviation spirit 50,000 sausage rolls and flown 505 sorties.'

By 16 April the ship had anchored at Leyte Gulf, and on 3 May she proceeded to Sydney via the unpopular Manus.

Leyte, [noted Charles] has been terribly hot. No wind, no leave, hard work, cruising watch closed up and grilling sun. Miles from shore. The ship became a cross between a knacker's yard and a sullage bin. We got out everything of immediate operational value to the other Carriers and took in hundreds of

10

empties, cylinders, long-range tanks which wouldn't fit and beer bottles. That was one 'good' at Leyte—a bottle of beer per day per man at 1/3d Australian, to be drunk on the flight deck, and about time too. 15 fighter pilots out of 41 left us for *Victorious* and *Formidable*.

Everyone left the *Illustrious* with regret.

It was no easy matter, [wrote Hanson later] to keep in real happiness a ship designed for a complement of 1,300 but carrying 1,800 officers and men; and a ship not designed for tropical service, yet spending month after month within 30° of the Equator. Yet Captain Lambe did it. We were universally envied as 'the happiest ship in the Fleet'; and at other times, particularly by our frequent guests, as 'the happiest hotel in the eastern hemisphere'.

His attitude permeated through his senior officers—all of whom were good or were *made* good by him right down to the lowest orders. And, no doubt because we were happy, there was a wonderful pride of ship and a truly terrific *esprit de corps*. To belong to a squadron in *Illustrious* gave a young pilot enormous status—certainly one that none of our sister Carriers ever attained. . . . He knew that most of us would have gone to the far side of Hell for him, and I am sure he loved us for it.

IV

It was at Manus, on the way to Sydney, that the ship's company had news of the victorious end of the war in Europe, the second time in his life that Charles had heard such tidings at sea.

A most beautiful day [he noted]. Pipe down. Big eats. Turkey. Spliced the mainbrace. At 18.45 mustered on the flight deck. I spoke for a few minutes, then a short thanksgiving Service, finally, 20 minutes after sunset, a *feu de joie* from every gun, with 100% tracer and rockets and Very's lights for 20 seconds. A wonderful sight. Everybody in very good heart.

Charles put some of his own reflections in a letter written to Peta on 7 May, the day before the event was celebrated.

Eighty per cent of the masses in every country all want the same thing, [he wrote] security, peace and work, and there is

no hope of a stabilized peace until each country is governed by
the people who want the same thing—who have the same aim
I mean. But before this uniting is possible I feel sure that there
has got to be a change of heart in the individual. We must *all*
be less greedy, less ambitious, less full of self-interest, less ready
to cut our neighbour's throat if we are to attain that unity.

Charles was immensely impressed by recent events in Burma,
which had been somewhat overshadowed by those nearer home.

I think the most wonderful news is the capture of Rangoon
which to anyone like me who knows the difficulties which were
raised seems absolutely miraculous [he wrote].
    I believe that that 14th Army Burma campaign will prove to
be one of the most brilliant in the whole war. In Washington
once I heard Wavell hold forth for 2 hours on how impossible
it was even to reach Mandalay from Assam. Now Dickie has
done the whole thing—and despite always being starved of
forces etc. It really is a triumph of the first order.

He also told Peta how pleased he was at the awards to his air
crews for Palembang. These included a Distinguished Service
Order, four Distinguished Service Crosses and four Distinguished
Service Medals. He himself received two separate Mentions in
Despatches for service in the Far East, one of them gazetted in
May 1945 and the other five months later.
    Charles loved his first glimpses of Australia, to which he
returned with pleasure, loved the country itself, and the warmth of
its welcome. Even in the few days he was there for the second time
he kept a look-out for the work of artists such as Russell Drysdale,
Frend, and Dobell. He got to know Drysdale well, over the course
of the years, and at this time bought a fine oil by Frend.
    The *Illustrious* sailed for home on 24 May, proceeding by way of
the Red Sea and the Suez Canal, in the passage of which, Charles
noted, the 'ship handled very well' despite having no centre
propeller. 'Very good pilot who sat in high chair in centre-line
with sound-powered telephone to the bridge. A tiring but most
enjoyable day.' The ship was home before the end of June.
    In July Charles made a B.B.C. broadcast which included an
account of some of his later experiences in the Okinawa campaign.

For the naval air crews upon whom fall the principal burden of
neutralizing enemy airfields it is a job which offers none of the

magnificent and immediate returns of the Taranto, or the *Tirpitz* or the Palembang operations [he told his audience]. It is a task which means months at sea with long hours and hard work. But it is a job which has two great consolations: the first is a feeling that we can hold our heads high and say that we are taking our full share in the vital American operations for the defeat of Japan, and the second is that, even on the other side of the world, we were getting letters from home delivered each time we went to replenish. . . .

As a postscript to his wartime commission in the ship, Charles cherished one souvenir of the *Illustrious*, a personal tribute which came to him from an anonymous poet from the lower deck. The words read:

> *We're all very fond of our Captain Lambe*
> *It doesn't matter if you're only an artisan*
> *Or a lacemaker from Nottingham*
> *Or a diamond polisher from Amsterdam*
> *Or just a plain inhabitant of Birmingham*
> *Or if you joined the ship at Durban*
> *Or if you can't fancy chopped ham or spam,*
> *Even if he tells you to scram*
> *He does it polite like as if he was a gentleman*
> *Not like some. And if you're in a jam*
> *There's no one we'd rather go to than Captain Lambe*
> *And see him personal.*
> *Signed Sam.*

Chapter Seven

FLAG OFFICER

THE surrender of Japan in August 1945, immediately following the dropping of atomic bombs on Nagasaki and Hiroshima, brought no rest for Charles, rather the reverse. Cunningham was still First Sea Lord, and was unlikely to suggest anything but a highly responsible post for an officer with experience both of high-level staff work and recent operations at sea. At the end of August, Charles was appointed Assistant Chief of Naval Staff (Air) with the acting rank of Rear-Admiral, which was made substantive two years later. His knowledge of the air would, so the Board of Admiralty considered, be invaluable in the difficult problems which seemed certain to arise after the war, when the Navy's claim to a greater share of the nation's air resources than it had ever enjoyed between the wars, or, indeed, since the original foundation of the Royal Air Force in 1918, would be pressed.

Work apart, it was everything to Charles that he could once again be with his family, and during the year following his return from the Far East he was made happy by the birth of a daughter, Louisa Caroline. His children were, indeed, one of the most important factors in Charles's life and from the time they could feed themselves they always had meals with their parents, no matter who else might be there. As for Andrew, during Charles's absence on war service, Peta had had the good fortune to discover Wester Elchies, at Aberlour in Morayshire, a school founded by Kurt Hahn partly as a preparatory school for Gordonstoun. There, Andrew began to flourish so well that in due course Peta and Charles became progressively more attracted by the ideas which Hahn was injecting into education, Charles eventually serving on the Governing Body of schools with which Hahn was associated, and in due course putting James under his care.

Elevation to flag rank, with its responsibilities, meant that Charles

had need to acquire a secretary. It was a matter over which he
was lucky, for he offered the post to James Pack, and a partnership
began which lasted for many years. There is no relationship in the
other Services exactly equivalent to that of admiral and secretary,
and there have been many productive combinations—Nelson's
with the two Scotts, Collingwood's with Cosway, Beatty's with
Spickernell, Cunningham's with Shaw, and a hundred more.
John Scott once said of Nelson that 'it is a happiness to be about
his hand', and that is precisely what Pack said he felt about Charles.
Pack had the advantage of war service alongside Fleet Air Arm
units, and, as Charles's earlier peacetime appointments were—
except for one interlude—concerned with flying, since he was
successively A.C.N.S. (Air) until 1947; Flag-Officer, Flying
Training, 1947–9; Flag-Officer Commanding 3rd Aircraft Carrier
Squadron, 1949–50 and Flag-Officer Air (Home) 1951–3, his
secretary's experience was of special value in days when the aircraft
carrier was a paramount arm. The interlude occurred in 1947,
when for some months Charles was engaged, with high ranking
officers of the other Services, on a report (which was never published), dealing with the huge subject of reorganization. During
that time he and Peta rented a house on the Paddington Canal
belonging to Lord Kinross, and had friends as neighbours such as
Lennox Berkeley and Heywood Hill.

Throughout Charles's career, not only people but themes were
apt to recur, sometimes more than once. One of the happier
renewals, when he first returned to the Admiralty, was contact
with the French, which had ended sadly a few years earlier in the
West Indies. It fell to him to conduct negotiations relating to the
transfer of the aircraft carrier *Colossus* to the French Navy. His
principal contact was Admiral Antoine Sala, who, so far as war
services were concerned, was almost Charles's counterpart, and
who had twice been decorated by the British for his part in active
operations with the navy of the Free French under General de
Gaulle. No one could have been a better choice than Charles to
help to heal the differences which had arisen during the struggle.
No one was more appreciative of his kindness, wisdom and tact
than Sala.

Son rôle dans les négociations qui devaient connaître un
heureux aboutissement fût prédominant [he wrote]. Son
intelligence rapide, son jugement très sûr, sa parfaite courtoisie,
son tact faisaient merveille.

For Pack, as Charles's secretary, initiation could have been a trying period, for he was much younger than the Admiral and fairly junior in rank.

The articled period was brief, [he wrote later] and after six months or so, I felt I had served my apprenticeship. I can claim little credit for this, for whatever my professional attainments, to a man of Charles's experience I must have seemed very 'green'. It was this same tolerance and understanding, which I have seen him hand out to others, which was now extended to myself. There was no condescension—the Secretary's viewpoint was always worth listening to, and sometimes he was flattered by having it accepted even though it was contrary to his own! An over-developed rank consciousness can be a failing with many naval officers. Never could this have been said about Charles; he had no time for keeping people at a distance and the Secretary stood to benefit from this characteristic most of all. . . .

It was the Fleet Air Arm more than any other branch of the Service that had reason to be grateful to him. His appreciation of the problems which at this time beset Naval Aviation, as it was then called, was complete. That there should be problems is understandable enough, for the Navy's responsibility for the Air Branch had been assumed only at the beginning of the war, since when it had been subject to mushroom growth. Its shore support in the way of airfields was inadequate, there were far too few long service pilots and observers, and there was a crying need for more robust aircraft which would stand up to the special requirements of carrier landing. He strove hard on their behalf and achieved wonders.

I think the most touching occasion I can remember was towards the end of his period as Flag Officer Air (Home) when he was able to say at a guest dinner held in his honour that the Admiralty had agreed to the title of Fleet Air Arm (which ought never to have been dropped) replacing the nebulous Naval Aviation. I am sure that the tumultuous applause which greeted this pronouncement was more a tribute to a man who had worked unremittingly for the air boys, rather than for the pleasure which the new title undoubtedly gave.

Another officer who had many opportunities, not only to observe Charles at work, but to share his problems, many of which were highly technical, was Rear-Admiral Sir William Jameson. He combined engineering skill with an intimate knowledge of, and the keenest interest in, twentieth-century naval history and some of its leading characters. Admiral Jameson's analysis of Charles's impact on naval flying could only have been contributed by one who was equally familiar with the subject and all its ramifications.

In 1948, [he wrote] when Charles Lambe came to Donibristle as the Flag Officer Flying Training, I was stationed at Arbroath. The Naval Air Stations in his command were scattered round the country from Lossiemouth in Morayshire to Culdrose in Cornwall. I was responsible for the supply of new and repaired aircraft and our duties were to some extent linked. It was only about twenty minutes by air between our headquarters; we were already old friends and saw a good deal of one another both on and off duty. After commanding the Third Aircraft Carrier Squadron in 1949 and 1950 Charles was at Lee-on-Solent as the Flag Officer Air (Home) and my immediate superior. It was during these years that we worked most closely together.

When he hoisted his flag at Donibristle we exchanged the usual official calls. I had lunch with him, and stayed on to see a fire-fighting competition which was taking place that afternoon.

The exercise, using the remains of an old aircraft soaked in petrol and oil, had been made as realistic as possible. The fire-fighters gave a spirited performance, quickly hauling the dummy pilot clear of the blazing wreckage and smothering the flames with foam. It was very well done, but it had also, under Charles's critical and enthusiastic eye, a special flavour. Life, when he was about, was never dull and always pitched at a slightly higher key.

The fire-fighting party of an air station is of vital importance, but their life is, it is to be hoped, monotonous. They must be ready for immediate action whenever flying is taking place, but are most unlikely, thank goodness, to have anything to do. This Micawber-like existence, can clearly become extremely boring, and the special clothing they wear makes it near-impossible for them to do anything else. As the days drag by it is not easy for these men to retain the enthusiasm and efficiency upon which, in a real emergency, everything will depend. Charles, talking to the sweating, grinning men after the exercise, made them feel that he knew all this even better than they did themselves.

He had a remarkable capacity for putting himself into other

people's skins. His interest in what was going on, whatever it might be, was genuine and his enthusiasm infectious. Whether he was taking part in an important meeting to decide future policy, or talking to a junior rating about that man's particular job, he seemed equally, and wholly, absorbed. He made people feel that they mattered. It is a priceless gift.

He was, as the Italians say 'sympatico', and to a quite extraordinary degree. He was quickly at home in any company or age group. His own interests were so wide that he had something in common with everybody. A sensitivity of perception, which may have been partly intuitive, put him instantly on to the right wave-length.

There was, in those years shortly after the war, a big job to be done with Naval Aviation. The war had very clearly shown where the main striking power of the Navy must lie. The carrier had displaced the battleship as the most important type of ship and the Fleet Air Arm had expanded enormously in size. It had drawn some of its strength from the regular Navy, but was, to a very great extent, composed of officers who had originally held short service commissions as aviators, and ratings who had joined the air arm, been specially trained for its particular needs, and served almost exclusively in aircraft carriers and on naval air stations. The air arm was the most important part of the Navy, but it had not been fully absorbed—an unfortunate and potentially dangerous situation which badly wanted putting right. There were a good many 'regular' naval officers, some in high places, whose blimpish attitude to the aviators tended to widen the rift, but the faults were not all on one side.

There is always a tendency in any branch for local loyalties to become too strong. Its members begin to think too much of the special skills which only they possess. This club spirit has its advantages, but must be kept within bounds or the Service will suffer. That the air arm spent much of its time in its own establishments ashore accentuated the difficulty, as did the fact that so many of its officers had come into the Navy direct from civil life. They suspected, not without some cause, that the regular, Dartmouth trained officers, looked upon them as horses of a different colour; aviators rather than sailors and 'not quite one of us.'

In an aircraft carrier, there is a genuine difficulty in integrating the air side with the working life of the rest of the ship. When flying is going on aircrew are very fully occupied, but at other times they had a good deal of time on their hands. The contrast can lead to misunderstanding, and the fact that their work is dangerous, highly concentrated and needs great personal skill may be forgotten.

This physical element, which has no exact parallel in the work of their messmates, is important. Pilots must possess and exercise skills and self-control which only other pilots can understand. Mind and body must be closely co-ordinated and danger faced, in varying degrees, each time they take an aircraft into the air, carry out a complicated mission, perhaps in bad weather, and land again. It puts them into the same sort of special category as, for example, steeplechase jockeys; members of a club which no one else can really join. This may be recognized by their non-flying brethren, but is not always fully understood. The non-flyers are aware that the flyers are less knowledgeable about ship matters than they are and have, by and large, fewer ordinary duties to perform. Thick-heads can assume that they are a superior form of flying chauffeur, no doubt very skilful in their own line, but hardly naval officers in the old established sense. This rift between flyers and non-flyers can be widened by differences in social background.

I am sure that Charles Lambe regarded the rectifying of this state of affairs as one of his major tasks during the time that I am writing about. His great reputation as a 'regular' naval officer and his unusual personal gifts made him an ideal person to put things right. There was also the important fact that he thoroughly enjoyed flying.

Those who have only flown in great air liners, where everything is done to create an impression of everyday ordinariness, will not appreciate how exhilarating flying can be. Neither will the unimaginative, using it as a quick but (to them) rather boring form of transport. He loved to sit in the co-pilot's seat of the twin-engined Expeditor which he used for official purposes, watching the country below unrolling under his feet. He would often take over with the dual controls and fly the willing, responsive little aircraft himself. He liked to take part in the problem of navigating in bad weather, when landmarks were completely hidden, and to share in the satisfaction of dropping down through the all enveloping greyness which would suddenly begin to thin, revealing glimpses of sombre, rain-soaked woods and fields, with the airfield he was making for coming into view ahead. It was even better fun in the second seat of a strike aircraft which could be hurled round the sky by its young pilot. It was exciting; it was often beautiful amongst the shining, towering clouds. It had 'the thrill which is almost fear' which he got on the polo field where he was so proficient. He often flew from his carrier flagship, enjoying the roaring departure off the deck, the rapid climb with *Vengeance* or *Triumph* shrinking to toy-like size on the sea below; the sight of the other machines of the flight edging into close formation behind either wing, apparently suspended in space behind the gleaming discs of their airscrews. He loved the plunge downwards in similated attack, with the aircraft almost vertical, and the tremendous swoop, body pressed hard into the seat, as it levelled off. The never-failing novelty of landing-on, with the narrow deck coming up ahead, tiny figures waiting, a growing sensation of speed and the final bump and wrench as the arrestor wires caught in the lowered hook, bringing the machine firmly to a stop. All these sensations he could share with the young men under his command. Their difficulties and joys were real to him. He knew what it all meant, and they knew that he understood.

On his journeying round his command Charles seized every opportunity of talking to and getting to know his aircrews, but these young men, comparatively few in number, are only the apex of the broad-based pyramid which makes up the Fleet Air Arm. Flying must be backed by an elaborate organization for control, communications, maintenance and repair. Charles's concern with these unglamorous, but essential, services was equally great. No one, however humdrum their job, was forgotten. He seemed to take as much interest in the galleys or stores as in the pilot training programme. 'Seem' is the wrong word. When he was talking to a rating engaged on some apparently simple task he became, for the moment, as wholly involved as if he was doing their job himself. This brilliant, artistic, highly-gifted man who was so perfectly at home at a high-level meeting attended by some of the best brains in the land, or talking to specialists about their own abstruse subjects, could also think like an aircraft mechanic of small general education struggling head-downwards in the cramped cockpit of a fighter with a recalcitrant bolt.

His instant grasp of technicalities outside what might be regarded as his expected range of knowledge was amazing. During his time at Donibristle the twin-engined night fighter Mosquito aircraft at Culdrose suddenly ran into serious trouble

with their Rolls-Royce Merlin engines. Engine failure caused
one fatal accident and was followed by a series of near-misses,
with pilots struggling back and landing on one engine—a very
tricky business with that particular aircraft at a place like
Culdrose with its hilly approaches and short runways. The Merlin engine was usually most reliable; there was no question of
faulty maintenance and the cause of failure was obscure. Finally,
after a great deal of hard work by the engineering staff, the
cause, which was due to a most unusual combination of car-
burettor setting and slight camshaft wear, was located. The air
engineer of Culdrose, Commander (as he then was) Illingworth
believed he had the answer, but the pilots, whose confidence
had been badly shaken, must be equally convinced.

Philip Illingworth decided that the best thing to do was to
explain in detail to his Captain, the Squadron Commanders
and other officers closely concerned, exactly what he felt had
happened. He had laid out in his office all the engine parts
involved—camshafts, valves, carburettors, flame traps, valve
springs—to illustrate his theory. He was sure he was right, but
could he convince them? For his pilot friends and messmates it
was, quite literally, a matter of life and death. Illingworth
describes what happened next.

'It was at this time that Admiral Lambe chose to visit us and
to join in the session. My first memory is my astonishment at his
grasp of the technicalities. He asked some very straight questions
and wasn't satisfied until he got clear and straight answers. But
my most vivid memory is of his immediate understanding of the
predicament of myself and my department in relation to those
who flew the aircraft. It was entirely due to his influence,
demonstrably professional and human, that after an hour's
session we were all convinced of, and confident in, the solution.
He then took trouble to talk personally to each and every officer
and rating in my department concerned with the work. That
night we started the biggest maintenance operation I can remember in peace time. Every engine was removed and stripped. . . .
Three days later we started flying again, and the trouble had
vanished.

'It's a simple story, but the officers and ratings concerned will
never forget it. We had had the opportunity to find out for ourselves that there was something very special about this man.'

His ability to go straight to the heart of any subject, from the
simplest to the most intricate, was one of his most notable

characteristics. He also had the gift, a very rare one, of thinking in first principles. At an important conference at headquarters he would often, with only an occasional remark, let others do most of the talking. But what he said sank in. Like the buoys marking the channel into a difficult anchorage his interjections guided the meeting towards the conclusion he wished it to reach. Those who had been in opposition would somehow find themselves supporting his ideas, or, better still, advancing them as their own.

One of his staff officers has recalled how his ability to illuminate the essentials of any problem reduced bulky dockets of official paper to a few homely phrases.

'I don't recall him ever having to write more than two or three lines on paper, sometimes only two or three words, to express his views and usually (with respect) hitting the nail bang on the head.' Another remembers how one day 'a slightly dishevelled Admiral in his shirt sleeves' walked into his office with a fat file in his hand, perched himself on the desk and said:

'Tony. I'm quite perplexed by all this bumph. What does it mean?'

He then proceeded to reduce the contents of the pile of 'bumph' to one or two essentials on which he gave a clear, concise, ruling. Suddenly it all seemed quite simple. You could *almost* have done it yourself.

'The atmosphere was always relaxed, with much laughter, but full of interest' is how another officer remembers Charles's periodical staff meetings.

Although the least pompous of men he could, on occasions, be exceedingly tough. Captain Kenneth Short, his chief of staff at Donibristle, recalls that 'his ability to give someone a rocket was electrifying'. Men near his own age and seniority, jauntily entering his office, were seen on occasion to emerge looking very much chastened. But, unlike many lesser men, he never found it necessary to stress the fact that he was not to be trifled with.

He was a good talker, but he was also a good listener, and he didn't mind admitting being wrong. One of the great dangers of success, particularly in a disciplined service like the Navy, is the partial vacuum in which the successful may find themselves. 'Where the Cabots talk only to the Lodges and the Lodges only to God.' Decisions are, and must be, made at the top, but if the worm's eye view is neglected they may be wrong ones. On a visit to one of his air stations Charles liked to break away and talk to the young men in his command. It was flattering to be singled out in this way, but at first a little alarming. The Admiral was, after all, a tremendous naval personality. Everyone knew the facts of a brilliant career—brains and ability which had brought promotion at an early age; difficult appointments in which he had distinguished himself—all the rather awe-inspiring paraphernalia of a closed community where seniors must be told they know best even if you don't agree. But a few minutes later that same tongue-tied youngster would be talking almost as freely as he would have to a contemporary. Just occasionally some rather uppish young man with ill-digested views would receive a shock—a quick glimpse of Charles's intellectual capacity. It would have been a little blinding if a lightning sense of humour, impish rather than malicious, had not turned what could have been a hurtful rebuke into a simple, and remembered correction. Everyone remembers Charles's warmth, humanity and charm, but there was never the slightest doubt, for all his friendly ways, that he was a man of quite exceptional ability.

The Lower Deck classified him, and it is, perhaps, the greatest compliment they can pay, as a 'thorough gentleman'. Socially the expression has, nowadays, little significance. A 'gentleman' is a respected leader who is brave, competent, compassionate and just; never blowing hot and cold and of complete integrity. Charles had all these qualities. Also, and this was most important, no one who was associated with him ever felt insignificant.

II

Opportunity for further sea service was given Charles when he took command of the Third Aircraft Carrier Squadron in 1949, just four years after he had left the *Illustrious*. He flew his flag in the light carrier *Vengeance*, serving under two successive Commanders-in-Chief, Admirals McGrigor and Vian, the first of whom wrote of him that he was 'an exceptional Flag-Officer with outstanding powers of leadership, youthful outlook, and great charm'. Vian, who already knew Charles so well, said of him that he was 'a national asset, whose great gifts and excelling talents are too well known to need comment from me'. He had, however, one qualification. Knowing Charles to be fearless himself, he wondered if he would always be ruthless enough in ordering his airmen to take justifiable risks when these became necessary. 'Would he,' asked Vian, 'in a tough war, be tough enough with his own side?'

This was the nearest approach to criticism which Charles had

had, during the course of his later Service life. It was a reasonable question, coming from such a man as Vian, but it worried Charles, who found this particular Commander-in-Chief an easier man to follow, in some ways, in war than in peace. He unburdened himself to Mountbatten, who was then Fourth Sea Lord. Mountbatten had sound advice to offer. 'A man who is as brave and physically reckless as Philip Vian is unlikely also to have been endowed with the other qualities which make for an easy Commander to serve in peace time. One thing however you need not worry about . . . during a long gossip . . . he did nothing but sing your praises.' Vian, as always, was sincere in what he said. He valued Charles, and showed it.

The *Vengeance*, as a flagship, carried an admirals' barge, and the barge entailed a coxswain. Here again, as with his secretary, Charles was lucky, for he picked upon a Leading Airman, D. J. Hammett, who in later years was promoted to commissioned rank. Mr. Hammett wrote:

I joined *Vengeance* as a Leading Airman in spring of '49 supposedly for Flight Deck duties, just at the time that the Admiral was asking for a volunteer from the ship's company to take over the job as his coxswain. I, as an ex-Leading Seaman, had had a great deal of experience in boats, so decided to apply for the position.

Less than half an hour after I had handed my request in to the Chief of the Deck, a messenger came down to the hangar where I was tinkering with a tractor engine to say that the Flag-Lieutenant wished to see me in his cabin immediately—I made my way aft and introduced myself and with little more ado was whisked straight in to meet the Admiral.

Admiral Lambe was seated at his desk where he had been working on some papers when Flags ushered me in and introduced me. I was acutely aware of the smudges of oil on my hands and shirt, but as I started to apologize for my dishevelled appearance, the Admiral stopped me at once and said he was looking for a Cox'n who would not be afraid of getting his hands dirty occasionally. We talked a little about my previous ships and experience and within a little while I felt completely at ease. Soon it was decided that I would start work immediately as his Cox'n, and so began the most interesting and enjoyable 5 years of my career—a year with the Admiral on board *Vengeance*, two years at Lee-on-Solent and another two in the Far East.

Naturally, as Cox'n to a sea-going Admiral, the barge occupied a great deal of my time. My introduction to it was not particularly auspicious. The barge had been sent to the dockyard for a complete refit. 'Flags' was a little worried about my lack of experience with twin-screw boats and had asked a midshipman with twin-screw experience to bring the boat out of the yard and give me a quick handling demonstration. Unfortunately, during the process he managed to run the barge full tilt into the Gosport ferry, the only other boat in the harbour, smashing the bows almost down to the water-line. I booted the petrified Mid out of the cockpit and took the near-sinking boat back to *Vengeance*, arriving just as the Admiral and Flags were returning on board. I left the Mid to explain to Flags as best he could, while I made arrangements for the barge to be hoisted aboard before it sank.

The next incident which stands out particularly clearly happened while *Vengeance* was anchored off the Isle of Arran. The Admiral and several other senior officers had been to dine with the Earl of Cork and Orrery. I had collected them from the jetty at the appointed hour and was returning to the ship. The night was moonlight and clear, my passengers dressed in mess-dress, some with boat cloaks stood waiting amidships whilst I brought the barge round in a wide 'Admiralty sweep', then reduced speed to come alongside the gangway, where the Commander, Officer of the day, Officer of the watch, Quarter-master and Bosun's Mate stood ready to salute and pipe the Admiral aboard. We were but a few yards from the gangway platform when suddenly a pair of naked legs appeared wriggling out through a port just under the gangway ladder—they were followed by a body clad in little more than a white shirt and a black bow tie, it then plopped into the sea close under my bow and struck out for the gangway. I had to go rapidly astern to avoid the swimmer, throwing the passengers into a confused heap as they grabbed wildly to retain both their balance and their caps. The swimmer obviously needed no assistance as he completed a dignified trip to the gangway platform which he mounted, and pausing only to adjust his shirt-tails to his satis-faction, climbed the ladder, gave a neat little bow to the gangway staff and vanished down the nearest hatchway before the gangway staff had recovered their composure. I was delighted to hear from the Quartermaster that the Admiral, when he arrived at the top of the gangway shortly afterwards, had said that it was the most comical sight he had seen for a long time and hoped that the culprit would be dealt with leniently.

There was one crew only for the barge, so we were on duty for as long as the boat was in the water—quite often this meant that we had little time to ourselves and sometimes no chance to go ashore. Admiral Lambe was very conscious of this, he was always most appreciative of the work that we did for him, for many of the functions he had to attend it was impossible to forecast what time it would end. This would often necessitate a long cold and uncomfortable wait for us in the barge, but he always apologized for keeping us waiting, and, after a late night trip would often invite me to bring the crew up to the pantry after securing the boat, where we would find a warming drink waiting for us. Once, during a visit to Norway, after a particularly long and busy period, during which neither the barge's crew nor the domestic staff had had a minute to themselves, the Admiral made arrangements to give us all a complete day off, provided picnic meals for us all and gave us free use of the barge for the day. This was a unique opportunity for us all to get away from the ship and explore some of the delightful little fjords and villages where we were made most welcome by the people—a day that we will all remember for a long time—little wonder that the crew were all fiercely loyal to their 'boss'.

The Secretary also had memories of an incident during the same visit to Norway, when the *Vengeance* put into Stavanger.

The mooring of the ship in a deep-water anchorage close to the shore of the fjord was assumed to be appropriate by the Norwegian harbour authorities. It proved inadequate, for, in a high wind, the forward mooring parted and the ship swung on to a canning factory.

The Captain of the *Vengeance* at this time was ripe for promotion and it seemed that this unfortunate incident, which in no way could be ascribed to his own negligence, might tell against him. Such had been known to happen before in a Service where promotion to Admiral is highly competitive.

It is a *sine qua non* that whenever a ship collides or grounds, a most detailed report is rendered to superior authority, and, to me at any rate, the need to do so on this occasion was inescapable, and such was my advice to Admiral Lambe. He would have none of it; he would prefer to protect a Captain of whom he

11

thought highly, and flout the regulations rather than place the Captain's promotion in jeopardy. I was, therefore, commissioned to proceed ashore to obtain the British Consul's agreement to stifle publicity, and to consult with the owner of the canning factory to enquire his views and enlist his sympathy.

But the best laid plans go awry, and it was a rude shock when the Consul told me that Reuters had lost no time in phoning him after the incident to enquire the exact details, and 'please how many people had been killed!!' The owner of the canning factory too, whilst extremely polite and co-operative, said that he would wish for a surveyor to assess any damage before he could agree to waive any claim—which seemed to me reasonable.

Crestfallen and feeling somewhat frustrated, I returned to the ship and reported my findings. The Admiral agreed that the incident must, after all, be reported in the usual fashion. Pleasant to relate, there was no unfortunate sequel and the Captain reaped his due reward and was promoted; but had not the odds been heavily stacked against him, Charles Lambe would certainly have turned a blind eye to the regulations in the Captain's interests.

The *Vengeance* must have been unique among flagships of her era in that Charles, now at last, as an Admiral, able to indulge his musical tastes as he wished, installed two grand pianos in his day cabin. It only needed the importation of a professional, a need which was met, on one of the cruises, by inviting Lennox Berkeley to go to sea with the Squadron.

I don't think, [he wrote later] one can say that Charles had any strongly marked personal taste in music. He just loved it with the enthusiasm that he brought to anything. What was remarkable was that while accomplishing a brilliantly successful naval career, he managed to keep up not only his interest in music but his piano-playing. His technique was competent, and his sight-reading astonishing for an amateur. He brought to his playing the extraordinary adroitness that he displayed in everything. I played duets with him many times and in many places—the most improbable of these being on board the *Vengeance*, in which I had the privilege of sailing with him to Gibraltar.

I can't remember exactly what we played—Mozart and Schubert I think. I have a feeling he liked best music of the classical period, but he was ready to try anything. What I remember chiefly was his enjoyment. He didn't approach music with solemnity but with delight, and this gave me a pleasure I have not always experienced in playing with professionals.

According to Charles, it was mainly Haydn that the pair of them played. 'He carried you along,' he remarked of his guest to Peta, 'and made you feel as if you really could play.'

Charles and Lennox Berkeley motored together from Gibraltar to Granada, and spent happy hours in the Alhambra. Berkeley returned to England in the last of the battleships—H.M.S. *Vanguard*—but without such musical celebrations as on the way out.

I can never thank you enough, [he wrote to Charles] not only because of the novelty and interest of everything I saw, but because of feeling the wonderful spirit and atmosphere that the Navy alone has, and of having for a moment, the illusion of being part of it.

Berkeley was then engaged on his opera, *Nelson*, 'and I'm quite sure', he added, 'that something of the atmosphere I absorbed will bear fruit in due course.'

The trip had an amusing sequel. A newspaper got hold of the fact of there being a piano-playing admiral, with instruments on board, and the editor assumed it was Vian. A rumour to that effect duly appeared, and the Commander-in-Chief was accused by his wife of concealing his accomplishment thoughout the whole of their married life! 'It has been the big joke all round the Fleet this week,' Charles told Peta.

Charles and Vian got on well, despite their differences in temperament, and in the autumn of 1950 they put in to the rarely visited Cape Verde Islands, described by Charles as 'all precipitous black and red rock, fantastic sky-lines, extinct craters and black beaches. Bare and barren everywhere except for many strange coarse plants and a few tamarisk trees. Sharks and giant rays prevent bathing except from special beaches.'

Charles and Vian went bathing together most days, and Charles drew portraits of the people in charcoal. 'Philip', so he told Peta, 'suggested I should make them remove their rags and do the little black boys in the nude! But it is their heads which are so appealing, not their under-nourished diseased bodies.'

On the last day, sports were held on the *Vengeance*'s flight deck in grilling sun. 'Tremendous attendance,' he wrote, 'and of course I had to run in the veteran's race 100 yards which I won, and was presented with a pair of crutches by the ship's company!'

III

In December 1950, Charles was made a Vice-Admiral, and in the
following year, when he was serving as Flag-Officer Air (Home),
with his headquarters at Lee-on-Solent, he was seconded as Flag-
Officer, Royal Yacht, for what was to have been the Commonwealth Tour of Their Royal Highnesses the Princess Elizabeth and
the Duke of Edinburgh, the Shaw Savill liner *Gothic* being adapted
for the purpose. He had been appointed A.D.C. to King George VI
in 1947, thus once more renewing immediate contact with the
Royal Family, and it would have been a particular pleasure for him
to have sailed for Australia on this tour with a Princess he had
known since her childhood, and a Prince who was not only a
naval officer by training, but a nephew of the man who had become
Earl Mountbatten of Burma. All plans were changed by the sudden
death of King George VI on 6 February 1952. Charles's flag was
struck at Mombasa a few days later, after which he resumed his
duties at Lee.

Peta had been given the privilege of remaining in the official
house during such time as Charles was to have been in the *Gothic*,
and there the family flourished. It was to Lee that Her Majesty
paid her first official visit to the Fleet Air Arm, Peta travelling all
the way to her Knockhill house in Fife to choose a turkey for the
visit, picking out the bird in the turkey-house in the dark by feeling
the plumpness of its breast, and having one of the scares of her
life when the bird got misdirected on the journey, arriving only
just in time.

At Lee, Charles acquired an admirer in the person of a young
Surgeon-Lieutenant, now Dr. Rodney Long, who wrote:

> At a gathering in London I met a well known artist. It came
> out that I was in the Navy and stationed at the Barracks in
> Portsmouth. 'Then you must meet my friends the Lambes', he
> said. 'They are at Lee-on-Solent. Ring them up and ask yourself
> over for lunch.' I pointed out that it was not quite the proper thing
> for a Surgeon-Lieutenant to do, to telephone an Admiral and
> invite himself to a meal! 'They won't mind in the least,' he said.
> Nevertheless I decided I could not possibly do this and there the
> matter ended.
>
> But back at the Barracks two days later I was told that Admiral
> Lambe wished to speak to me on the telephone. He said: 'I hear
> you were asked by a Derek Hill to ring us up. You haven't
> done so. I must therefore order you to lunch with us tomorrow.'

And so, on that memorable Sunday, I took the ferry across to Gosport where Admiral Lambe had arranged for his car to meet me. The driver was a leading seaman; as we motored towards Lee-on-Solent I told him that although I had once met the Admiral officially, I was worried about this social encounter, and could he please tell me what he was like. It was some time before he spoke, as if he were searching for words, and then, with a firm look at me through the driving-mirror, he said simply, 'I can't answer your question, Sir, but if I tell you I would die for him, does that help?' It was the most wonderful tribute I had ever heard, and my fears vanished.

That Sunday at Lee-on-Solent was the turning point in my life, and on numerous occasions since I have asked myself why. I think it was because Charles Lambe, from the first moment I met him and for the first time ever, made me feel a person in my own right. He had this extraordinary capacity for making lesser people feel that they counted, that what they said mattered, even that they were important. It was, for me a deeply moving experience that he, of all people, with his vast commitments, his many interests and the huge claims on his time, should care for me, be concerned with my problems and offer wise counsel and warm friendship. No wonder he aroused such devotion in those who served under him; no wonder there was often a 'lame duck' staying in his house.

By any standard Charles Lambe was a remarkable man. In my view he was unique. He was *in* the Navy but in a strange way not *of* it. Although he had a brilliant career, and reached the highest rank, it was hard to think of him as a Naval Officer even when he was in uniform. There was about him an air of absolute completeness, to which the Navy contributed only a portion.

When I remember him, as I often do, it is not in isolation. I first met him in the company of his wife and children and even afterwards, in my mind, he was inseparable from them because they were so much a part of him. Those who knew him best as a professional sailor (and perhaps never came into close contact with his family) must have seen him in a different light. But those who were privileged to be included sometimes in that enchanting family circle were conscious of the main source of his strength and inspiration.

On those occasions when he had to come to London alone on official business from places abroad, he preferred to relax with those friends to whom he could talk about his adored wife and children. He was a wonderful father and he could never conceal (indeed he was proud to reveal) the joy and delight he found in Peta. She was not the conventional naval officer's wife. This she could never have been, this Charles never wanted her to be. If she failed to distinguish between an admiral and his flag lieutenant Charles was amused, not annoyed!

I have never known a marriage such as this—where one partner so illumined the other and where together they transmitted their happiness so excitingly to others. People, places, ideas and things never failed to fascinate and absorb them. Their total involvement in all that went on around them, wherever they were, made them unforgettable (even legendary) figures in many parts of the world. What they achieved together in an international sense in the sphere of human relationships, during the various high appointments Charles held, can only be guessed at.

Constancy was one of the qualities I admired in him and pretentiousness was undoubtedly one of those he abhorred in others, for in him there was none. Whether talking to a humble rating or an exalted celebrity he was always exactly the same. There was, in that fine voice, no hint of superiority or deference. Once I was with him when he was guest of honour at a swimming gala. He was met by a smooth lieutenant-commander (with a double-barrelled surname) who escorted him, sat next to him and was unbearably unctuous. Charles behaved impeccably, betraying not the slightest boredom or irritation but right at the end, when saying goodbye, he transposed the two parts of the surname and let his voice fade away as he spoke them. It was a gentle, yet telling, rebuke.

And then I recall vividly with what effortless charm he talked to me when, as a junior Surgeon-Lieutenant, I had to appear before him in his cabin in H.M.S. *Vengeance* concerning an enquiry into the death of a sailor. I was desperately nervous but he understood that and put me at ease immediately. That was before I met him socially, and the aura of greatness which surrounded him then never faded in after years, even when I knew him well.

In spite of all the adjectives of praise which could be lavished upon Charles Lambe he never emerged as a man too good to be true. He was too modest, too human—to great—for that. He must have influenced many people in his lifetime. I do not believe one could be found who would say he was not influenced for the better.

IV

It was at Lee, on New Year's Day 1953, that Charles had news that the Queen had appointed him a Knight Commander of the Order of the Bath. This was in recognition of his services to naval aviation, and it was a fitting prelude to his next appointment. In March 1953 it was announced that he was to go to Singapore, where he would fly his flag as Commander-in-Chief, Far Eastern Station.

Chapter Eight

COMMANDER-IN-CHIEF

WHILST he was in the *Vengeance*, Charles acquired a Flag-Lieutenant, John Edmondson, now Lord Sandford. He was a remarkable officer who, many years after being transferred to entirely different spheres of activity, provided a comprehensive outline of the general conditions which faced Charles when first he arrived to take up his responsible post in the Far East. As so often, Charles was lucky, for the officer concerned was able to set the scene clearly and, moreover, to sum up what was done during Charles's time at Singapore. His achievement was not negligible, however much later events may have modified or altered the picture.

It was no surprise that Charles Lambe's first encounter was not his first round of official calls on his fellow British Commanders-in-Chief in Singapore [wrote Lord Sandford]. The first salute he got from South East Asia was a garland of frangipani on Bangkok airport, and a welcome from a Thai guard of honour. This happened before he had even arrived at his headquarters in Singapore. This was, of course, a dreadful breach of protocol. It was totally unexpected. He enormously enjoyed it. It was a profound symbol of the next two years.

In the spring of 1953 it was as though the Far East stage was in the hands of the scene shifters. General Templar still presided over the Malayan 'emergency' but the Communist terrorists in the jungle were on the run.

In Indo-China prodigious efforts by the French colonists had not prevented the Viet Minh amphibious commandos from permeating most of the rich ricefields of the Mekong Delta around Saigon. And they had not succeeded in checking the universal spread of graft and corruption. Dien Bien Phu would

At the coming-of-age of King Constantine of Greece, Athens, 1958

*14.   With General Lauris Norstad, Supreme Allied Commander, Europe, at Paris, 1958. A̶
Lambe was then Commander-in-Chief, Allied Forces, Mediterranean*

*15.   The Board of Admiralty in session, 7 April 1960, l. to r. Ian Orr-Ewing, M.P.,
Admiral Durlacher, 4th Sea Lord; Vice Admiral Walter Couchman, Deputy C.N.S.; Charles E. I̶
1st Sea Lord; Sir Clifford Jarret, Under Sec. to the Navy; Lord Carrington, 1st Lord of the Adm̶
Sir John Lang, Permanent Sec. to the Navy; (the late) Vice Admiral Sir St. John Tyr̶
Bart.; Admiral Sir Peter Reid, Naval Secretary; Vice Admiral Copeman, 5th Sea Lord.*

*C.E.L. had his first heart attack during this meeting; the last one he ever attended. He was ta̶
hospital next day*

16. *Charles Lambe as artist: Misida Creek, Malta*

17. *A scene at Malta*

fall within twelve months. The Huk rebellion, inspired by Chinese communists in the Philippines, had almost been stabilized. Indonesia was independent, struggling but quiescent. Borneo was still a colony divided between the Dutch and the British.

In the north of the 'Far East Station' the United Nations had been fighting their first major battles. They were now engaged in bringing hostilities in Korea to a halt along the 38th parallel. The Panmunjon armistice would be signed during the summer. This was the changing scene confronting the new Commander-in-Chief, Far East Station.

Once ceremony and protocol in Singapore had been satisfied, C.E.L. set off to see his fleet in action in Korea 3000 miles away.

By 1953 R.N. ships and aircraft had been fighting in Korea under United Nations Command for many months. The land battle had now become stabilized across the Korean peninsula, and the flanks of the land front were being supported at each end by naval sea and air forces. The U.S. 7th Fleet took care of the right flank. The rest, made up mostly of ships of Commonwealth navies, took care of the left flank operating under Rear Admiral Clifford of the Royal Navy.

This first visit was full of delightful surprises. It was a delight to discover the British naval base HQ at Sasebo established in H.M.S. *Ladybird*, an ancient Chinese river gunboat. It was a delight wherever he went in Korea to be constantly bumping into the Bishop of Croydon, Bishop to the Forces, in his purple cassock, and Lady Reading (Chairman of the W.V.S.) in her green uniform, who both happened to be visiting British troops at the same time. It was a surprise to be flown back from the front line in a light aircraft which used the main street of a little Korean village as its runway!

The surprises and delights that await anyone making their first visit to Japan and to Korea are a feast in themselves—the further novelties to be found inside a United Nations command added considerably to the richness of the Far East mixture.

Before leaving Korea and Japan for his own headquarters back in Singapore, C.E.L. received an invitation from Admiral Radford (then C-in-C Pacific and about to become Chairman of the U.S. Joint Chiefs of Staff) to break his journey at Manila, in order that the British and American Naval Commanders in Chief might meet and confer together informally.

This early tête-à-tête was the first of many attempts by C.E.L.

to play his part in reconciling British and American attitudes in the international affairs of the Far East and South East Asia.

These radical difficulties were increased for C.E.L. by the practical difficulties of having two American Commanders-in-Chief to deal with, General Mark Clark (later General Hult) C.-in-C. Far East in Tokyo and Admiral Radford (later Admiral Stump), C.-in-C. Pacific in Pearl Harbour.

And Commonwealth relations were not much easier. Australian, New Zealand, Canadian, United Kingdom and other Commonwealth units of all three Services had been effectively integrated as a Commonwealth Force in the United Nations Command in Korea. But as the prospects of a truce grew brighter at Panmunjon the prospects of continuing this Commonwealth harmony in defence elsewhere in Far East or South East Asia grew bleaker. All this, C.E.L. sought to combat with all the considerable tact and persuasion he could muster. Her Majesty's New Zealand ships were the first to respond to an appeal to assume a full share in naval duties in South East Asia—in the defence of Hong Kong, on patrols in the Formosa strait, in defence of British ships and on patrols off the coasts of Malaya against smugglers and terrorists. And in due course Her Majesty's Australian ships also came to take more interest in South East Asia and to be better prepared and equipped to deal with affairs in that part of the world.

But C.E.L. did not for long find it easy to urge his case for a staunch defence of South East Asia upon his Commonwealth colleagues. Once the armistice in Korea was over, pressure to reduce U.K. commitments in the Far East began to build up. The military demands of NATO, the need for economies in the UK defence budget, the need to reduce the length of unaccompanied overseas service in the Far East Fleet, all combined to reduce the size and effectiveness of the Far East Fleet and to make UK pretensions to a real stake in the defence of South East Asia look rather thin. Furthermore, they made defence discussions with our Commonwealth partners, and particularly with our American allies more and more embarrassing for C.E.L. and his United Kingdom colleagues. Not that the maintenance of large naval forces in the Far East would have solved everything.

The fall of the French fortress Dien Bien Phu in Vietnam in the spring of 1954 drove home sharply and grievously the lesson that the contest in South East Asia would not be won by force of arms alone. The loss of Dien Bien Phu taught that neglect of economic problems, social issues and the political aspirations of the Asian countries was perhaps the surest way of losing the contest. Our United Kingdom responsibilities and our experience in these fields in Malaya now stood us in good stead.

It was fortunate also that at this juncture there were in Singapore, in the persons of Malcolm Macdonald, the Commissioner General for South East Asia and C.E.L. as Commander-in-Chief Far East Station, two people uniquely sensitive towards the men and women of the countries to which they were accredited.

Each gave the other the greatest support in gaining the affection and trust of the Chinese, Malays, Indians, Thais, Filippinos, Cambodians, Vietnamese and Indonesians whom they met and with whom they worked.

None of these Asians were interested primarily in military matters and only a few in diplomacy. It was therefore good that there should have been in Singapore when the South East Asia Treaty Organisation came into being in September 1954, a British Commander-in-Chief who could build his international relationships through his membership of the Singapore Orchestra, his study of Balinese music, through his enjoyment of tropical birds and Chinese food, and a hundred and one other social and personal contacts beyond the military and European set.

When C.E.L. came to Singapore in 1953 the files of his office were already replete with defence plans and military agreements, variously labelled AWZAM, ANZUS, 5 Power Agency, B.D.C.C., UN Command Korea etc. etc. By the time he left in 1955 another shelf labelled 'South East Asia Treaty Organisation' had been added. Perhaps the military power on this SEATO shelf did not at first amount to much, perhaps, to begin with, the political strength of SEATO counted for little. But the mutual trust and affection between those of Asian and those of European stock in SEATO on which all was based had been firmly established. C.E.L. had played no small part in building this.

Lord Sandford spoke of Mr. Malcolm Macdonald, the man who, two years earlier, when he had been United Kingdom High Commissioner in Canada and Charles was on his wartime mission to Quebec and Ottawa, Charles had thought 'a *very* nice person'

who he 'would love to know well'. He had his wish. As Com-
missioner-General in South East Asia, Macdonald also had his
headquarters in Singapore, and the two men grew to be close allies.

Army, Navy and Air Force Commanders-in-Chief met me one
morning every week for conference in a body called the British
Defence Co-ordination Committee in the Far East [Mr.
Macdonald wrote]. We considered all the most important—and
sometimes most difficult—current Service-cum-civilian problems arising during those revolutionary times in that vital
region of the world.

Lambe's contributions to our discussions were invariably
distinguished. He could always balance judiciously the sometimes rival claims of British military, civilian and political
interests, and also harmonize them with the aspirations of the
local Asian peoples. His counsel on numerous matters touching
such delicate questions as the emergence of Indonesia and
several other countries into national independence, the then
virulent civil war being fought in French Indo-China, the
reconciling of the Malay, Chinese, Indian and other racial
communities' interests in potentially free and united Malaya,
and the relations between Hong Kong and China, was always
thoughtful, ripe and wise. Naturally he was no more invariably
right than the rest of us; and he had his occasional prejudices.
These were a part of his essentially human make-up. . . .

One reason why Lambe was so good was that he had a
liberal mind. It never got stuck in ruts; it was always ready to
be flexible without abandoning firm principles; and it was
constantly up-to-date in his comprehension of and adaptability
to a significantly changing world. At the same time it was not
easy-going, loose or superficial. And his hard head was justly
influenced by a warm heart. His thoughts were influenced by
sentiment—but never by sentimentality. And although his
arguments could be gently but firmly destructive of a case
which he considered bad, they were always constructive in
their presentation of alternatives.

He combined the brain of a sailor with the mind of a statesman, and was passionately concerned for the development of a
peaceful, friendly, higher human civilization.

II

Charles's more personal impressions of the background of his
future activities were sent to Peta in a series of letters to England,

written before she joined him. He enjoyed his first visit to Bangkok almost as much as anything he experienced during his spell in the Far East. On 16 March 1953, he wrote from there on his way to Singapore:

I'm sitting in only a towel on my verandah after breakfast, right at the top of the house overlooking the busy river with temples and pagodas beyond. We dined with a cousin of Prince Chula's last night. House full of lovely early Siamese lacquer and serene Buddhas in stone. Ladies in short evening dresses of Siamese brocade. Wonderful food and wine.

Earlier, Charles had seen some 'glittering classical Thai dancing'.

This was the State Ballet—a gala performance with all the stars in my honour. There was one princess—a niece of Chula's—who was incredibly beautiful and the most superb dancer who—being royal—cannot dance in public but who would otherwise be the local Fonteyn at 16½. At the end she came forward and gave me the garland of jasmine and frangipani from her ear and I fell madly in love!

First impressions of Singapore were very different.

The city is *vast* [he wrote on 21 March], a mixture between California and Woking. The trees and vegetation indescribably beautiful, the houses like film stars 'homes' and Government House like a villa built by the Ministry of Works in the middle of a tropical Richmond Park.

When it comes to this [Admiralty] House, words fail me. It is a sort of Malta Auberge—primitive beyond words. The Admiralty has partitioned off corners of some bedrooms to make bathrooms—and the partitions are simply 8 foot high screens in rooms 20 feet high! The floors everywhere are dark stained wood—there are no doors—or windows—and there is *no* privacy. All the furniture is oak—mostly polished—and all the chairs and sofas throughout the house are pink and white flowered cretonne.

The kitchen is minute—there is a wine cupboard—there always is—but otherwise no scullery, no larder, no china cupboard, no anything so far as I have yet seen.

The food so far is poor wardroom standard. The orchids—some beauties—and the bananas and the pineapples in the

so-called garden are my solace. So too are the Java sparrows
and the golden orioles. But the garden is a London park. . . .
There is an all pervading smell of mould everywhere except
in the heated cupboards in which clothes are reported to remain
quite all right. John [Edmondson] is wonderful. Absolutely
sweet and tremendously efficient and I should be cutting my
throat already if it were not for him.

By the end of the month, Charles had pretty clear ideas of how
he would transform the place, not forgetting the drawing-room
which he described to John Hill, whose advice on re-decoration
he sought, as 'like the lounge of a very old transatlantic liner'.
One of Charles's earliest visitors was Louis Kentner, the first of
many musician guests.

A small, slightly bald, dark Hungarian, [he told Peta] who
looks about 50 but must be younger. He is very gay and a nice
guest. Practises hard on the piano which at once went out of
tune but is being done today. He is touring the Far East and
Australia and New Zealand for four months without a single
sheet of music!

Almost as soon as Kentner had gone, Charles was off on tour.
Hong Kong he described as a huge Gibraltar with Chinese instead
of Spaniards. 'But it's not restricted like Gib—far more scope both
physically and socially. Lots of interesting people. Madonna lilies,
bougainvillea, dahlias and hollyhocks everywhere.' Then Japan,
including Tokyo 'like a Yukon gold-rush mushroom city with a
lot of Philadelphia superimposed'. Then, in H.M. cruiser *Newcastle*,
to the coast of Korea, where the Navy was still actively engaged.
Ashore, Charles stared through glasses 'at Communist dug-outs
from our hill-top across to theirs, with the hill-sides ablaze with
petunia-coloured wild azaleas like heather in Scotland, and
weather like a Mediterranean spring'.

Yesterday, [he wrote on 21 April to Peta] I transferred by
high-wire breeches-buoy to a destroyer and then to our carrier—
the *Glory*. Rushed all over the ship and, in the afternoon, I flew
in a Firefly on a strike—bombing shore targets. Very exhilarating. Everyone in an awful stew about my safety but there was
no opposition. . . . It's all really rather fun except that everybody is so awe-inspired when I appear that it is a hard fight to
make them relax.

The Korean countryside gave Charles a shock of surprise and pleasure.

I've been staggered by the beauty of Korea and its people [his letter continued]. The landscape is rather Tuscan in form but more arid and less fertile. Wonderful wild flowers appearing everywhere. The snow only gone in the last month. Cold wind but brilliant hot sun. The people are very square and stocky— rather impassive but rather beautiful. The children are lovely.

He also paid a visit to the American command in the Philippines, where he astonished a Marine officer in whose jeep he was riding by insisting on stopping to look at and pick a 'silver grey green woolly anemone with a dark wine coloured flower clothed with silken hairs and golden stamens. Quite lovely.'

Louis Kentner returned to Singapore from a visit to Hong Kong the same day as Charles, and was again his guest. 'He is giving four recitals of Beethoven Sonatas,' he told Peta. 'The first one last night was wonderful. I went with Van Hien—the local conductor—and his wife and Malcolm Macdonald and we all had supper afterwards in the garden of the Raffles Hotel.' Next day, 5 May, Charles and Kentner lunched with Macdonald. 'The latter and I find ourselves very much in sympathy,' he told Peta. Inevitably, Charles and Kentner played duets—Haydn was the choice, as it had been with Lennox Berkeley in the *Vengeance*. A week later Charles reported:

I've found an awfully nice youngish army doctor called Robert Hill who is a very good clarinettist. He came to supper and was very thrilled at having his accompaniments played by L.K.— brilliantly.

Early in June, Charles flew home for the Coronation of the Queen. He was in the Abbey, Peta in the crowd in the Mall with the children, for although she would have been given a seat inside herself, she wished the family to share her experience. She and Charles had so little time together—though Peta was on the eve of her own departure to Singapore—that it was from 'over France', on 6 June, that he told her that at the Buckingham Palace party he had a talk with both the Queen and the Queen Mother, 'also Dickie *at last* introduced me to Nehru, which was fascinating. I should have loved a long talk but it was impossible.'

Peta's journey out was by sea to Aden with her younger children, then on by air via Bombay and Colombo. Her impressions of the Far East were at first overwhelming, and her introduction to Admiralty House abrupt.

Of course, [wrote Charles to the family's friend, Hugh Drake, on 28 June] I was not expecting the earlier arrival, so there was a dinner party of 22 the next night here and a tennis party of 30 yesterday. But years of training in the great manors of England came to the surface and the Lady of Admiralty House slid gracefully into her exalted position and dispensed charm and graciousness from a little cotton day-dress—all she had brought.

Oh the wonder of it all [wrote Peta in a postcript to this letter]. It's like living in the tropical house at Kew with the Zoo tropical birds thrown in. On the divan of our bedroom is the most exquisite head of a Malay policeman painted by Him [Charles]. High time I came home!

The wonder continued.

Here, [wrote Charles to Hugh Drake early in September] all is a fantasy. I am quite staggered at the ease with which her ladyship has donned the royal mantle. The vast house is organized on a sort of 18th century basis. One never quite knows who is staying with us, let alone who may come in and out during the day—or night.

Levées are held on a chaise-longue (basket) on our verandah— an exquisite oriental Sarong being worn outside the night dress for greater security. The children, Chun Hao, the Chinese Steward and the Flag Lieutenant are usually in waiting with note-books and pencils to note the royal commands. Doctors, dentists, hair-dressers, basket-makers and carpet-sellers attend from time to time just like the first act of Rosenkavalier.

The other day she suddenly rose up and went and bathed with Andrew [who had by then arrived from home] at the local swimming club and swam with rubber frog-man's flippers on her feet! Wonders will never cease.

We went for a week up the east coast of Malaya in the *Alert*, my warship-yacht. Andrew, the children, Jo Hill, Jimmy and Eloise Pack, their three boys and John Edmondson. The whole house was moved—furniture, pictures, silver, trunks of clothes, cushions, bowls of flowers and so on. A Marine orchestra of twelve musicians, an interpreter in all Malayan languages, cinema projector and a library of films all came too. It was like Beckford moving from Fonthill ... I got a glass of squash thrown in my face when I referred to her ladyship as Lady Docker.

Socially, she has started at the top this time, and is working down—an unusual technique for her. She has enslaved Malcolm MacD. as a first step and bouquets, wireless sets, rare Javanese hangings and so forth are poured at her feet by either him or his wealthy Chinese friends. All Malcolm's Foreign Office staff with their Greek or French or Austrian wives are included in the conquest and she is now taking stock of the situation before launching her next campaign.

Livestock was another ingredient. Hammett the coxswain waged a constant and sometimes losing battle with white ants, and at one time, he wrote 'we had on our books a bull-dog, pony, cats, gibbon, parrot, cockatoos, turtles and an assortment of tropical birds'. Fifi, the gibbon, was a special favourite with both Charles and Peta, delicate and apt to chills as she was. Admiral E. B. Ashmore, who then commanded the *Alert*, noted that 'cruising on his bridge required an eye alert not only to the usual accompaniments of sea-watching but also the sea birds'. Charles, wrote his captain, 'attacked that badge of servitude, the hat. We were allowed to salute bare-headed, and so to leave or return to our ship—though few of us could emulate the distinction of the Commander-in-Chief's disembarkation fondly clasped round the neck by Fifi.'

During Charles's stay in Singapore, John Edmondson was promoted, and a younger officer, Martin Sands, took over as Flag Lieutenant.

Organizing the social side of the Admiral's life occupied a great deal of my time [he wrote]. Entertainment on the cheap or thoughtlessly arranged was intolerable to him, but he avoided having to do more of the planning than he need. [Charles, who had done this work himself, years before, for Admiral Brock in the Mediterranean, knew all about it.] I found from experience that about the only time of day he was disposed to think about parties was while he and Lady Lambe were breakfasting in their bedroom. So began an almost daily ritual in which I would

12

appear during breakfast when they couldn't very well escape, perch on the end of the bed and flourish guest lists and menus.

They enjoyed having people to stay and a stream of more or less distinguished and fascinating guests visited Admiralty House. Inevitably visiting admirals of various nationalities predominated, but they often found themselves sharing hospitality with such as Dr. Boris Ord, then Organist at King's, Claudio Arrau the pianist, Graham Greene, Stephen Spender, the daughter of an exiled Vietnamese Prime Minister, Freya Stark—or perhaps a passing ambassador. They ebbed and flowed, but the house was seldom entirely devoid of guests. The domestic staff normally coped extremely well as, like everyone who came into Sir Charles Lambe's orbit, they were invariably treated with warm understanding and courtesy; but once the Chief Steward complained mildly when he had to serve breakfast in eight different rooms.

Peta herself described her life in different terms and equally graphically, in a letter to Victor Stiebel.

I work harder than I've ever done in my life and, of course, with less strength. I have to combine the duties of the manageress of a flourishing but select hotel, a hostess in the Edwardian grand manner, and a hospital visitor—i.e. sailors in wards with ghastly accidents, officers' wives with miscarriages (endless those) and psychiatrics (fascinating those) and, most tricky of all, and of course tragic, an officer in a private room reading Simenon in French, about to go to prison.

Then there is Poppy Day which I am supposed to organize for the Navy. Oh! and I nearly forgot the constant giving away of prizes to sailors, boy scouts and Asian schools (rather fun that after the first doz.) and receiving huge bunches of orchids, and Chinese youths squatting very close with cameras; then I have to be a mother too, but never a wife, that at least there is no time for, and so to bed and oh! thank God for the phenobarbitone at the end of the day!

III

One of Charles's earliest letters in 1954 was to Hugh Drake, describing an official visit to Macao, that fragment of Portuguese empire spared, like Hong Kong, from absorption, mainly perhaps because of its use as an entrepôt.

P. was not really well enough to sail with me, [he wrote] so I sailed away in the *Alert* and had 24 hours of guns, guards, bands and banquets. The Portuguese were awfully nice. I met an elderly lady all in black with black bird of paradise hat and asked her if she had been long in Macao and Portugal and she said—in rather guttural tones—Ah yes. You see I am pure Portuguese except for my behind. My behind is half Spanish and half French. That made my visit.

A few months later, after Charles had made yet another tour which included Hong Kong, Tokyo, and even Pearl Harbour, to which he sailed in the cruiser *Newcastle*, Peta found that the heat was affecting her in a way which she described as a 'slow, progressive and hardly perceptible decline of health, a wasting away of the energy and a sleeping paralysis of the will'. She amplified her description in a way which will be found true by all who have lived long in the tropics.

The siesta slowly eats into the day and now tends to last all the afternoon. Now I never go into the garden as I used to in the first months. I hate the sun and long to have the blinds down all day. After tea until 9 p.m. are the worst hours, there is not a breath of air and all the heat of the day rests on the house like a furnace, one is beyond thought, and can barely breathe to keep alive. The children by then are tired and cross and need all one's patience poor darlings.

Her letter, begun in May, was finished late in June, when she felt able to describe Charles's musical exploits. He had become President of the Musical Society, and was its life and spirit.

He sings bass in the choir [Peta told Drake], of course surrounded by beauty. They have just given two superb performances of the St. Matthew Passion in the Cathedral here, and four soloists from Europe came out. I had the tenor called David Galliver to stay, and the pianist who is a very famous man, Dr. Lofthouse, great Bach expert and harpsichord player. Well! they were absolute heaven.

David has a voice such as I have never heard, to make you die and cry and exult, pure Italian. This wonderful voice would go soaring through the house from 7 a.m. to midnight—for three weeks this went on. The other soloists were Dutch. . . . They rehearsed for 5 hours a day, they sang opera arias and

Brahms and gave 3 concerts as well. I gave wonderful supper
parties of Singapore intelligentsia, and the children came to all
performances and were entranced.

That was long ago, but we never cease entertaining, a dance
for 300 young officers, and then a concert in our house for 100
Asians, Malcolm Macdonald and the Bishop's wife! A Bach
3-piano concerto was played (one piano by C) and a Chinese
lady gave solos.

Charles himself amplified Peta's account of the performances of
the St. Matthew Passion, which he thought 'had magic', in a
letter to Stewart Perowne. 'A choir of about 120, at least half
Asians, Chinese, Indian hindoos and Malay moslems with a Sikh
playing second French horn.' He added later: 'at a concert at
Admiralty House I played one piano in the Bach D minor 3
piano Concerto with a small string orchestra. Now I'm working
on a Mozart Trio for clarinet and viola and piano for another.'

Meanwhile, there was a visit by two French cruisers. The
Admiral and twenty-four French officers came to dinner, followed
up by another at the French Consul's ('pure Balzac'), and a
farewell lunch on board the *Gloire*:

pure 19th century plush and engravings of Toulon, lobster and
wines and champagne and les politesses without end. We were
all given a brooch and a medal when we left and la Marseillaise
and the tears nearly rolled down my cheeks [wrote Peta].

For both Charles and Peta, one of the highlights of their stay
in the Far East was described in a letter written by Peta to
Victor Stiebel in September 1954. It was a visit to 'the fabulous
turtle islands off the coast of Borneo, the most exciting thing I have
ever done'. The Lambe family flew in an R.A.F. plane to Kuching
in Sarawak, taking with them a cassowary for Tom Harrisson,
Curator and Government Ethnologist, and once of Mass Observation, who was in charge of the island they were to visit, in
addition to a lot of pigeons.

State drive into town preceded and followed by Sikh outriders.
Centre of town, all get out. Charles in full regalia inspects guard
of local police, all wonderful looking Dyaks, Kenyas and
Kelabits, in other words, head-hunters, but tamed for the
moment into rigid attention in beautiful Victorian white and

dark blue uniforms. Then all step into a beautiful white sampan with plaited palm-leaf roof and are paddled across wide river by cross-legged, seated Malays in regal white and blue velvet Sonkhas (Malay national headdress.)

Up the steps of the Governor's Palace on the other side and there greeted by the Governor himself, Sir Tony Abell, a charming, cultured and amusing bachelor. There we were in the demesne of the Rajah Brooke and nothing has changed at all. Handshakes, including James and Louisa, with a row of smiling, turbaned and saronged servants. Long low house, all on ground floor, ceilings decorated by Chinese in Italian manner, black and white raised plaster birds and animals, mostly peacocks and dragons. Heat stifling.

Dinner party of locals v. funny. Two days there, then Tom Harrisson took us in a wonderful old-fashioned steam boat to his islands, six hours at sea, wonderful, blue and calm, looking back at high jagged peaks inland. Anchored off-shore and were rowed in to a white dazzling sandy beach, banked high by storms. The island, as one had always imagined tropical islands, beach backed by fringe of cocoanut palms and then impenetrable jungle.

A beautiful Malay boy welcomed us by putting a lei of frangipani round my neck and a tiny one for Louisa too. Tom's house a dream—tiny, built of wood and thatched with palm leaves . . . cocoanuts were brought and opened for us, and later raw fish caught and eaten with onion and fresh lime juice. Later still a whole boat-load of Sea Dyaks arrived, invited by Tom, and when it was dark they began to play their wonderful throbbing tom-tom music, the women and children seated on a square of carpet they had put on the sand. Five chairs were garlanded and put for us to sit in and later, after the men had drunk much arak, they began to dance in front of us. Louisa and I were wrapped in carpets against the strong wind and the sand that blew. Only the men dance and always apart—never touching— a strange primitive African, yet sophisticated, rhythm. All absorbing and fascinating, their faces ending in almost a trance-like look.

Then at 11 p.m. the real object of the visit began. The female turtles had arrived and were already up on the beach laying their eggs. . . . They are huge, 4 or 5 feet long with very big sad faces and green shells. When it is dark they walk up the beach 40 or 50 in one night and they dig a hole 2 feet deep with their flippers. This process takes about an hour. If you go near them during this time, they go down to the sea again, but once they begin to lay, you can shine torches in their faces or scream in their ear or sit on their backs, and they cannot move—they seem chained to the spot by some strange unseen force. To sit beside these creatures on the sand in a hot tropical night and watch their round white shell-less eggs dropping one by one until 120 in number are reached is one of the most moving and thrilling experiences I have ever had.

During this time they groan and pant and sometimes tears roll down their cheeks; then the final covering up and getting themselves out of that deep hole is a feat which seems impossible, but somehow or other, during the hours of darkness the impossible is achieved and these creatures of the deep, who only come on land to lay their eggs, once more reach to the sea.

When dawn breaks, there are always some stragglers, who had been unable to find a suitable spot and are still laying; the whole of the beach is churned with deep troughs and undulations and scarred with tank tracks where they have made their way to the water's edge. The eggs are left in the sand, for the mothers never return, and in two months time hundreds of little turtles hatch out of the sand and walk straight to the sea, never to tread foot on land for 15 or 20 years.

James and Louisa each sat on the back of a turtle at 7 a.m. as she moved down to the sea. At 8 we stepped into a boat and were rowed away from that enchanted island, inhabited only by Tom Harrisson, turtles and Imperial Nutmeg Pigeons. A few hours later, and it all seemed like a dream.

And so home to Singapore with four baby turtles in a tin and a beautiful Dyak knife and spear for James and an exquisite hat for Louisa made out of plaited straw and coloured beads and silver sequins made by a tribe called Melanus, and 1 lb. of the best pepper in the world for me.

An interesting postscript to the visit was printed, nearly five years later, by the *Daily Mail*, which reported that the cassowary which Charles had taken to Harrisson had been given to the Hamburg Zoo. 'It arrived there yesterday' stated the paper on 24 March 1959, 'having eaten in transit 5 cwts. of bananas and 1 cwt. of rice. In Sarawak it ate 300 bananas a day with snacks of snails, snakes, stones and kittens in between.'

If for the Lambe family Borneo was one of their best adventures, there were many others—for instance, Saigon, which so impressed Peta by its French atmosphere, Angkor Wat, one of the sights of the world which came up to every expectation, Bali, where the paintings particularly interested Charles, Penang, and Malacca, with its remnants of Portuguese and Dutch architecture. Peta had the chance of a flight to Australia, which gave her as much pleasure as Charles had found on his wartime visits, and always there were friends coming and going, Steven Runciman, for instance, who joined the Lambes in the *Alert* on the way back from a look at Rangoon early in February 1955. Runciman was in Singapore nearly a month, 'a very unobtrusive but charming guest'. as Charles told Hugh Drake, 'full of lovely gossip and anecdotes'.

As early as August 1955 the Lambes were laying plans for a return home via various friends, including Freya Stark at Asolo. Like Peta, Charles was by then beginning to feel the heat, writing to Perowne that 'the hand won't even slide on the paper' and confessing in the same letter 'the glamour of the East has had it for me!'

Before release, he had many more official visits to make, including a final one to Hong Kong, but the day for farewell came at last, except that some at least of the many pets were to be taken back to Europe by their devoted owners, including the ever-popular Fifi. Arrangements for departure—pets included—fell largely to Hammett, the coxswain. They were successful after:

much form-filling and argument, with supplies of food obtained, special cages made, and stewards bribed. All went surprisingly well, the pets arrived in the U.K. fighting fit, and were taken to Edinburgh Zoo to await collection by the Admiral, only to be lost in a disastrous fire the day before he was to have claimed them.

Mr. Hammett continued:

Admiralty House looked strangely depressing as personal belongings were taken down and packed away, ornaments, paintings, children's toys and the much-travelled baby-grand piano vanished one by one into the crates and were trundled away by the lorry-load. When finally the time came for the departure of the Admiral and his family, not only the whole of the domestic staff but all their families turned out spontaneously to bid them farewell—their sarongs, cheong-sams and saris making a lane of colour down the long drive.

Most of the staff had served many years in their present jobs and had seen the coming and going of several C.-in-C.'s, so one might have expected that their oriental inscrutability would be subjected to little strain—but on this occasion even Chun Hao, the Chief Steward, found himself overwhelmed, whilst the amahs and many others were openly in tears.

IV

If it is the personal rather than the official side of Charles's time in Singapore that has been emphasized, it is because the public aspects of Far Eastern affairs, in so far as they relate to the Navy, have already been indicated by Lord Sandford. Events have followed one another in swift and sometimes bewildering fashion ever since, for the East continues, as ever, in transition.

Leaving matters of high policy to be wrestled with by his successors, Charles and his family returned to Europe by sea. A comfortable German ship, the SS. *Schwabenstein*, took the Lambes to Genoa where they landed early in May 1955. There they had a letter from Stewart Perowne, which told them that although he himself would be away, his wife Freya Stark was looking forward to welcoming them at Asolo.

> We were so stunned by the sights and sounds and smells of Italy after two years in the Far East [wrote Charles in a message to a friend], that everything else went out of our heads. It was cold and wet at Asolo, but Freya and her guests were vastly stimulating after such a long spell away, and I managed to paint a bit.

Freya Stark, unlike her husband, knew Charles only in his later years, 'but his steps in friendship', she wrote, 'as in everything, were rapid and sure, and he would risk himself in the vulnerable paths of affection with the same self-reliance that so many people keep for their battles, and so few for their ordinary lives'.

Analysing his qualities further, she said:

> He would take hold of our problems, however trivial, and one could almost *see* the mind focussing—no half or absent-minded contribution, but the whole of a vivid intelligence put to our small service—filling in a picture like a draughtsman with clear and certain strokes, to a solution so rapid and so secure that its

authority appeared unquestioned. There was no one whose advice could be more completely trusted, because of this full measure of honesty and rapier-like efficiency combined.

After a brief visit to other friends in Italy, the Lambes motored home across Europe. Peta spent June in London house-hunting, settling in the end for what Charles described as 'a tiny mews house in Stafford Place, a cul-de-sac opposite the Westminster Theatre', which became the family's London home for the rest of Charles's life. He was by this time a full admiral, and after a necessary spell of leave, it was announced that his next appointment would be as Second Naval Member of the Board of Admiralty and Chief of Naval Personnel, which entailed over-all responsibility for the human as opposed to the material side of the Navy. Charles was well fitted for such a post, and as Lord Mountbatten was to be in office as First Sea Lord, two very old friends could devote themselves, in close association, to the problems of the Service to which they belonged. Charles was also appointed an Extra Naval Equerry to the Queen, thus continuing his by now long association with the Court.

Chapter Nine

SECOND SEA LORD

AS WAS proper, official secrecy surrounded the deliberations of the Board of Admiralty, which since Charles's time has become part of an integrated Ministry of Defence, but even within the bounds of a personal memoir, an idea may be given of the scope of his work, and of his effect on some of those who came into contact with him.

When Charles first took over his new duties, his deputy was Admiral Sir Laurence Durlacher. This was fortunate, for Durlacher had already served as Charles's Chief of Staff in the Far East, knew his ways and admired his methods. 'He had a remarkably quick brain allied with an extremely sound judgement,' he wrote. 'These two qualities are, unfortunately, frequently not found together. He also had great charm of manner and an instinctive sympathy and feeling for the points of view of others.'

Charles had need of all his gifts, for the problems facing him were considerable. In peacetime—or what passes for such—there is a constant struggle between the Treasury and the Service Departments, the Treasury fighting for economy, the Services for their needs, well knowing that once an emergency arises they will be expected to produce miracles from starved resources. Perhaps such a battle is inevitable, but it is none the less exhausting.

Admiral Durlacher, from his point of advantage, set down some of the current issues with the same clarity as Lord Sandford described conditions in the Far East during Charles's tenure of command.

> The Second Sea Lord, [he wrote] as Chief of Naval Personnel, is responsible for all matters affecting the recruitment, training and welfare of the officers and men of the Navy, and at the time of Charles's arrival a great many problems were besetting us.

A major reorganization of the officers had recently taken place, with the introduction of the 'General List' for officers of the Seamen, Electrical, Engineering and Supply and Secretarial branches, and the controversial decision had been taken to divide officers of the Seamen branch on promotion to Commander into the 'Post List' and 'General List'. Only the former would be entitled to sea-going jobs. This required a fairly profound change in the attitude of officers who had hitherto, not unnaturally, expected a proportion of sea-going throughout their careers. Charles handled the results of this decision with great skill and understanding.

His chief concern, as his Secretary, James Pack, well remembers, was to try to ensure that those who made the Navy their profession took to it the same sense of dedication which had been found among the best officers of earlier generations. With opportunities becoming so circumscribed, the attitude that the Navy was 'merely a job', the prelude to another and perhaps a better one later on in life, had to be combated. This was not easy, but the quality of many of the officers of the present generation is a proof of his success, and of that of his immediate successors.

Officers were not the only problem.

A serious manpower shortage amongst ratings was also manifesting itself [Admiral Durlacher continued], and in 1955 a committee was set up under the chairmanship of Sir Henry Wilson Smith to investigate the causes of this shortage, and was given very wide terms of reference to recommend any changes they thought necessary in all aspects of service including length of engagement, recruitment and pay. I was a member of this committee and a review of the problem was made specially urgent in view of the decision to abolish National Service in the near future.

The work of this committee and the subsequent inter-Service and inter-Ministerial discussions lasted many months and culminated in the fairly drastic changes which appeared in the 1956 Pay Code. During this lengthy and difficult period I was sustained by the complete support and wise counsel of Charles, who of course had many other matters to deal with.

He was an ideal Second Sea Lord in that he combined a clear and logical mind with a true humanity and understanding of the needs and feelings of both officers and men.

Admiral Durlacher's testimony is well borne out by Mr. G. Andrews, formerly a Chief Yeoman of Signals. He not only wrote a full tribute to one important aspect of Charles's work, but gave an idea of why he was so highly regarded by men of the Lower Deck.

My first meeting with Admiral Sir Charles Lambe [wrote Mr. Andrews], was in March 1956, on board H.M.S. *Tyne*, then the flagship of the Commander-in-Chief, Home Fleet.

At that time H.M.S. *Tyne* was at Gibraltar, and Admiral Lambe was heading a top level visit to both the Home and Mediterranean Fleets, who were in harbour. This was at a time when the morale of the Fleet was at a very low ebb, and Admiral Lambe as Chief of Naval Personnel was clearly determined to find out for himself what many of the Lower Deck were thinking and why. To do this he talked to men on the mess decks or wherever he could find them. He was unaccompanied and I believe it is true to say he was the first Chief of Naval Personnel ever to act in this way.

To me it illustrates the kind of person I later found him to be, for, to say the least, he was a very remarkable man. My first meeting with him was as unexpected as it was stimulating and rewarding, whilst it brought about a chain of events which for a considerable period caused various repercussions throughout the Fleet and indeed amongst many retired Admirals, not to mention some senior Civil Servants of the Admiralty.

Prior to our meeting, I was concerned for many months with a scheme to improve the lines of communication between the Lower Deck and Their Lordships, and had already had my proposals turned down at lower official level, much to my bitter disappointment and temporary disillusionment. By some strange circumstance, however, Admiral Lambe came to hear about the scheme, and although I did not know it at the time, this was the reason I was summoned to see him in a small unostentatious spare cabin of the flagship.

I was not even given a lead, but after a few minutes I suddenly realized I had the opportunity of a life-time, and for the next hour and a quarter I had the undivided attention of the Admiral, who was apparently impressed, albeit somewhat shocked by the implications of the scheme proposed. Admiral Lambe then said he would give serious thought to what he had heard. I left his cabin walking on air but in all truth I thought it probable I should hear no more.

My fears were unfounded, for the Admiral was no ordinary man, and within weeks a scheme of 'Personnel Liaison' was started, which today is still in operation and is now known as the 'Second Sea Lord's Personnel Liaison Team'. Had it not been for the foresight and high moral courage of Admiral Lambe, I am almost certain that this valuable contribution to the improvement of Service conditions would not be in operation, and all thinking men of the Lower Deck should be grateful to him.

This then was how and why we met and I can say in all humility that we became great friends, and the more I saw of him the more my respect grew for him. From the moment of our first meeting, I had no doubt that I had met a kind and understanding man, and as I was to learn later, one who had the interests of all humanity at heart.

The same year that we met, my wife and I lost our youngest daughter under tragic circumstances, and I firmly believe that had it not been for the real understanding and personal sympathy shown to me by Admiral Lambe, I and therefore my wife, could not have withstood the long ordeal ahead of us. There was in fact little material help that anyone could give, but I was able to draw great spiritual strength from this wonderful man and I shall always feel spiritually richer for having known him. . . .

One of his secrets was his natural attitude to men like myself; he never talked down to anyone, for as great and accomplished as he was, he displayed a natural warmth and directness which could put anyone at their ease.

He also possessed a warm sense of humour and I shall never forget one remark he made to me when I was summoned to his office at the Admiralty. With other senior officers, we had been discussing the pros and cons of my scheme, and when the meeting was over Admiral Lambe said: 'Well Andrews, you have really convinced me, and you must now leave it to me to decide how the scheme must be operated,' to which I replied, 'I am putting all my faith in you, Sir,' and immediately the Admiral said, 'I know, Andrews, you keep on telling me how to do my job!' I'm happy to say there was a humorous twinkle in his eye when he said this.

On another occasion about two years after the schemes referred to had been in operation, I had to face a different ordeal. The Press got to know of the scheme and I was instructed to attend a Press conference, my first and I hope my only one. On completion of this, Admiral Lambe walked in and asked me how I had been treated and I replied 'Quite well Sir', upon which he said, 'Well done, Andrews.'

Much to my dismay the following morning, I read my newspaper to see that the Admiral's remark (he was then Second Sea Lord), had been completely altered to read: 'Keep it up, George, you are doing fine.' However, when I saw the Admiral some time later and remarked on this he gave a dry chuckle and pointed out that if and when I had as much experience of the Press as he had, I would no longer be surprised at such sensationalism.

During the last few years of the Admiral's life, Mr. Andrews came to know Charles and his family well, and they wrote to one another on occasion. Charles's letters are remarkable in their clarity, honesty, and directness, and Mr. Andrews felt what many have felt about them, and why so many have been preserved.

Amongst my most treasured possessions are several personal letters from Admiral Lambe, and in this age of stresses and strains, when it is so often easy to lose faith and heart, I simply re-read the letters and in some strange way I am mentally refreshed again—such was the impact that this man made on my life. . . . To know a great man is to know enrichment and whatever else happens to me in this life I shall thank God for the privilege of having the friendship of Admiral Lambe.

II

At the time when Charles first served on the Board of Admiralty, Lord Mountbatten was steering the Navy into the nuclear age. The advantage of having Charles as his principal naval colleague was immense. Well as they knew one another, Mountbatten realized that Charles would allow no personal consideration whatever to affect his thought on large issues. He would always get a straight opinion, and one with reason behind it. Whenever the two men were in London, Charles, in company with the Board as a whole, breakfasted with Mountbatten at least once a week, and Mountbatten is on record as saying that he regarded Charles as his principal adviser, and that all major policy decisions were arrived at together. Flattering as this could have been to anyone less independent, it imposed an additional strain on one who, ever since his return from Singapore, had enjoyed less than his usual health. Charles was beginning to feel the toll of years of responsibility and command.

He would in fact have been glad to retire at any time after his term of duty in the Far East, and no one was better qualified to enjoy leisure—but the idea was simply not permitted. Nelson once said: 'As I rise in rank, so do my exertions', and this was as true of Charles as of any other high-ranking officer with the experience and brains to meet continuing demands and all too often recurring crises. For instance, the Anglo–French Suez adventure occurred during Charles's spell at the Admiralty, an affair which he considered totally impracticable and morally indefensible. He did his best to resign over the question but was finally persuaded not to do so. For a time at least, the operations themselves put a considerable strain on all Service resources.

There were, however, one or two refreshing interludes, among them a cruise in the royal yacht, *Britannia*, made in March 1957 a few weeks before a State Visit to Copenhagen in which he was to take part as Senior Service Officer. On 11 March, Charles wrote to Peta from H.M.S. *Tyne* to tell her:

... we had four lovely days in the *Britannia* steaming eastward. Nothing very exciting or new about the exercises but it was very restful and at the same time stimulating being with the Duke. We discussed everything under the sun and I must say he has a most refreshing and provocative approach to everything. ...

When the *Britannia* steamed up close to the *Tyne* I was whistled across the intervening gulf on a jackstay—much to the delight of all. ... Dined in the wardroom last night. Saturday night at sea—sweethearts, and wives etc. Had to make a speech to the sailors after prayers this morning and have just visited all Chief and Petty Officers messes to hear what they have got to say about new pay etc. ...

The May visit to Denmark was Charles's third time in Copenhagen. He had first been there as a midshipman in the *Wryneck* in 1919, on his way to what was then the Baltic theatre of operations. He had gone again as a commander, when he had just been through the trials attendant on the abdication of Edward VIII. On this occasion he could look forward to a little enjoyment as was indicated in a letter to Peta from the royal yacht on 19 May.

A lovely calm sunny day today but it was blowing hard when we embarked at Hull. You would have hated the boat trip off—sluicing tide made it difficult.

The Queen and Prince Philip came aboard at 5 and we sailed down the Humber at 6—the Queen wearing dark blue trousers, brown shoes, a sort of pilot cloth reefer and a head-scarf. Lots of cheering and hooting of ships. By then the wind had dropped and the sun shone and it was v. nice. I sat on the Queen's left at dinner—Selwyn Lloyd on her right. She was very gay—quite untired after 6 hours of Hull.

After dinner when the ladies had gone, Prince Philip told the story of his reunion, when the Queen arrived at some airfield in Portugal. You remember the broadcast described how he went on board before she disembarked, and that the blinds of the aircraft's after compartment were drawn? Well, when Prince Philip entered he found the whole compartment filled with people with long beards. The Queen, the Foreign Secretary, and all the Household—all looking like Makarioses!

Rather nice to hear that they have some fun. Extraordinary that the Press have never heard the story.

The actual visit, begun grandly, when the guns of Elsinore fired in salute across the Sound from the Castle of Kronborg (just as they did in Hamlet's time) was described by Charles as 'gruelling but rather lovely'.

It all started [he told her], by the Danish Suite arriving on board at 8.30 the morning of our arrival. We had to get to know each other over breakfast! I have really enjoyed it all very much and my tummy has stood up splendidly to lobster and champagne— whilst longing for cod and Tuborg—and it was only last night that we did not get to bed till 2 a.m. due to a supper party given by their Lord Chamberlain after the gala at the ballet . . .

We lived on the top floor (old servants rooms) of an exquisite 18th century rococo palace all done up very cleverly by Queen Ingrid, with sentries all over 6ft. 6″ (8ft in bear-skins) and specially chosen for their looks standing on every landing.

Sat next to Queen Ingrid (Prince Philip the other side) at lunch in an 18th century hunting lodge in a beech-forest, called Ermitagen today. Long discussions on Industrial and Interior decoration design and modern painting and so on. All very easy and rather stimulating. She seems a wonderful person.

It all looked very Tissot last night on board here the *Britannia*. Fireworks across the harbour after dinner. By about midnight there were still thousands of people to cheer as the Queen and

Prince Philip left by car for the King's country palace, Selwyn Lloyd looking rather like Nelson in white breeches and blue and gold lace coat.

Charles had not been home long before he was made a Knight Grand Cross of the Order of the Bath (G.C.B.) in the Queen's Birthday Honours List.

III

In the autumn of 1957 the Commander-in-Chief, Mediterranean, Admiral Edwards, who was also head of Allied Naval Forces in that area, became seriously ill, and it was necessary to relieve him as a matter of urgency. Peta was in Scotland with her children when Charles told her the news by telephone. 'I bet they'll make you go!' she said laughingly, to which Charles answered: 'Nonsense—I'm much too old.' But they did. Three days later Charles rang and said: 'You were right. They want me to go to Malta straight away. What about it?' Peta replied: 'Of course we must go. How terribly exciting!'

It was indeed a man-sized job, for naval affairs at Malta had inevitably fallen into some disarray, and there were political crises throughout the Mediterranean: in Malta itself; in Cyprus; in Greece and Turkey; in the Lebanon; in French North Africa. The task before Charles was first to restore internal matters as quickly as he could, and then, in concert with his country's Allies, to cope with external events. He would be the first officer for a very long time to have commanded, in peace, both the principal British overseas stations.

Lord St. Vincent once remarked that naval command in the Mediterranean 'required an officer of splendour'. His own great era had provided a succession of such men, Hood, St. Vincent himself, Nelson, and Collingwood among them. What none of these precursors had ever been required to do was to assert, by personal example, leadership of disparate Allies, among whom the French were known to be restive under the existing set-up, and prepared, under General de Gaulle, to look very hard indeed at the whole North Atlantic Treaty Organization.

To face his new tasks, Charles had various advantages. He had known and loved Malta since his youth. He spoke French well, and Italian reasonably, and his seniority and experience would be respected by all with whom he dealt. He had in Peta a wife not only

13

familiar with the most appropriate way of running Admiralty House in an overseas station, but one whose knowledge of languages and love for southern Europe would prove invaluable. Moreover, in Rear-Admiral Christopher Bonham-Carter he found a Chief of Staff with whom he would see eye to eye as truly as he had done in Singapore with Admiral Durlacher.

Charles had a short spell of leave in Scotland before the flight to Malta, much of it spent being ill in bed. The two doctors who were consulted both prescribed a long rest, but somehow he persuaded them that he was well enough to go. 'If you must, you must,' was their final verdict, 'provided you live the life of a country parson!'

The journey out, with Peta beside him, was made early in November, Peta being thrilled, just before their arrival from darkness, to find Malta blazing with lights. For her, it was a happy return after a very long absence. 'I had the feeling', she wrote, 'that they really were glad to see us—not the usual official standing-to-attention kind of welcome at all.' The pair drove at once to Admiralty House, Valetta, which was one of the finest buildings in the island. It dated from the regime of the Knights of St. John, and had a magnificent double staircase, exquisite painted ceilings, and a large courtyard. The Lambes knew it of old, and soon it was very much their home.

Chapter Ten

RETURN TO MALTA

THE enforced period of vacuum at Malta had been particularly trying. The preliminaries to the take-over by Charles are perhaps best described by Admiral Bonham-Carter, an officer who had much to do with what, to outward appearance, was a smooth transition, but which, under less capable direction, might have been otherwise.

Admiral Bonham-Carter wrote, about this difficult period:

Until Charles Lambe took over command of the Mediterranean Fleet and the N.A.T.O. Command of that area, I had hardly met him. As Chief of Staff to Admiral Edwards, I had experienced certain difficulties, owing to the Commander-in-Chief's illness. It was not a happy time, and the involvement of the N.A.T.O. Command made matters no easier.

Admiral Edwards went home to the United Kingdom for medical treatment and, for understandable reasons, there was an enforced delay before a successor could arrive. In the meantime, the Second in Command took over the British Fleet and a sort of interregnum existed. A headless and entirely unsatisfactory body of which I was, of necessity, an important though unhappy part.

After some three months of this I learnt, I forget how, that Charles Lambe was to succeed to the Command. I didn't know him, as I've said, but I suspected I knew of him a great deal more than he knew of me, as is found to be the case between the Senior and the Junior.

So I wrote to him. I remember I wrote in manuscript from my house in Malta and tried to tell him with all the frankness I could command that I had been made the Chief of Staff to Ralph Edwards whom I knew and liked. The affair had finished sadly, and I felt very strongly that he should in no way feel that he was obliged to keep me, no choice of his, as his Chief of Staff for any reason of sympathy to me or my future in the Navy.

In reply I received one of the most charming letters, also in manuscript, of my life. Charles had complete knowledge of our difficulties. He said, in effect, that, although he didn't know me, he knew enough about what I had done to want me as his Chief of Staff.

We met in Rome, where he achieved a week or two's leave. At once we were at home with each other. In no more than five minutes he had asked all the pertinent questions concerning the Mediterranean Fleet and I only hope I answered them adequately.

He arrived in Malta. Everything changed. He made it crystal clear to me that he expected me to run the every-day matters of the Fleet, and that he would run the N.A.T.O. Command and the immense political responsibilities which have gone with the command of the Mediterranean Fleet since before Nelson. On this basis we worked in tremendous amity and I can only hope I never failed him.

The headless command of the Naval Forces in the Mediter-ranean was transformed in a week and all could see it. Charles re-established the British reputation in the N.A.T.O. Command, which was vital, and took no time at all to achieve it. Here was not only a sailor but a statesman, as many of our best products have been.

Charles's appointment was dated 11 November 1957. He and Peta lost very little time in settling in to Malta: then he was off, with a small Staff, on an official visit to Turkey. This he described in a letter to Peta which was begun on 29 November at the British Embassy, Ankara, and was continued: 'In the air en route for Izmir', a place which in his earlier days in the Mediterranean had been known as Smyrna.

Ankara was exhausting but really rather wonderful [he wrote]. Tremendous reception from the Turkish Armed Forces. Very comfortable huge modern Embassy. Wonderful Italian major-domo called Tiziano.

Tea with the President (who sent two boites of caviare); called on Prime Minister Menderes—most amusing dynamic person, talks excellent English and chuckles in a rather horsey, race-course way. Ministers of Foreign Affairs and of Defence present.

Reception for all Generals, Admirals etc. in an hotel first evening (splendid buffet supper), huge lunch party at Embassy yesterday and dinner party last night. . . . In my bedroom were books by Freya, Paddy Leigh Fermor, Patrick Kinross, Steven Runciman etc., etc.—all rather like home. . . .

I must say I like the Turks enormously and I certainly could not have had a friendlier reception. They are very staunch friends, one feels. Despite the heavy programme (the worst item was the Press Conference but it proved less alarming than I feared) I am feeling fitter and stronger every day. . . .

There was hard frost and thick mist yesterday, and the surroundings of Ankara reminded me of Spain—that same rather bony elephant-hide look. Very attractive. Stunted stone-pines and poplars in the valleys and huge flocks of biblical sheep and mohair goats. Buffaloes too—smaller but just like the Chinese ones.

After the visit to Turkey came almost equally important ones to Athens and Naples. The political atmosphere in Greece was clouded by difficulties over Cyprus—the wish of many of its Greek inhabitants to be united with the Mother Country, the natural hostility to this of the Turkish inhabitants—indeed the whole question of the future of the island, and of the British base, was delicate. That was the reason why Charles's visit was by air, not in his yacht, the *Surprise*.

The Athens stay was of unusual interest, indicated in a letter sent to Peta on 1 December, when events and contacts were fresh in his mind. The recent death of Prince George, of the Greek royal house, and a 'natural reluctance to play up the presence of a British Admiral (Cyprus)' had helped to make the visit 'comparatively restful'.

All in all [he wrote], it has been a great relief to have some time to myself. Though various Ministers on whom I called have been very friendly, they are obviously most anxious not to provoke publicity or any comment from M.P.'s or the Press. But they all go out of their way to apologize and to say how important it is that Cyprus shall not be allowed to cloud the traditional Anglo–Greek friendship—particularly naval friendship.

We dined at the Embassy the first night. Much talk of Freya and Steven. . . . This Sunday morning I got out to the small Byzantine church at Daphni—in the hills about 7 miles from Athens—to see the mosaics which I have always wanted to see. They are quite the best quality I've ever seen and if Ravenna approaches them they must be staggering. Very quiet whites, greys and blues but magnificently drawn and strangely moving—11th century.... I don't think any of my entourage have yet recovered from this revelation of my strange tastes!

Then lunch with Princess Andrew. She was alone, in her usual grey habit, in a small flat in a block. No servant, but the lunch had been sent up from a restaurant. She padded back and forth from the kitchen and never drew breath and I could have sat and listened to her reminiscences for years but alas! she had to pop off to Piraeus for the arrival of Pr. George's coffin at 4 p.m. so I had to leave early.

She said she was 73 and enjoyed doing everything for herself. In an ectasy because she goes to Sandringham on Thursday and hasn't spent a Xmas with her son Prince Philip for 14 years. Then a lot about the German occupation. She and (I think) Princess Nicholas stayed in Greece, being widows. Food almost unobtainable till her sister Queen Louise managed to get some diamonds to her which she sold well. Then she faced starvation again until she moved to her brother-in-law's house where they had stocks of beans and chick peas. No bread.

Then the Queen Mother of Rumania heard of her plight and sent a truck of black flour (which the Greeks could not cook properly) and some cooked butter. People dying in the streets from starvation. The Germans used refuse bins to remove the corpses and then all the streets were covered in refuse.

They were reduced to 2 plates of beans and water for the servants (because they worked) and one plate for herself.

The siege of Athens was very exciting. She had lived through so many wars (world and Balkan) that she does not notice sniping. 'An old war horse' she said. 'Of course the Balkan wars were quite different—gentlemen's wars—they were great fun. I thoroughly enjoyed them.'

Then much talk about her childhood in Malta when Prince Louis of Battenburg was a cruiser Admiral. Of the awe in which she held Admiralty House and all Admirals. And then she described the horror she felt when Prince Philip told her she was to have an Admiral attached to her as Equerry for his wedding. All the old awe returned and she expostulated hotly that she could not face it—at which Prince Philip laughed—and that was my introduction—Charles had been the Admiral Prince Philip had chosen!

Charles went by air from Athens to Naples, at which port he was able to make the cruiser *Birmingham* his headquarters. It was from the ship that he wrote to tell Peta of the later events in his tour.

> All is now over [he told her on 5 December], and I can relax for a bit and I have survived very well.
>
> All the way from Athens there was snow and it seemed to get thicker and thicker as we flew over Apulia and approached Naples. Vesuvius looked like Fujiyama and everyone shivering in an icy wind!
>
> The first day was heavy going with calls on everyone including the Archbishop, the Prefect and the Mayor but all very welcoming. The Consul General came with me and was astonished at the Mayor's cordiality. The whole Town Council turned out and I was presented with a really lovely book on Napoli. The Mayor is Sg. Lauro of the Flotta Lauro and a very anti-everything politician so it may have done some good.

Charles saw 'Nerone' at the San Carlo Opera when in Naples, and had this to say about it:

> ... fascinating—very long, very gloomy and nobody but me enjoyed it. Rather derivative, bits of Wagner and Debussy and rather like Les Troyens in scope and staging but not much easy music. Toscanini put it on in 1924 several years after Boito's death and it is wonderfully orchestrated.

Charles told Peta he had had to speak Italian all through one of the lunches. 'Everyone very pleased at my efforts,' he added. Alas, he could not say the same of the cookery for the return party which he gave on board:

> ... *nauseating* after all the wonderful food ashore. I felt ashamed. The duck was bitter and cooked in some disgusting fat and rather high. The potatoes were in little fancy whorls and baked hard in the hot cupboard and needed a sharp bang with a knife before you could penetrate and the pancakes round the caviare had obviously been made before breakfast. The ice-cream alone was good, and that I'm sure came from ashore.... Sometimes I despair.

Charles's cry was one of a long succession of such, uttered by food-conscious British admirals entertaining foreign guests. He need not, perhaps, have taken the shortcomings quite so much to heart, for Neapolitans visiting a British cruiser scarcely expect the cuisine to which they are accustomed. Food is not altogether what they go for.

As the long association of Charles with James Pack, who had been his Secretary since soon after the end of the war, ended with Charles's departure from the Admiralty, Pack was among those to whom he wrote from the *Birmingham*, telling him of the first fortnight at Malta, which he described as 'pretty intense'. Peta, so he reported:

> ... was quite extraordinary—tireless, calm and enjoying it all. She obviously felt right on top of it and confident, which I would not have believed possible 10 years ago. . . .
>
> Gosh! The NATO problems! Though the naval party work quite wonderfully together and sink their jealousies in the common effort, every military solution is beset by national susceptibilities. Greek and Turk. Italian and French. But I must say they all seem to warm to the British and I could not have had a more cordial reception.
>
> The Italian admiral here—my subordinate commander—is a charming but slightly shy bachelor. I am showered by presents too. Even in Athens we were none of us allowed to pay our hotel bill—and what do *we* do when they come to Malta? Unless they stay at Admiralty House they pay their own way and we give give them a second-rate dinner.

Charles gave Pack a recollection of Turkey missing from his letter to Peta.

> The visit [he wrote], was rather alarming because you have to stop in the middle of inspecting a guard and shout 'Mehaber Asker!' and they shout back 'Saoul'. I was so busy trying to remember this when I arrived at Izmir and also memorizing the name of the USA general who was meeting me that I nearly shouted 'Harkins' at the guard and shook hands with General 'Mehaber!'

Pack was one of the first to hear of Charles's plans for reorganizing his command.

> Malta has been very cold and wet, [he wrote later]. Fires all day and fur coat at night for Peta. But we've got the house nice. Maltese stewards very different from Chinese.

I like Christopher Bonham-Carter both as a person and as Chief of Staff. He and I have already planned a complete reorganization of all the Staffs on Far East Station lines. . . . But this is not being achieved without violent resistance—as we had before. But I'm determined to do it and save 23 Staff officers.

I must say I find my experience in the Far East is invaluable here. One can start off with a bang and not have to feel one's way.

Charles could have added, had it been necessary, that much of his work as Second Sea Lord had involved just such reorganization as he described. Under conditions where every officer had to be made to count, unnecessary staff appeared a crime. He may well have remembered a saying of Andrew Cunningham's: 'Reduce to the irreducible minimum—and then cut by 15%!' His letter ended with an enclosure he had received from the Director of Naval Intelligence. This was entitled:

WHAT THE SOVIETS THINK

The Appointment of Admiral Lambe

The English Admiral Charles Lambe has been appointed C-in-C of the English Mediterranean Fleet and of NATO naval forces in the Mediterranean. He replaces the English Admiral Edwards, who is handing over his post, according to the Foreign press 'for health reasons.'

Lambe is a warm supporter of the policy of a position of strength. When he was in the Far East he took a very active part in planning the fight against the national freedom movements of the peoples of South East Asia. With the aim of 'demonstrating forces' this Admiral more than once went at the head of a detachment of British warships into the ports of the lands of South East Asia, and in February 1954, at the climax of the struggle for national freedom in Indo-China took part in joint U.S.–Anglo–French naval manoeuvres in the South China Sea which were plainly provocative.

The appointment of Lambe who is a specialist in terrorizing freedom loving peoples, to his new post in the Mediterranean takes on a special significance now, when the imperialist forces are preparing to interfere again in the affairs of Arab countries.

SOVIETSKI FLOT. 15.11.57

One of Captain Pack's children was Charles's godson and namesake. 'I feel Charlie really ought to know the truth about his godfather,' he wrote.

II

Charles paid a flying visit on duty to Paris and London in January 1958, and while in London saw Mountbatten and heard rumours, not for the first time, of what was likely to be his future. At the end of the month he wrote to tell Peta of

> . . . the hell of an evening alone with Dickie. Lots of fascinating news about internal crises. . . Dickie wants, I think, to postpone any show-down until I am available to relieve him as First Sea Lord. I got the impression that he is determined to hand over to me and I again told him I don't want the job. Anyway Dickie agrees that we can't have another change of NATO C-in-C for a year or so.

In point of fact, Charles was to retain his Mediterranean post for just over a year from the time he wrote to Peta. Although not long, this was enough to restore relatively harmonious workings in the command, and to establish very cordial relations with Allied commanders. Among those with whom Charles dealt was the French Admiral Antoine Sala, with whom he had made friends in London soon after the ending of Second World War. It was Admiral Sala from whom came the most memorable tribute to Charles's work during the course of the year 1958, for the whole of which his energies were given to Mediterranean affairs.

In the earlier months of that year, Admirals Sala and Auboyneau faced serious disturbances in Algeria, which entailed visits by French naval forces to both Algiers and Malta.

> In difficult circumstances [wrote Admiral Sala], Sir Charles Lambe evinced exemplary lucidity, tact and breadth of vision. He mastered problems, and spread confidence around him. He received us with his usual charm and courtesy on board H.M.S. *Surprise* and at Admiralty House.
>
> This old palace, haunted by the shades of so many famous British admirals, served as the background of my last official meeting with the man whose valour equalled that of the greatest of his predecessors, and who was shortly to succeed, for alas too brief a time, to the highest post in the Royal Navy.

Charles's more private view of Admiralty House was put in a letter to Hugh Drake which he wrote during the course of the summer. He was beginning to feel 'submerged by the life', and he added:

... Peta is continually battling with the problems of the house and the vast staff. After endless energy has been expended on getting them to cook or serve something in the right way or on getting them even to do something as basic as making the beds correctly, a fortnight passes and—hey presto, it's all back to where it was before. Like special hybrid rhododendrons they all go back to ponticums in a flash—or at least that is how it seems to her, though actually the transformation since we have been here is unbelievable—but it is hard and continual work.

We have a new Chief Steward, elderly and square, who wears naval white shorts from a gigantic tummy, and every time Louisa sees him she giggles. He is very genial and benign and is a sort of cross between Balaieff (do you remember the Chauve-souris after the First War or were you too young?) and a teddy bear, and is so busy saying, 'Yes, my lady', and 'No, my lady' that he never takes anything in.

He is supported by an *army* of stewards who rush madly off (desperately keen) to do the wrong thing as quickly as possible so that they can pack up and go home to their dumpy wives and *vast* families. Then there is an English Chief Petty Officer coxswain who follows her everywhere with a notebook and never stops talking and even follows her into her bedroom. And *of course* they all tell her everything about their lives and she, fascinated but exasperated, still has never learnt how to *escape*.

Marine sentries guard the door and click their heels and salute smartly whenever you go in or out and if you come back driving the car yourself they rush to open the wrong door and let the dogs out under the traffic or all the parcels fall out into the street while they stand strictly to attention.

Peta, so Charles reported, had been away at Ischia for a week by herself, and had returned refreshed. She and Charles had had one or two summer sorties from Malta—to Crete, Izmir and Athens, 'for the coming of age of the eighteen-year-old Crown Prince', now King.

Despite the very tricky political situation [he continued], we were invited by the King and Queen, and it was a fantasy. We—

and Makarios—dined with Their Majesties in the Palace garden
and afterward a State Ball amongst flood-lit cypresses and pools
and pavilions and masses of diamonds and white satin.

Then we drove off next day with only Martin Sands, Flag-
Lieutenant, in our own car to spend a night at Delphi followed
by a huge limousine containing 8 plain clothes police. But we
saw—and photographed—some wonderful places: Daphne, the
waters of Lethe, the Plain of Thebes and the place where three
roads meet, where Oedipus slew his father unknowingly—and of
course Parnassus, remote and rocky and aerially blue. Kindness
and friendliness everywhere, despite Cyprus.

It was always 'despite' something, during Charles's time in the
Mediterranean. Malta itself was in political turmoil, Prime
Minister Mintoff in and out of office, and at last the Constitution
suspended. But whatever the political temperature, which at times
led to rioting and once at least caused Admiralty House to be
stoned, when the future of the great Dockyard seemed to be an
impossible stumbling-block, personal relationships between Lambes
and Mintoffs remained as warm as they had begun in London,
before Charles ever took up his appointment.

Charles was also fortunate in his relationship with the Governor
who represented the Queen at the time he was at Malta. This was
Major-General Sir Robert Laycock, who at the height of the war
had succeeded Mountbatten as Chief of Combined Operations.
Incidentally, Laycock was relieved by Admiral Sir Guy Grantham,
who had been in the same batch as Charles of early promotions to
Captain.

There were comedies too. On one occasion, so Martin Sands
recalled:

> ... at what promised to be a very dreary and laborious lunch with
> some Yugoslav dignitaries, the Admiral related how one of his
> predecessors on a visit to Dubrovnik had been taken for an
> afternoon drive by a Yugoslav Admiral.
>
> They both spoke poor French, but had to make do, as it was
> their only common tongue. On returning to his ship the British
> Admiral summoned one of his staff to commit to writing what
> he understood to be an agreement he had made, on the drive,
> about providing the Yugoslav Navy with anti-submarine
> training facilities at Malta.
>
> It later emerged that the Yugoslav Admiral was simultaneously
> asking one of his staff to enquire tactfully of the British why their

Admiral was seeking oil fuel storage arrangements on the Dalmatian coast!

They had both merely tried to make polite conversation about the scenery, and neither had the foggiest idea what the other was talking about.

From then on, the lunch became a riot of improbable and barely understood story-telling!

Fortunately it was not all foreign 'dignitaries', and ambiguous conversations in French. There was the British Fleet to look after, and Charles's inspections, often as thorough as they were unconventional, soon became renowned.

> He had a remarkable flair for putting sailors at ease [wrote Sands]. Once on a tour of a cruiser's engine-room he came upon a grizzled old stoker who was evidently the child of an earlier age, but nevertheless still at the bottom of the ladder. Enquiring if the man had ever sought higher rank he was met with a mischievous smile and the bland reply: 'Oh no Sir, after all you've got to have a proletariat, haven't you?'

Needless to say, there were also musical activities, this time a quartet whose earlier efforts, particularly that of a rather portly violinist, were apt to cause merriment to Louisa, when, as she sometimes did, she peeped at the rehearsals through a curtain, and there were young people in love, in whose welfare Charles took the strongest interest. Martin Sands, the Flag-Lieutenant, was one of them: David Checketts, an Air Force officer who was a much valued member of the NATO staff, another. The Admiral was consideration itself to them both. 'When my future wife came to Paris while we were there for a NATO conference,' wrote Sands, 'he made it clear he didn't wish to see me after a short morning's work,' and it was the same elsewhere.

As for Checketts, Charles's behaviour to him after he had had the misfortune to involve the Commander-in-Chief's gleaming barge in a fracas with a rock, was, so he felt, unforgettable. When the rather dishevelled miscreant presented himself at Admiralty House and confessed, Charles's first remark was—'Anybody hurt?' When relieved on that score, he offered the young man a drink and told him that long ago he had done the same thing himself. 'Had it been me,' an exalted member of another Service told Checketts, 'you'd have been Court-martialled.'

Checketts and the Admiral had a bond in their love for dogs. In the Far East, it had been Glen the bulldog, who adored crowds and noise, and who would lie on his back, all four legs spreadeagled, in the centre of the floor, snuffling happily, and generally the centre of attention. In Malta it was Charles's ageing wire-haired dachshund, who had grown infirm, but whom Charles could not bear to put down. Mrs. Checketts, soon after she arrived at Malta as a bride, offered to take the dog over, and her last memory of Charles was of him after parting from his favourite in a Malta street, the tears streaming down his face.

III

The very nature of Charles's post—Commander-in-Chief, Mediterranean—and in charge, simultaneously, of the Headquarters of the Allied Naval Forces in the area, entailed ceaseless travel, visits, and large-scale entertaining both at Malta and on board H.M.S. *Surprise*. This ship, when the Lambes were afloat, carried varied additional staff from Admiralty House, Valetta, and a great many furnishings, official and personal. Like the *Alert*, she was a converted frigate, and she had actually served as the royal yacht at the Queen's Coronation Review of 1953.

Early in 1958 Charles and Peta sailed in the ship on a visit to Rome. While in the Italian capital they lived at the British Embassy with Sir Ashley and Lady Clarke, the ambassador and the admiral, both musical, playing piano duets, and making the very utmost of their Italian contacts. 'I have been told', wrote Peta in her diary, 'that during our time in the Mediterranean, British–Italian relations have been more cordial than for many years.' The fact that the Lambes knew the whole country so well, and liked the people so much, was an obvious ingredient in their success. So was their love of opera.

Their progress from Civitavecchia, where the *Surprise* berthed, to Rome itself was a matter of some excitement, for they were provided with a motor-cycle escort, with out-riders—three in front, three behind. 'We drove at sixty miles an hour with the car boxed in, and everything fell flat before us,' wrote Peta in describing a progress lasting twenty minutes which could, under normal circumstances, take more than two hours.

The visitors had the same escort on their way from the British Embassy to the Vatican, where they had a private audience with

the Pope. They had been given this privilege once before, when
Charles had been in command of the 3rd Aircraft Carrier Squadron.

> This time [wrote Peta], I suppose because Charles was higher
> in rank, we were ushered straight into the Pope's private office
> where he sat at a desk and we sat in front of him on two chairs. . . .
> The minute we got into the Presence, it really was an extra-
> ordinary feeling. Although he was rather a political Pope, he was
> a very holy man and a very good one and one felt all that
> when one was with him. He talked to us for over half an hour,
> which was a great honour, and he gave us each a little medal
> and a rosary.

The next important visit was to General Lauris Norstad, who
was at that time Supreme Allied Commander, Europe, and who
lived in a beautiful house at Versailles, where the Lambes felt very
much at home. The General, who was seven years younger than
Charles, with whom he got on famously, looked positively boyish,
and proved to be a delightful host.

In May, the Lambes made a journey to Libya and the Western
Desert, an area which impressed Peta as few places have ever done
before. In August, Field-Marshal Montgomery visited Malta, and
was a guest at Admiralty House. 'I was won by his charm and
gentleness of manner,' wrote Peta. After a night ashore, Montgomery
sailed off in the *Surprise* with Charles and other senior officers, and
watched a number of exercises and manoeuvres, including beach
landings, the efficiency of which he seems to have approved.

Early in September the Lambes were invited to Algiers by their
friend Admiral Auboyneau. They had known their host when he
had been the French Commander-in-Chief at Saigon. 'A very
colourful person, with great charm and integrity,' so Peta described
him, her memory going back as far as the days of the war, when he
had first come over to London to join de Gaulle.

Algiers was sad.

> This was my first visit [wrote Peta], and the first thing that struck
> me was—here is this large French town with beautiful buildings,
> shops etc and *no one* in the streets. So immediately one had the
> feeling of sadness; sadness for an epoch which was slowly
> disappearing, sadness for the misunderstandings which had
> brought this about. We had already seen the disintegration of the
> French Empire in Vietnam, and now here it was happening

again in Algiers. There was real hatred abroad in the streets and
the very few Algerians one saw had probably just been placing
time bombs under a table in some cafe or shop. I went to the
hairdresser and noticed that the doorway and entrance had all
been shattered, and a few boards were laid across the entrance.
I asked the proprietor how recently this had happened, thinking
perhaps he would say last week but he said 'C'etait l'année
derniere, Madame.'

Later the Lambes visited the Arab quarter in the middle of the
town. They were accompanied by an armed guard of four soldiers,
for there had been so much sniping at Europeans that it was not
considered safe. On their last evening, the Auboyneaus gave a
large party, the guests including Generals Salan, Charles, and
Massu, all of whom later became involved in a plot against
de Gaulle, of whose Algerian policy they disapproved.

Among the last official visits was one to Spain, which gave Peta
an experience of bullfighting, and, where she saw some wonderful
Picassos.

Summing up the impression made on him by these and other
visits Charles told James Pack something of what he felt to be the
failure of the Western Allies in putting their 'image' across
successfully.

> As a result of a year here [he wrote], I am sure that we are
> failing to counter the enemy's most potent weapon—namely
> Radio Moscow, Radio Cairo and Radio Damascus—simply
> because nobody at the top will yet believe that it is deadly, or
> will look far enough ahead.
>
> *Before* we provide for nuclear war, we should provide a political
> plan for Africa to unite them all—perhaps with Western backing,
> and we need to put it over by all forms of propaganda, black and
> white, as a counter to Cairo's appeal. Without this the un-
> developed people will fall into the other camp and won't *want* to
> be saved by the West. And the armed forces can only save them
> if the majority *want* to be saved.
>
> In the meantime, Libya, the Sudan and the peoples of Africa
> are in the front line and what are we doing to counter the
> Egyptian schoolteachers and Radio Cairo in these Countries?—
> Nothing.
>
> I'm sure this is the crux of 'Defence' for the next 10 years, *not*
> V-bombers, *Victorious*es, or nuclear missile firing submarines.

The Veneto near Asolo

19.   *Admiral Sir Charles and Lady Lambe at Admiralty House, Malta 1959*

And it was to Pack, a few months later, that he wrote his last letter from Malta, after he knew for certain that he would become First Sea Lord in May 1959, relieving Mountbatten, who would be made Chief of the Defence Staff.

My flag comes down tomorrow [he wrote on 2 February], and we are waiting for the Bingleys [Admiral Sir Alexander and Lady Bingley] to arrive this evening. All is swept and garnished and the house stripped and bare.

We had about 600 people to say goodbye on Saturday night. Peta and I stood and shook hands from 7–11 p.m. We fly away from Hal Far on Wednesday after spending tomorrow with the Bingleys. I feel very sad but at the the same time a bit light-hearted at the prospect of a holiday.

It's been the hell of a month. I have been to Naples, Athens, Ankara, Izmir, Algiers, Paris and Rome to say goodbye. Here too it has all been farewells, with several hundred letters to answer and an invasion of packing cases. Peta has stood up—just—though she is continually asthmatic. But that will clear up when we get to Rome.

The Lambes had been lent a lovely house in Rome by some American friends, and had hoped to 'lie up there' for several weeks. But it was not to be. They had barely a week in Italy before they had to return to England for a niece's wedding. 'I don't see any long clear spell during our two months freedom,' added Charles, and he was right. He only enjoyed snatches here and there until he took over the duties of 'Lord Commissioner of the Admiralty and Chief of Naval Staff'.

The very first to welcome the Lambes back to England was Lord Mountbatten, who told Charles that the Queen particularly wished to see him. 'She remembers you so well from the time you were Equerry to her father,' he said. 'The idea is that the four of us should go to the theatre together,' The party took place a day or two later—scrambled eggs and smoked salmon in the Queen's private apartments at Buckingham Palace, and a very happy evening, Peta noting how amusingly the Queen could converse about current affairs.

A more formal occasion came a few weeks later, when the Lambes were bidden to a State Banquet in honour of the Shah of Persia. 'A fairy-tale assembly,' so Peta described it, 'with fantastic gold plate.' She herself sat next to the Commander-in-Chief of the

14

Iranian Navy, who knew no English, but she soon found out that
as he had done some of his training in Italy, he spoke Italian well.
'We had a most interesting and agreeable evening,' she wrote,
'talking in Italian about everything under the sun.' The Lambes
found the Shah 'very handsome, with tremendous charm, and
very much an Emperor'.

Soon they were to be caught up in official duties and in the
varied, arduous and unceasing social life which high office so often
entails, for early in May 1959 Charles took over his new
responsibilities.

Chapter Eleven

FIRST SEA LORD

AT THE age of fifty-nine, some forty-two years after he had joined the *Emperor of India* as a midshipman, Charles became First Sea Lord and professional head of the Navy. It was a post which he had not sought, and which he accepted only through the pressing persuasion of Mountbatten and others who thought him the best equipped man for the post.

The position of First Sea Lord, enviable to an officer of ambition, to one who is primarily attracted by the exercise of power, had far less appeal for Charles, to whom high command had come early. He had fulfilled such ambitions as he possessed. Blissful as the very idea of retirement would by this time have seemed to him, he was a man of courage and experience who would not easily have forgiven himself had he refused what was, in fact the greatest challenge. As it happened, his acceptance was tragic, since he very soon overtaxed his strength, but in the earlier months of his tenure he was sustained by the knowledge of how invaluable his counsel would be to his friend, the Chief of the Defence Staff, and by the signs he received on every hand that his appointment was popular in the Navy.

The post of First Sea Lord is always onerous. In war, the holder is largely responsible for naval strategy, upon which in an island nation the fate of the country will depend. In peace, the struggle is almost equally arduous, since it involves securing what the holder believes to be every essential maritime need, in the face of economic and political pressure. Side by side with the Whitehall struggle, and regular meetings not only with Admiralty colleagues, but with the heads of the other Services, there is the constant call of social duties. The life has taken a heavy toll.

Very shortly before the Second World War, Sir Roger Backhouse collapsed in harness. His successor, Sir Dudley Pound, wore himself out at the Admiralty, and even Lord Cunningham, who had been ready enough at the age of nearly sixty to stand up to continuous bombing, and to facing the ruin of his Fleet in the fighting off Crete, had to retire to Haslar during the course of his Admiralty tenure, due to protracted strain.

Lord Howe, in the days of the old sailing navy, used to say that sixty was too old for active command at sea. Admirals usually attain a position when they are called upon to fulfil the highest rôle too late in life for their own well-being. Certainly this was so with Charles.

On relinquishing the office which he had held for some four years, Lord Mountbatten stated in a Press interview that he considered the most significant event with which he had been concerned had been the decision to apply nuclear power to submarines, the most important vessels of which class were henceforward to bear the names of former capital ships, the first of them being H.M.S. *Dreadnought*.

The step involved the necessity of close liaison with the United States, and here Charles, with his long familiarity with that country, and with his many friends across the Atlantic, was happily placed. He had got on excellently with Norstad, who had been responsible for United States affairs in the Mediterranean as in Europe generally, and it was the same with Admiral Arleigh Burke, with whom he was most closely concerned during the earlier months of his Admiralty appointment.

Charles served with two First Lords. The Earl of Selkirk was in office until November 1959, when he was replaced by Lord Carrington, who for some three years had been British High Commissioner in Australia.

One had only to meet Charles Lambe for a short time, [wrote Lord Carrington] to realize that here was somebody of great capacity and personal charm.

One of the drawbacks from which naval officers are inclined to suffer is a lack of contact with people in other walks of life, the professions, and society generally. This is of course very largely because, particularly in the old days, they spent such a long time at sea. I think it is a drawback because they do not start off with the same circle of acquaintances that can help influence things when they get to the top.

Charles Lambe was very much the exception to this. He knew everybody and had the entrée everywhere, and the Navy greatly benefited from this. I think it was partly because he was naturally gregarious and friendly, and partly because everybody liked him. . . . I know I was profoundly impressed by his grasp of naval affairs. He was excellent at meetings because he was articulate and forthright, and I have no doubt that, had he lived, he would have been an outstanding First Sea Lord.

If the two overseas Commands he held had demanded almost continuous travel and ceaseless activity, professional and social, Charles's new post was not a whit less onerous in this respect. Within a few months of taking over from Lord Mountbatten, the Lambes were away on a crowded visit to Canada and the United States.

On 27 October 1959 the First Sea Lord and his wife flew to Canada by way of Iceland and Goose Bay—'deep frozen snow everywhere, and a wonderful welcome', Peta noted. Three days were spent in visiting various Canadian naval establishments, but one afternoon was snatched to visit the National Gallery, where the work of a number of painters, particularly that of James Wilson Morrice made a great impression. 'The effect of seeing all this great and, to us, totally new painting was truly uplifting,' wrote Peta. Lady Garner, the wife of the British High Commissioner, also drove Peta, while Charles was working, to a lake set among the hills near Ottawa, where the colouring of the surrounding maples was at its best, and where they were able to see beavers at work shifting logs to build their houses.

Admiral Arleigh Burke, who then held the post corresponding to that of Charles in the Navy of the United States—Chief of the Naval Staff—sent his private aeroplane to fly the Lambes from Ottawa to Washington, where they were the guests of Admiral and Lady Thistleton-Smith, both very old friends.

Charles was next invited to take the passing out parade of the cadets at the Naval Academy, Annapolis, a very great honour which was much appreciated. 'Various anthems were sung at the end,' noted Peta, 'including "Way Down in Dixie", and I was fascinated to see that only the Southerners stood up when this was played, and when they played the "Stars and Stripes", only the Northerners stood up.'

While Charles was attending to naval business, including a visit to the nuclear submarine *George Washington*, Peta took the chance of spending the night with a lawyer friend in Philadelphia who had been in the Navy and had met Charles during the war. The talk turned to hunting. 'Do they wear red coats here?' asked Peta, in all innocence. Her host looked at her as if she were mad. 'How could you think they wear red coats?' he replied. 'Of course they wear brown.' 'Because of the soldiers?' asked Peta, history coming to her aid. 'Because of the soldiers, yes.'

The Lambes had not long returned home before it was their turn to entertain Admiral Arleigh Burke, and an easier and more appreciative guest could not have been imagined.

Burke noted that Charles was an early riser, like himself, and in the course of their friendship he found, as Mountbatten had done when he and Charles were together at the Admiralty, that 'many matters were discussed over a cup of coffee before breakfast', when the minds of both men were at their freshest.

In the turmoil after World War II and Korea, [wrote Admiral Burke] many changes were occurring in the composition and equipment of the navies of the world. Their functions remained the same as they had throughout the ages, but the equipment with which to carry out those functions was changing at a greater rate than ever before. Atomic weapons had come into existence. Nuclear power was being tried in submarines. This necessitated great changes in the equipment for anti-submarine warfare. The aircraft then being developed were vastly different from the aircraft of just a few years before. Great changes in radio and radar and in all electronics were rapidly overtaking equipment just recently developed.

The one element of naval power which was not changing rapidly was the need for knowledgeable, experienced, capable and inspiring officers and leaders.

After I returned from the Pacific in World War II, I knew a few of the officers who had served in other navies in other areas during that war. By the time I had become the United States Navy Planner in 1953, the name Charles Lambe was synonymous with an excellent officer of the Royal Navy. However, it was not until I became Chief of Naval Operations in 1955 that I became familiar with the qualities of Admiral Lambe. . . .

When Admiral Mountbatten knew that he was to become Chief of the Defence Staff, he informed me that his successor as First Sea Lord would be Admiral Charles Lambe. At that time Admiral Mountbatten stated that Lambe was one of the best officers who had ever served in the Royal Navy, and from what

I had learned from United States naval personnel who had known Admiral Lambe, I agreed.

Most of the personal contact between myself and Admiral Lambe occurred in 1959 when he was First Sea Lord and I was Chief of Naval Operations of the United States Navy. There were many problems which confronted our two navies. We conferred in London and Washington and Paris, and we exchanged correspondence. Both navies, as well as the other navies of the world, were in the throes of constant re-evaluation, re-organization, and re-assessment of new weapons systems. The new equipments did a magnificent job, but they were all tremendously expensive, and so one of our mutual problems was budgetary. How could we maintain the proper balance between being ready for eventualities in the near future, and the development of fleets which would be effective in the distant future?

To arrive at proper solutions to these problems required the closest sort of co-operation among the Free World navies. It also required complete mutual confidence among the uniformed leaders of the navies. Admiral Lambe and I were very fortunate in that we admired and respected our opposite numbers in the other navies. It was in this field of building mutual confidence that Admiral Lambe was extraordinarily successful. His gentle nature and understanding of people did more to create confidence in his Navy even than his great knowledge of naval affairs and new technical developments. Because of his extraordinarily fine personal characteristics, most of the necessary arrangements between the two navies could be accomplished informally and with complete assurance not only that the agreements would be kept meticulously, but that the necessary mutual understanding would be maintained and enhanced.

For example, in May of 1959, the Royal Navy had committed itself to the building of the Dreadnought class of submarine which was based on the United States Polaris submarines. The exchange of complex technical information was a sticky enough problem, but the training of personnel—shipyard personnel, shore-based personnel, ship-board personnel, was nearly impossible to solve. On the part of the Royal Navy they needed the experience which United States people had accumulated without going through the expense and the false starts which we experienced. On our part the training of additional people put a severe burden not only on our school system and our ship-board training facilities, but also in our normal operating people. The fact that this could be accomplished was largely due to the understanding of Admiral Lambe.

In the latter part of 1959 we had many discussions on our mutual problems, such as the value of navigational satellites; the naval command relationship within NATO; the establishment of mutually advantageous facilities for units of our fleets, including Holy Loch for the United States Polaris submarines; the nuclear weapons policies of NATO and our various Allies; the gradual withdrawal of the Royal Navy from the Indian Ocean area, and the necessity for the United States to fill the vacuum that the British withdrawal would create. The remarkable thing about the discussions of all those confidential and serious matters was that our opposites in the other navies were kept informed, informally, of our discussions, so that we all could maintain confidence one in the other.

Charles Lambe was a great naval officer, but he was also a great friend. He was quiet and reticent, but his very presence created a warm atmosphere in which his foreign associates conducted their difficult negotiations with calmness and mutual respect.

II

The ardours of Charles's final post in the Navy brought him certain consolations. He could have his beloved family around him whenever he was not on one of his official visits; he could renew friendships; and he could even rejoin the Bach Choir, in which he had first sung when a very young officer on courses at Greenwich. He was appalled when he had to pass another test, at what he considered so advanced an age, but survived the ordeal, and enjoyed every moment under the baton of Dr. Jacques.

Charles even refused an official dinner party to which he had been invited by the Prime Minister because the date clashed with a performance which the Bach Choir were to give at the Festival Hall, though he attended the Government reception afterwards.

The Lambes lived at their house in Stafford Place instead of within the Admiralty. This arrangement was made all the easier because No. 10 Downing Street was being renovated at the time and during the process the Prime Minister moved into Admiralty House, the First Lord taking over the First Sea Lord's flat, which adjoins the Admiralty Arch straddling the Mall. The Lambes had a Wren cook. During their visit to the United States she went on a Cordon Bleu course at which she did so well that she later took a prize at an exhibition at Olympia.

Entertaining was incessant and it started at breakfast, to which other Sea Lords were regularly invited. There were two reasons for this practise, which had been started by Lord Mountbatten. The first was that many people, Charles among them, are at their best in the morning. Another was that interruptions were so inevitable during the course of a normal day's office work that a leisurely meal followed by a walk through St. James's Park to the Admiralty was as good a way as any of conducting business.

For some months the Lambes had a charming addition to their household in the person of Lysette Nguen Van Tam, the daughter of a President of South Vietnam. She arrived suddenly, with the words 'My father sent me to stay with you', and she was at once adopted as a daughter. She was to study at the Courtauld Institute, and she came (via Paris) with so many new clothes that the Customs could not believe they were not for resale. Charles testified to her character in Court, and was able to explain a very natural misunderstanding.

The year 1960 opened with a cold spell, during which there was a grand scale wedding to which the Lambes were invited. It was that of Pamela Mountbatten.

It was one of the coldest days in the winter [wrote Peta]. Snow was falling the whole way. There was a special train, and everybody had on their best hats, and when we arrived we were taken in a bus as near as possible to Romsey Abbey, which was not very near. We had to walk the rest of the way in thick snow and so by the time we got into church my hat was filled with it. It was brown tulle turned upwards, and when we got into our seats I looked round and just behind me was Noel Coward and we started to get the giggles as he was a very old friend, and that was rather a dreadful beginning.

It was a most beautiful wedding, and after the church ceremony we all went back to Broadlands where there was a huge and wonderful reception. Unfortunately, the moment it was dark, all the lights went out so everything happened by candlelight. Suddenly one came on friends one had not seen for twenty or thirty years.

Edwina Mountbatten looked terribly lined and tired, but she left England soon afterwards on a tour of the Far East in her rôle as Superintendent-in-Chief of St. John's Ambulance, and that was the last time either of us saw her. She died in North Borneo a few weeks later.

The news of the death of Edwina was broken to the Lambes by the Duty Commander at the Admiralty, ringing on a direct line to Stafford Place. Charles was asked to go round at once to Lord Mountbatten with whom he spent most of the day. Lady Mountbatten's body was brought home to England for burial at sea, and Charles was the first up the gangway before the ship made her way out of Portsmouth. 'I used to be very frightened of her when I was young,' wrote Peta of Edwina. 'She seemed to be so wonderful—glamorous and efficient: how efficient! She was a great help to me before we went to Malta, in telling me a little about the Maltese and what she felt ought to be done, and she was always right.'

III

The crisis of Charles's life came suddenly, in March 1960, when he was asked by the Prime Minister, Mr. Harold Macmillan, whose trust he had won, to go to Australia to convey the news that Britain did not intend to proceed with the costly and complicated rocket project known as Blue Streak, at least in the way originally planned. It was a matter which much affected Australia, since the rocket would have been tested in that country, and abandonment of work upon it would almost certainly involve a good deal of unemployment. In the normal way, the mission would have fallen to Lord Mountbatten, but the very recent death of his wife made the assignment out of the question.

The whole tour which was entailed was at once delicate in its nature and involved in its travel. It would have taxed the strength of a far younger man. It included a two-day visit to Singapore, then a flight to Djakarta, before the round of Canberra (where Charles had to make a statment before the Australian Parliament), Melbourne, Sydney, Woomera, and Rum Jungle. New Zealand was to be included, and a return made via Singapore, Bangkok, and Delhi.

Peta accompanied Charles to Singapore and Djakarta, Peta staying at Djakarta as the guest of the Indonesian Navy, while Charles proceeded on his tour of Australasia. Although this was successful, it was so strenuous that by the time Charles reached

New Zealand he was in great pain from a series of heart attacks, of which, however, he never spoke.

While in New Zealand, despite his distress, at least one typical piece of thoughtfulness did not go unnoticed.

> Wellington was greeting him at a reception given by local notables in the Town Hall [wrote Sir William Jamieson]. The assembly was a large one with many important people crowding round their principal guest. In the corner of the big room a small four-piece female orchestra, all in their late fifties, was gallantly but ineffectually, trying to make itself heard above the roar of conversation.
>
> Charles had had a long and tiring day, and still had an official dinner, with its speeches, ahead of him. When the time came for him to leave the hall he suddenly turned and said: 'I must say goodbye to the musicians.' Back he went through the crowd to shake hands with and thank each one of those surprised but delighted elderly ladies.

Malcolm Macdonald had a glimpse of Charles at Delhi on his return flight, and was shocked at the change in his old friend. 'His journeys had been too hasty and hectic,' he wrote, 'and he looked not only tired but unwell. His natural vivacity and personal charm could not disguise the fact that he was physically unfit. A few days later I heard that he was dangerously ill in hospital in England.'

It was true. Peta returned from the Far East on 7 April, and within a few hours went with Charles to Covent Garden during the State Visit of General de Gaulle. Charles's first serious heart attack had occurred that very morning, during a meeting of the Chiefs of Staff. Another occurred in the Opera House itself. It was so grave that it was apparent that he could no longer hope to carry on, though his resignation was not formally recorded until 23 May.

Although he had at last tried his wonderful strength too sorely, he never for a moment resigned himself to incapacity. He was taken to the Millbank Hospital, where he found the care so good that as soon as he was allowed to do so, he made a drawing, by way of a thank offering to the staff, of the main entrance to the building Ever creative, he also began some 'Notes on his life' for the benefit of his son James and his daughter Louisa. These were pencilled into a large, loose-leaved notebook, but they only reached the year 1910, when he joined Horris Hill. He saw friends, who still seemed to draw as much refreshment from him as he from them, and there was at least one occasion—since he was near the Tate—when he visited favourite galleries in a wheeled chair with the more artistic of his two half-sisters, Dorothea Weatherby. On 10 May 1960, shortly after his collapse, the Queen approved his appointment as Admiral of the Fleet, 'in special recognition of outstanding services during a long and distinguished career.'

During the summer, Charles convalesced at Knockhill, a home where he always felt happy. There he began embroidering a carpet in petit-point, this time based not on a design of his own, but on one by William Morris, which he planned would take him six years to complete.

On 28 August 1960 Peta drove Charles to Edinburgh to hear a performance of 'I Puritani' but the effort was too much, though he would not have had it otherwise. He died at Knockhill next day, 'just at the beginning of his life', as his successor, Admiral Sir Caspar John, wrote in a letter to Mountbatten.

He was buried on 2 September at Forgan Old Churchyard, this being the first ceremony to be held in that ancient place for many years. It honoured Charles's wish to be laid at rest in the traditional burial ground of his wife's mother's family, the Stewarts of St. Fort.

A firing party from H.M.S. *Cochrane* led the procession with arms reversed. The blue jackets were followed by Royal Marine buglers from Portsmouth. Among the mourners were Earl Mountbatten; Admiral Sir Caspar John and members of the Board of Admiralty; the Chief of the Imperial General Staff, and the Air Officer Commanding-in-Chief, Coastal Command. The service was conducted by the Chaplain of the Fleet, the Venerable John Armstrong, who preached a sermon at a Memorial Service at St. Martin's in the Field on 27 September which will be quoted in its place. This final service was attended by a great congregation, including a representative of Her Majesty the Queen.

Chapter Twelve

THE TRIBUTE OF FRIENDS

CERTAIN phrases in that stirring 44th Chapter of *Ecclesiasticus* which begins: 'Let us now praise famous men ...' seem particularly fitted for Charles, summing up his attributes in a way that no personal view could equal. *Ecclesiasticus* refers to: 'Leaders of the people by their counsels, and by their knowledge of learning meet for the people, wise and eloquent in their instructions: such as found out musical tunes, and recited verses in writing. . . .'

Of the many tributes which Charles attracted, a number have already been quoted to illustrate his life and his character in action: others seem more fitting in a summing up. And who could better lead the way than Freya Stark, so wise a person, so fine a writer?

> One could not help noticing [she wrote] when Charles Lambe died, what a Renaissance atmosphere there was in every friend's remembrance of him. It was the many-sidedness of his brilliance that dazzled. Everything he touched was given some of that 'life enhancement' which he carried like a sort of aura about him.
>
> As a naval man the praise must be left to the chorus of his colleagues and successors; but as an artist, a musician, and even an embroiderer—for he did beautiful stitching in his spare time, designed by himself—as a general expert in the art of living and in the management of human beings, he still belonged to the non-bureaucratic ages and would have shone and felt at home in any court or council of the old civilized world of Europe from the 15th century to the era of Napoleon.
>
> He carried a climate which one may call the splendour of living, of which I believe everyone who came to know him was

conscious. But what I most remember is something quite different. I think of it *because* it was so different—a quality rarely combined with the other gifts he had in such abundance. One could describe it as a sort of concentration of conscientiousness; he would bring it to bear on all questions that came to him, great or small. It appeared in conversation—the quick grasp, the lightning appraisal, one flash in a swift and accurate mind— and the judgement not only imaginative but supremely balanced and reliable. . . .

He had a gift for intimacy with all sorts and varieties of people, regardless of nationality or race. It is something, in a rather restricted age, to remember someone as vivid, as individual and universal as Charles Lambe.

That gift of intimacy with such varieties of people, of which Freya Stark spoke, is supported by an observation by Rear-Admiral P. W. Brock, who knew Charles well at more than one stage of his life, and who spoke of 'the remarkable balance between his general affability and pronounced reserve, but with various people admitted on various levels and to various depths, on the strength of common tastes or interests in one or other of a number of fields.'

It would be difficult to work for one man so long [wrote Mr. Hammett, once Charles's coxswain] without learning something, and with Admiral Lambe there seemed something new to learn every day. His interests were so many and so varied that it was difficult to find a subject about which he did not have a working knowledge. He would apply himself wholeheartedly to anything that he did and yet was never too tired or preoccupied to remember to give a few words of encouragement and appreciation to those working with him.

I will always consider myself fortunate to have known and worked with him so long—the example he set us has been my ideal and a great help to me ever since.

Admiral Sir Alexander Bingley, when attending a ceremony in 1963 in H.M.S. *Vernon*, at which a portrait of Charles by Edward Halliday was presented to the ward-room, said that he:

. . . was the best persuader, the best maker of a case, the best diplomat that I have ever met.

He said what he believed and he believed what he said. He never did a crooked thing, not even in the Whitehall jungle battle. He never let anyone down and never dodged a responsibility. He was always ready to listen to the views of others, however far below him, intellectually, they might be, and not only to listen, but to change, and admit that he had been wrong, if he had.

Finally there was his sympathy and genuine interest in people. Whoever he was speaking to—Royalty, the captain of a ship, a member of a petty-officer's mess he was visiting, Maltese Dghaishaman, that was the person he was interested in and his problem was, for the moment, the most important thing in the world.

Music had been among Charles's earliest loves, and of the qualities he brought to his music, Lennox Berkeley, who had been his much-appreciated guest on board H.M.S. *Vengeance* in the 3rd Aircraft Carrier Squadron wrote:

The thing that stood out most in Charles's love of music was the excitement and pleasure he got from it. It was not that he liked in particular the more pleasure-giving type of music in the ordinary sense—on the contrary, I suppose his favourite composer was Bach—but that his approach to music was to find enjoyment in it. Moreover, he discovered it for himself; an excellent sight-reader, he would get hold of the scores of music he liked and study them at the keyboard, so that his musical opinions were first-hand rather than ideas assimilated from books or programme notes. He loved to play piano duets with musical friends. The extraordinary adroitness that he had in everything had enabled him to acquire an adequate technique for this. I have a vivid recollection of playing every type of music with him.

It must have needed no little determination for him to keep up his music while pursuing a brilliantly successful naval career. A man who can take the conventions and rigid discipline of a naval officer's life in his stride while at the same time not merely taking an interest in, but actually practising the arts, is indeed rare. It was this vitality and versatility that made him the fascinating and unforgettable character he was.

Mr. Malcolm Macdonald characterized Charles's qualities in considering matters even wider in scope than those of the Navy, saying that his mind was 'touched by an understanding of political, international and human problems which gave it a much deeper sagacity. This sprang from his instinctive, sensitive, sympathetic knowledge of people of different classes, creeds and races—which in him was a jewel of a quality.' Sir William Hayter endorsed this view.

The same qualities of free, unprejudiced judgement that he brought to bear on defence questions also informed his approach to politics [he wrote]. He was far from sharing the unquestioning acceptance of Conservative policies that tended in his time to prevail in the Services. He approached politics with an open mind and came up with some surprising results; for instance he was often unexpectedly sympathetic with Soviet demands, not out of weakness or appeasement but because he thought them justified.

Though there was this quality of hard, unprejudiced clarity about his thought he was delightfully easy and agreeable company. There was no subject that it was not a pleasure to discuss with him. When illness forced him to retire from the Navy, those of his friends who did not realize how serious his illness was hoped selfishly that his release from official duties would enable them to see more of him. We in particular were counting on seeing him more in Oxford, where he would have fitted perfectly. It was a hard blow when we realized that he would never come.

Admiral E. B. Ashmore recalled Charles's 'generosity and trust, but in retrospection I owe him most for his example of a gay, versatile and unselfish spirit.' Admiral Ashmore recalled that once when Charles's flagship was on a visit to Leghorn, he called the officers together and told them 'in his stimulating and simple way of the beauties of Florence and of those treasures which gave him most pleasure and which he therefore commended to us'. And of Charles's own qualities as a painter, Lord Haig, as friend and fellow artist, had this to say:

The memories I cherish of him are clear-cut because of his strong personality—a personality which to me was significant and sympathetic. We shared an artistic make-up imposed on a Service background—a background which was both native and natural. In spite of our difference in age, I felt at home with him. To be with him meant communication which was beyond mere talk and beyond the world around us.

Sketch of Louisa Lambe aged six, and her dog Linnet

21.   *Admiral Lambe at a press conference, Melbourne, March 1960*

Not that our common interests in music and painting, farming and landscape, Service life and Service men did not provide food for a great deal of discussion. He adopted a rather complex attitude to life, which varied from his Socialistic political leanings to the rather right-wing views which he had as a landowner and a member of the Royal Naval Polo Team. The complexities of his make-up were symbolized in the two pianos in his day cabin in H.M.S. *Vengeance*—pianos which gave him emotional release and spiritual refreshment after duties on the flight-deck. In his cabin prevailed the same civilized atmosphere as reigned in his home on shore.

The watercolours and drawings of his which I have seen are serious and intelligent studies of landscapes and people, recording places he knew and visited. Their treatment in line and wash, particularly in the interpretation of landscape, is not unlike Edward Lear. His drawings of heads gave him a chance to observe the solidity of structure and to communicate with sympathetic insight his sense of character. The conception or interpretation was always based on truthful observation of nature without much flight of fancy or imagination. His artistic handwriting was like his ordinary handwriting—strong, regular and balanced. But the interpretation was far from being bogged down in a laborious recording. The feeling of his brush or pen was allied to profound formal conception. His powers of intellectual analysis were allied to the feelings of someone who knew and felt music, the sister art, at which he was far less of an amateur. I can safely say, though, that he had the talent and make-up of a painter, and that if he had concentrated his time and energy on developing his talent in painting, he would have become a very good artist indeed.

More important is the knowledge that Charles enjoyed his painting. His mastery of simple techniques enabled him to go out and say without the frustration of the normal amateur who tries to say and do too much with too many colours and too many brushes. One can't escape the sheer efficiency of the man, or the clarity of his purpose and vision, or, above all, the shrewdness of his outlook.

To me he was a lover of solitude partly because of his inner completeness and self-sufficiency, partly because he liked doing things as an individual. It was because of his lone wolf attitude that his soul as an artist was able to be nourished and grow. It was tragic that on the completion of his task as a naval officer

15

he was struck down before he had time to enjoy and develop further the great gifts and resources which are denied to so many who enter retirement after a distinguished career.

I last saw him sitting in a concert hall during the Edinburgh Festival a few days before he died. I had not seen him for several years, since he had been in the Far East or since he had been First Sea Lord. Superficially he retained his interest in life and in the music we had been hearing, about which he talked with appreciation and knowledge. But he was behind the barrier which divides those who live and those who know they are about to die.

I thought of the kingfisher-like creature I had met at the beginning of the war in a cloudless autumn before the onset of those heavy responsibilities which proved too strenuous for his artistic make-up. Charles was one of those who gave their lives for their country—a great gentleman and a true artist.

Another artist, this time Victor Stiebel, saw Charles in a highly individual way, yet he too went to the heart of the matter.

He had in abundance all the talents that were required for his life as a professional sailor plus that extra coating of star-dust that distinguishes the top man from his lesser brethren. I am sure that if, as a child, he had been asked what he wanted to be when he grew up, he would have answered 'The First Sea Lord'. It was natural for Charles to succeed.

Because it seemed that he lacked nothing (he had good looks, personal charm, adequate funds, prowess at most sports, and a real appreciation for the Arts) he might easily have been considered something of a bore. That he wasn't was due to the fact that he had, at birth, been given by the good fairies a splendid bonus—an enquiring mind, a mind that probed diligently into the highways and the byways of any interest that came within the circumference of his life. It was this extra quality, this constructive seeking that gave Charles his real value. Without it he would never have been able, when C-in-C Far East Station, to establish in Singapore a string orchestra composed of local inhabitants, which he watched over like a Nanny, or to paint his delicate water-colours, or to play so lovingly his piano, or to embroider with such skill his rugs and chair-covers, or to hang in his warship cabins the works of Picasso and Augustus John, or when in London to sing so happily with the Bach Choir or to study with enthusiasm the habits of the roses that he grew in his Scottish garden.

I think that Charles derived more pleasure from choosing for his wife a moonstone ring than from his professional successes. After all, almost anybody can become a First Sea Lord.

Sir William Jamieson had a pageant of memories of 'Charles at work and play'. They included:

> . . . dancing a reel at a Highland ball; steering a difficult meeting to a sensible conclusion; talking intelligently to experts on all sorts of subjects. Never in a hurry, or discourteous, however busy he might be. Suddenly totally absorbed in something unusual he had seen or heard. Causing the faces of those around him to light up by some witty, apposite remark; staring out of the window of his aircraft at the beautiful world around and below him. Making everybody feel a little larger than life.

Sir William, in his tribute, quoted a letter from a fellow officer who wrote of Charles: 'In my time in the Service I never met a more charming or more brilliant senior officer. He reduced me for the only time in my life to abject hero-worship.'

It seems fitting that final valediction should come from the sermon preached at the Memorial Service in St. Martin's in the Fields by the Chaplain of the Fleet.

> Far too often goodness exists without charm, and charm without goodness—but in Charles Lambe goodness and charm were united, and therein lay the secret of his character. . . . Although he himself was blessed with many talents, he was never indifferent to or intolerant of those with few. To each and every one he gave his due.
>
> During the early days of his illness he was tremendously grateful to receive refreshment of mind and soul through the laying on of hands, and his moments of Holy Communion were a deep and moving experience of the goodness and mercy of God.
>
> Few men can look back on their lives and say that they were wholly good and every moment well spent. Charles Lambe could, but he would have been the last person to have said so.

Admiral of the Fleet Sir Charles Lambe, G.C.B., C.V.O.

SERVICE CHRONOLOGY

1900   Charles Edward Lambe born at Stalbridge (20 December).

1917   H.M.S. *Emperor of India*. Midshipman.

1919   H.M.S. *Wryneck*. Service in the Baltic.

1920   H.M.S. *King George V*. Acting Sub. Lieutenant
        H.M.S. *Leamington*. Service in Ireland.

1921   Sub. Lieutenant.

1921   H.M.S. *Raleigh*. West Indies and United States.

1922   Lieutenant. October: Courses at Cambridge.

1923   H.M.S. *Excellent*, for courses.
        H.M.S. *Benbow*: service in Mediterranean.

1924   H.M.S. *Queen Elizabeth*, Flag-Lieutenant to Commander-
        in-Chief, Mediterranean.

1925   H.M.S. *Vernon*, for courses.

1929   H.M.S. *Stuart*: service in Mediterranean.

1930   H.M.S. *President*, for Staff College. Lieutenant-Commander.

1931   H.M.S. *Vernon*.

1932   H.M.S. *Hawkins*: service in the Far East.

1933   Commander. H.M.S. *Vernon*, for special course.
        H.M.S. *Coventry*: service in the Mediterranean.

1935   H.M.S. *Vernon*.

1936   Naval Equerry to H.M. King Edward VIII.

1937   Captain. Naval Equerry to H.M. King George VI.

1938   H.M.S. *Curlew*, in command.

1939   C.V.O. New Year Honours. H.M.S. *Dunedin*, in command.

1940   Assistant Director of Plans, Joint Planning Staff.

1941   Deputy Director of Plans.

1942 British Admiralty Delegation, Washington.
Director of Plans, Admiralty.

1944 C.B. New Year Honours.
Flag Captain and Chief of Staff to Rear-Admiral, Aircraft Carriers, Eastern Fleet.
H.M.S. *Illustrious*, in command (October).

1945 Mentioned in Despatches (May) Admiralty: Assistant Chief of Naval Staff (Air) Acting Rear-Admiral.
Mentioned in Despatches (October).

1946 Special Duty with Director of Plans, Admiralty.

1947 A.D.C. to H.M. King George VI.
Rear-Admiral. Flag-Officer, Flying Training.

1949 Flag-Officer, 3rd Aircraft Carrier Squadron.

1950 Vice-Admiral.

1951 Flag-Officer, Royal Yacht. Admiral (Air) Home.

1953 K.C.B. New Year Honours.
Commander in Chief, Far Eastern Station.

1955 Second Sea Lord and Chief of Naval Personnel.
Extra Naval Equerry to H.M. Queen Elizabeth II.

1957 Commander in Chief, and NATO C-in-C, Mediterranean.
G.C.B., Birthday Honours.

1959 First Sea Lord and Chief of the Naval Staff.

1960 Admiral of the Fleet (May). Resigned due to ill health (23 May).
Died at Knockhill, Fife (29 August)

ACKNOWLEDGEMENTS

Lady Lambe's original plan was that her husband should be commemorated in a privately printed volume containing appreciations from his friends in many walks of life. A number were in fact collected, and these were included among the very large collection of papers which were put at my disposal when, after some time had gone by, it was felt that the general interest of the Admiral's career justified a full-scale biography.

I am most grateful for permission to make use of the material assembled, and offer thanks to those who have helped to make this work fuller than it could otherwise have been. My acknowledgements are alphabetical, as this seems the least invidious order when indebtedness is so various. Thanks are due to: Mr. George Andrews; the Ven. John Armstrong; Vice-Admiral E. B. Ashmore; Mr. Lennox Berkeley; Admiral Sir Alexander and Lady Bingley; Rear-Admiral Sir Christopher Bonham-Carter; Rear-Admiral and Mrs. P. W. Brock; Fleet Admiral Arleigh Burke, United States Navy; Rear-Admiral Sir Anthony and Lady Buzzard; Sir Michael Carey; Mr. H. L. Carr; Lord Carrington; Squadron-Leader David Checketts; Viscountess Cunningham of Hyndhope; Admiral Sir William Davis, who kindly provided the draft of his article on Admiral Lambe which appears in *The Dictionary of National Biography*; Dr. Ronald Doig, for a most useful summary of manuscript material; Mr. Hugh Drake; Admiral Sir Laurence Durlacher; Air Chief Marshal Sir William Elliot; Captain Derek Empson ; Instructor Rear Admiral Sir John Fleming; Admiral J. H. Godfrey; Earl Haig; Mr. D. J. Hammett; Mr. Norman Hanson; Mr. Tom Harrisson; Sir William Hayter; Mrs. Howard-Vyse; the late Sir William Jamieson and Lady Jamieson; Admiral of the Fleet Sir Caspar John; Lt.-Commander P. K. Kemp; Mr. James Knapp-Fisher, my publisher; Sir John Lang; Dr. Rodney Long; Mr. Malcolm Macdonald; Sir George Mallaby; Admiral of the Fleet Earl Mountbatten of Burma, for the tribute with which the book opens, which appeared originally as a notice supplementary to *The Times* obituary; Major-General Sir Robert Neville; Mrs. Norfolk; Captain James Pack, for the loan of letters; Mr. Stewart Perowne, for a similar kindness, and for impressions of an astonishing man; Captain S. W. Roskill, for a generous account of Admiral Lambe's Service life and for valuable information about the series of post-war Naval Courses at Cambridge; Sir Steven Runciman, for his most perceptive Foreword; Admiral Antoine Sala, of the French Navy; the Rev. the Lord Sandford; Commander Martin Sands; Vice-Admiral B. B. Schofield; Captain John Stanning; Freya Stark; Sir Michael Stewart; Mr. Victor Stiebel; Vice-Admiral Sir Geoffrey and Lady Thistleton-Smith; the late Admiral of the Fleet Sir Philip Vian; Mr. Mark Wilcox, and Admiral of the Fleet Sir Algernon Willis.

My principal collaborators have, of course, been Lady Lambe and her family, and my wife.

O. W.

INDEX